REAT 1983

CHONGJIN 9-46-10-50
Chu-Ul 12-2-50
Myongchon
Kilchu
Songjin 12-9-50

ngnam

NSAN

U.S. Navy
LST St. Wind

SCALE OF
MILES
0   80

Kumgang San

KOREA
600 MILES LONG
135 MILES WIDE

38°

1-50

JL

56

EASTERN SEA

Kuryonpori
12-11-50

PUSAN

THE THREE DAY PROMISE

A KOREAN SOLDIER'S MEMOIR

BY DONALD K. CHUNG, M.D.

FATHER & SON
PUBLISHING

This book published and manufactured by Father and Son Publishing, Inc., 4840 Tower Road, Tallahassee, Florida 32303.

Library of Congress Cataloging-in-Publication Data

Chung, Donald K.
   The three day promise.

   1. Korean War, 1950-1953—Personal narratives, Korean. 2. Chung, Donald K. I. Title.
DS921.6.C45 1988   951.9'042'0924 [B]   88-13240
ISBN 0-942407-06-7

Printed in the United States of America

First Edition

4th Printing, 1995

THE THREE DAY PROMISE

A KOREAN SOLDIER'S MEMOIR

Don. K. Chung

For my mother Kim Ki-Bock,
Friendship, and Peace

INTRODUCTION

For almost four decades I have been privileged to witness first-hand the indomitable courage of the Korean people—first, as their fighting partner during the Korean War, and then as a friend who witnessed their superb national regeneration in latter years. The Koreans are imbued with the quality I tried to pursue during my own military career, something I call "The Will to Win."

Dr. Chung's book is a unique contribution to the history of the Korean War, and it is also a case-study in Korean courage. What many Americans do not realize is the degree of the indignities to which the Korean people were subjected the first decades of this century, when they were occupied by the Japanese. No sooner were the Japanese expelled than Korea had to fight off a new invader, the Soviet-dominated puppet regime of the North. Dr. Chung gives a vivid picture of that war, in which I played a role as Commanding General, Eighth United States Army Korea (EUSAK) from April 1951 through January 1953.

One episode is strong in my memory. The Korean army had some problems the first days of my command, chiefly because it lacked trained officers and equipment. I had a long and candid talk with the president, Syngman Rhee, and I told him, in effect, that the Koreans would have to do the brunt of the fighting. President Rhee nodded. I should not worry. He would inspire his army to fight. And he did.

My admiration of the Korean people is unbounded. I commend Dr. Chung's book to any citizen interested in the long friendship of our people.

James A. Van Fleet
General, USA (Ret)

PROLOGUE

At six o'clock on the morning of February 6, 1982, Richard and Alexander woke me with cries of "Happy Birthday, Dad!" Each handed me a birthday card commemorating my fiftieth birthday. I had reached another major milestone in my life, and I wondered how I was going to feel about it.

That evening, after what amounted to a daylong celebration, with wonderful birthday cards and remembrances from my employees, colleagues, friends and even members of my Sunday school class, my family took me out to a prime-rib dinner at our favorite restaurant in Newport Beach. This had been our family tradition for birthdays since we moved to Long Beach in 1972. As occurred every year, I recalled my earliest birthdays before World War II, when Father took me for borscht and meatballs at a small Russian restaurant in Harbin, a large city in Japanese-occupied Manchuria.

My fiftieth was a good birthday. Nothing unusual happened, and all the customary good feelings attended the day. After the boys went to bed, however, I felt that I needed to have some quiet time to myself for the remainder of the evening. I went into my study and played some of my all-time favorite music on the stereo. There was only a dim light over the stereo as I sat in the farthest corner of the room to reflect on my past.

*

I remembered the last time I saw Mother, as she handed me a small bundle containing fresh socks and three days' supply of rice. I remembered the buzz of emotions in my head as I strode to the main road from our house for what I thought would be only a three-day parting while North and South Korean soldiers fought over my little town. My mind flashed to random scenes of violence and waste during my nearly three years as a combat infantryman in the South Korean army. I thought of my arrival in Seoul, the capital of South Korea, in the early evening of July 27, 1956, after my discharge from the Republic of Korea Army, exactly three years after the end of the Korean War. The ROK Army had released me to face civilian life with one month's extra pay after five years and eight months' active duty, including two years and seven months' service with a front-line infantry combat reconnaissance company. There were no veterans' benefits or pensions; I had had to survive on my own. I had no home or family to which to go, and the money ran out after the first week. Yet, somehow, I managed to support myself, even to re-enter the medical school, from which I eventually graduated as my class valedictorian.

Following my graduation from medical school, I had ventured from Seoul to St. Louis, Missouri, on September 17, 1962, a single man with no attachments. I had $50 cash in my pocket and a small suitcase holding all my meager possessions. Despite this inauspicious new beginning—one in a long line of new beginnings—I eventually received training in one of America's finest medical centers. Later, I co-authored several medical textbooks, taught at several medical schools throughtout the United States, was honored by my hospital with its "Teacher of the Year" award, and conducted or participated in innumerous medical seminars through the years.

Despite my humble beginnings and numerous detours, I had achieved an "American" measure of success. To all outward appearances, I was a highly successful man at the top of my profession. I seemed to possess all the things by which success, particularly as a physician, is usually measured.

I should have been content and happy as my fiftieth birthday drew to a close. I was warm and safe in my own hideaway, listening to music I truly cherish, thinking of things safely in the past. But I remained sad—sad to the core of my being.

Exactly fifty years earlier, Mother had delivered me following seven hundred days of ceaseless prayer and seemingly endless wishing for a son to carry on the family line. Mother had then devoted her entire life to me, nursing me through serious illness, ceaselessly doing her humble best for eighteen of my fifty years to help me grow up to be a "big man."

Though war and politics had kept us apart for thirty-two years, I reflected on all those intervening birthdays and intervening years, on how, at each milestone, I had proclaimed to myself, "This is the year I am going to locate my family and fulfill the last promise I made to Mother: 'I'll be back in three days.'"

War and politics had prevented me from fulfilling that promise. An "iron curtain" lay between my family in North Korea and my closest access to my former home.

How terrible, I thought over and again that night of my fiftieth birthday, that the old business of ideological differences prevented sons and mothers from sharing their love in person rather than through the ether, in the mystical mode I had had to employ over the growing distance in time. I did not once know for certain all those years, if Mother, Father or my three sisters were even alive. And they knew nothing of me since I had taken those terrible first strides away from all of them in the bitter Winter of 1950.

The stereo continued to play, and I wallowed in my sentimentality. I had listened to those songs many times over the years, but they had never moved me so deeply as they did in the waning hours of my fiftieth birthday.

As much as I want to
I cannot return to my home village
Deep in the mountains
Under that thousand-mile-distant sky.

In this strange land
I am always lonely, always crying;
I miss the home so
That is there only in dreams.

In the many years since I left
I wandered through different lands.
When can I meet my parents, brothers, sisters again
In the home that is only in my dreams?

I found myself miserable and crying. When I had visited South Korea in 1979, I had found that many of the refugees from my hometown had already died. Since then, my best friend and former roommate had also died in South

Korea. Like me, he had been the only son. He had not been able to fulfill his lifelong dream of returning to his family in North Korea.

My heart was breaking; I was afraid to admit that my parents had certainly died by now, and that I would probably die in America, this wonderful but nonetheless strange land, before I would have the opportunity to visit with what remained of my family in North Korea.

Another song followed, and I drifted into a waking dream about my elderly, gray-haired mother sitting in her backyard, looking at the southern sky toward the 38th Parallel, the far-off "iron curtain" that kept us apart.

Ah, why can't you come back home?
    Because a mountain is blocking you?
Ah, ah, why can't you come back home?
    Because water is blocking you?

Didn't we travel free in our homeland before?
    Now we are thousands of miles apart,
        In separate nations.
In every dream, every night, I wander
    I search the Thirty-eighth Parallel for you.

Ah, when the flowers blossom
    Are you coming back home?
Ah, ah, when the snow begins to fall
    Are you coming back home?

Who was it set up the three words:
    Thirty-eighth Parallel?

I kept thinking that Mother did not even know that I was alive and well. I could not go on any longer, listening to those sad and defeatist songs. I turned off the stereo, and then I sat and cried for a very long time.

I vowed, as I sat with tears streaming from my eyes, that I was somehow going to visit my hometown in North Korea, and that I would write a memoir dedicated to Mother. I had thought about such a trip off and on for many years, but I had allowed friends who had come south during the Korean War to dissuade me. They had always been able to argue that such a trip might jeopardize the lives of my family, or even my own life, for I had deserted "the cause" when the first opportunity arose.

On this night of my fiftieth birthday, after looking back at the good life I had been living in recent years, and with many thoughts about my wife and two sons, I realized that I could not rest, and certainly could never count my life a success, until I had directed my total energies toward requiting the decades-long pain I had inflicted since reneging on my promise that I would return home to Mother in "only three days."

I knew what I had to do.

It had been a long day, my fiftieth birthday, and a new beginning.

PART I
From Manchuria to North Korea
(August, 1945 - September, 1950)

CHAPTER ONE

The dull pain began before daybreak, spreading swiftly over my abdomen. It was soon accompanied by a bloated sensation and nausea more severe than I had known in my thirteen years. By noon, my body seemed to be consumed in fire; the pain was excruciating. All the while, Mother became increasingly alarmed at the rapidly-progressing illness of unknown origin that was wracking her only son.

Mother did not know the cause of my illness nor what to do to alleviate the pain or other symptoms, but in time she sensed that she must take swift, decisive action. She ran into the street outside our house, waved down a horse drawn taxi and bundled me into it. As the team of horses galloped over the cobblestone streets of Harbin, the gregarious Russian teamster rambled on endlessly about himself. As he spoke of his experiences I could barely follow through the waves of my pain, I could feel my face twist under the pressure of stifled cries evoked by each small bounce of the taxi.

By the time the Russian cabby reined in his horses before the Chinese herb doctor's office, I was doubled over from the pain, vomiting and retching. The doctor asked a few perfunctory questions as he palpated my stomach, but even the practiced, gentle probings of his fingers sent fresh waves of indescribable pain through my body.

After considering the symptoms and telling Mother that I had a bad case of stomach cramps, the herb doctor held a five-inch silver needle to the flame of a lamp. I was absolutely terrified, for I had never seen an acupuncture needle. The practitioner swiftly located the exact center of the pain with his left index finger, then

17

slowly and surely slid the needle into my pain-taut abdomen. The relief was immediate. I could even feel my face relax into an involuntary smile of sheer gratitude. The herb doctor next prescribed three packets of herbal medicine and instructed Mother to apply hot compresses over the stomach area for the next ten hours.

When we got home, Mother placed a hot-water bottle over my stomach and tucked me into my bed beneath thick blankets. Then she boiled the herbs down to a bowlful of thick, dark-brown extract and insisted that I drink it all. It was very hot and had an extremely bitter taste, by far the worst thing I had ever tasted, before or since. I held my nose, shut my eyes and took it all down in one disgusting gulp. Mother popped several raisins into my mouth to neutralize the bitter taste.

Early that same evening, I turned a deathly pale shade as cold sweat ran down my face in tiny rivulets. The pain was back, stronger now than it had been at dawn. My knees were drawn up to my chest because it simply hurt too much when I tried to straighten them out. Mother's short-lived joy turned to a deep anguish. Uncertain and fearful, she just sat and clung to my hand, the hand of her only son.

Vivid memories raced through Mother's mind as she sat anxiously at my bedside.

*

Kim Ki-bok was seventeen years old in 1920 when her parents arranged her engagement to fourteen-year-old Chung Bong-chun, who lived on a mountainside farm about two miles from her home. Mother's family lived in Taehyang village, near Chu-ul, a farming town of some 10,000 souls on Korea's far northeastern coast. Taehyang's population of only a few men, women and children was widely scattered along the mountainous coast.

Many of the village children had to walk two or three miles to the district four-year elementary school, a one-room straw-thatched building no different on the outside than any of the other buildings comprising the central village. Classes were held at night under kerosene lamps because the students were needed to work on the family farms during the day. Not all of the children received even the rudimentary education offered at the tiny school. Though education opportunities were by no means reserved for boys only, Mother received no formal schooling, and she never learned to read or write.

Bears, deer, wolves and even Siberian tigers often roamed at the outskirts of the village and its satellite farms. Stories were told of people who had been killed by tigers.

Her wedding ceremony took place just a few weeks after the announcement of her engagement. All of the villagers and outlying farmers were invited to see the bride unveil her face for the first time before her new husband. It was a time of celebration, with ample food and rice wine.

Following the ceremony and celebration, Mother moved to her new husband's home to undertake the traditional full year of service to her new in-laws. Mother was lucky in at least one regard: her mother-in-law was a kindly and considerate woman. Even so, Mother faced heavy responsibilities in the service of her new in-laws. When she was not busy cooking or sewing, she was at work in the fields. Once each week, she carried farm produce to the village market to trade for clothing, shoes and other necessities. During the two-hour walk to the village, the heavy burden was piled atop her head or tied to her back.

Donald Chung, M.D.

Mother was very careful to uphold all the traditions in her new home. She was modest and humble, observing the protocol of never looking her elders directly in the face. She did all her housework without being told. She spoke in a quiet voice so as not to be heard more than two feet away. While she slept with her young husband, there was neither romance nor affection in their intimacy. All this was accepted as being her lot in life.

The newlyweds soon had a daughter. Then a second daughter, who died in infancy. A third pregnancy resulted in yet another daughter. This unbroken sequence of female babies caused Mother great anxiety. Father was the eldest of five sons (he also had four older sisters), and his sons would perpetuate the family line. Mother felt guilty at not having given birth to a boy, and she worried ceaselessly about her position in the family, for a wife and daughter-in-law who could not produce necessary male heirs was in a tenuous position.

It was after the birth of the second surviving daughter that Mother began getting up well before dawn to climb a nearby mountain overlooking the sea. For over seven hundred consecutive mornings, she kneeled upon the mountain and prayed to Amita Buddha to send her a baby boy. Even after she became pregnant again, she continued to climb through rain or snow to offer her ceaseless prayers.

Anxiety built up steadily in the house as the birth approached. When Mother finally went into labor, no one in the house spoke, lest they tempt fate. Even the cattle stabled beside the house stood quietly through the long hours.

At two o'clock in the morning of February 6, 1932—the Year of the Monkey—a small head covered with black hair began to emerge from the birth canal. With her own mother's skillful assistance, Mother gave birth without any complications. The baby cried loudly

20

while held upside down by the legs. At that moment, Grandmother gave a loud shout of joy, "It's a boy!" Everyone in the house rejoiced.

As was the Korean custom, several pieces of red pepper braided into a straw rope were hung in front of the house to signify that a boy had been born. For the first twenty-one days, neither Mother nor the son left the house or were shown to those outside the family. This was to protect them from any possible infection. The family named the boy Dong-kyu. "Dong" was written in the Chinese character for "east", and "kyu" with the character for "star".

Despite the early precautions, I was not a healthy baby. I suffered from frequent fevers, and sometimes even lapsed into comas. Mother continuously worried about my health. She consulted a succession of *mudang*, women shamans, who came to the house in strange costumes to dance around me. Their incantations, however, failed to cure my many illnesses.

When I was two years old, Mother finally consulted a sorceress, who recommended that, in order to calm the evils threatening my life, I should be adopted as the fifth son of a family with the surname Hong. Our relatives searched far and wide for a family that could fulfill those specifications, and they eventually found one in a village about four miles farther back in the mountains. This family took me in and renamed me with their family name.

After only two months with the generous Hong family, I was fully recovered and so returned to Mother. A short time later, she took me and my two elder sisters away from Taehyang to join Father, who had gone to seek new opportunities in Harbin, a large and prosperous city in Manchuria, which, like Korea, had been conquered by the Empire of Japan.

21

CHAPTER TWO

Harbin, the capital of Pinkiang province in Manchuria, is located on a boundless, absolutely flat plain on the south bank of the Sungari River, which is navigable for six months of the year by ocean steamer. During the warm months, the city's numerous beautiful gardens and flowing waterways attracted many tourists from what was then the mainland portion of the Empire of Japan—Manchuria and Korea—and, indeed, from the Republic of China and nearby Russian territories. Most important, Harbin was a major commercial center that provided seemingly endless vistas for advancement by Koreans, whom the Japanese had economically and politically repressed in their own homeland to the south.

The Harbin of the 1930s was considered a cosmopolitan "international" metropolis with its population of about 700,000 native Manchurian Chinese, the ruling Japanese, White Russians who had arrived in the wake of the Bolshevik Revolution and Koreans who migrated to Harbin throughout the years following the Japanese invasion of their homeland. Each national group lived more or less in its own distinctively-built section of the city, though intermingling was fairly widespread, particularly in the realm of commerce.

Naturally, the ruling Japanese dominated city life. The Chinese and Russians were not severely affected in their daily lives by the Japanese rulers, but the Koreans were. As in Korea itself, most aspects of Korean culture were ruthlessly suppressed, including the reading and writing of our distinctive language and our nation's entire store of literature and art. Indeed, all Koreans were forced to adopt Japanese names as part of the program to forcibly assimilate the Korean people. Another important area of Japanese domination over Koreans could be found in educational opportunities; early elementary education was open to Korean children, but the only "good" high school in the city enrolled Japanese and only the most-advanced and most-assimilated Korean students. Even with constant reminders of our inferiority in Japanese eyes, Koreans in Manchuria were better off in many respects than Koreans in Korea. Here, at least, we *might* get ahead.

My family emigrated to Harbin in 1934 for much the same reason most Koreans wound up there— economic opportunity. Father hoped to establish a permanent home in Harbin.

*

Mother and Father had drifted far apart by the time I was born. In fact, Father left for Harbin well in advance of the rest of the family. I am certain his early departure had its practical reasons, such as finding a job, but the proof of his motives was discovered as soon as Mother, my two older sisters and I arrived to find Father living in relative luxury with a concubine. The situation was not uncommon in Asia, so there was no overt social stigma, but people are people, and the rejection did have its impact upon the excluded majority of the family. Though the family was cared for after a fashion, Father never lived at home during our years in Harbin.

Father had only achieved a fourth-grade education, but he was an extremely sharp individual with tastes well above his early station in life and a fearless determination to get ahead. He went to work as a clerk for the Harbin district attorney's office, and soon managed to establish a secure niche for himself because of the good impression he was able to make. For example, Father never owned a watch, but he was an

24

habitually punctual man, arriving at his office at precisely eight o'clock every morning.

One way Father got ahead resulted from the arrival of an endless stream of Koreans bent upon smuggling valuables from Korea to sell in Harbin. Opium and gold were two popular staples of the smuggling trade. Many of the smugglers were apprehended and since Father was the only Korean working for the prosecuting attorneys, he was endlessly contacted by relatives of the prisoners, who naturally offered bribes in the hope Father could get the smugglers freed or, at least, influence the length of sentences. At each new year, the family received mountains of rice and other foods, not to mention valuables and even cash. Father repaid these gifts as often as possible by indeed influencing decisions at the district attorney's office. More than once, his own relatives were spared harsh sentences for their abortive smuggling activities.

Father's position and pliability resulted in our living a safer, more-prosperous life than might otherwise have been our lot, but his devotion to his concubine kept him a distant, often harsh figure in my life. He regularly visited with us, and demanded of Mother her wifely duties (my youngest sister was born in Harbin in 1939), but those visits were rarely pleasant. Father was extremely demanding of me, his only son. While he left me to live my days in a world dominated by Mother and my two older sisters, he harshly demanded "manly" behavior of me.

My early childhood was victimized by ailments including a form of incontinence that I now realize was caused by the deep psychological pressures of my uncomfortable and unconventional family life. Still, as would most children who knew no other way of life, I was extremely proud of Father's amazing success, and even of his elegance of dress and manner. He had come a long,

long way from his humble beginnings, and I managed to bask in his ever-pulsating glow.

Years later it occurred to me that he might not have been as indifferent to us as we suspected, but could have felt a certain inferiority despite his apparent success. Not once in the seven years I attended school in Harbin did he attend a school function in which I participated and to which the parents were invited—and expected—to attend. I suspect he avoided the schools because they were known to be the places where educated people gather. But on the other hand, he rarely participated in *any* child-oriented activity. When he did take me out, on a father-son basis, it was either to the racetrack, to which he was mildly addicted, or to one of his favorite restaurants. On rare occasions, particularly on my birthday each year, he took the family to my favorite Russian restaurant so I could enjoy my favorite Russian borscht—a hearty soup consisting of meat stock, cabbage and onions colored red with beet juice and served with a thick dollop of sour cream.

Mother achieved no hint of glamour from her occasional encounters with Father. She remained a down-to-earth, practical, farm-raised woman. Her total lack of formal education in no way lessened her remarkable common-sense approach to all of life's grave and small crises. She carried on, no matter what, and in today's jargon would be called a "survivor." While the discipline Father exerted upon me seemed to spring from some basic disapproval of me as a person, or as a crude and inconsistent means of showing that he was engaged in my upbringing, Mother's roughly-administered spanking with a broomstick always seemed to have been given for a good reason: to punish unacceptable behavior I had committed. Such occasions were invariably accompanied by the same kernel of folk wisdom: "A habit formed by the age of three will continue until eighty."

Mother recognized her lot, and with her native stoicism accepted it. Her material well-being, if not her emotional needs, was somewhat protected by Father's windfalls during those years in Harbin. She accepted Father's obvious devotion to his concubine as well as his absence from our home.

She was, in all ways that matter, the center of my life, and I always sensed that I, her only son, was the center of hers in a way that went far beyond the Korean customs establishing the relationship between mother and elder son.

Regardless of Father's occasional windfalls, he was paying to run two households, so he was able to pay only half of our living expenses. Naturally, it fell to Mother to make up the difference. For ten to twelve hours a day, regardless of the extremes of the Harbin weather—long, freezing winters and short hot summers—she worked as a helper at the corner grocery store, fighting the weather every step of the way with her fragile strength. Besides this arduous daily work, she cleaned homes, took in ironing and needlework, and even chopped wood to sell to customers who hoped to ward off the chill of the winters. Because of her exposure to the weather in all its vagaries—the bitter chill of winter and the blistering heat of summer—her face was a leathery tan whose only cosmetic was work- or heat-induced sweat! I can see her now, wearing the homemade, full, sack-style black cotton trousers, common even today in mainland China, which were the most convenient type of apparel for her back-breaking labor. As time went on the joints of her fingers became swollen and deformed from severe arthritis for which she never resorted to any type of medication, bearing the pain in her indomitable way. I imagine she suffered greatly every day of her life, but we never realized it for she never complained; neither did she

27

show any hatred or animosity toward Father, at least in the presence of us children.

My oldest sister, Moon-hee, was just completing elementary school when I entered the first grade. Since Mother spent most of her waking hours supplementing our income, Moon-hee took much of the burden for my care upon her shoulders, bathing me and attending to many of my needs. In many ways, the second parent I otherwise lacked.

My second sister, Ok-bong, was a fairly aggressive tomboy type, a typical middle child. She was extremely bossy and constantly picked fights with me.

The baby, Jung-hee, came when I was seven years old. I never felt I lost any ground to her, for I was well-established in the family and, most important, I remained the only son. Jung-hee was largely raised by Moon-hee, by then a young woman in her own right.

*

That first week of August, 1945 was the beginning of an excruciating experience for me. Far from subsiding under the ministrations of the Chinese herb doctor, the pain in my gut washed over me in waves of bitter agony. I was deathly ill, and Mother was wholly at a loss for means of helping me. Close to midnight Father returned from a business trip. Immediately he realized the gravity of my condition, so he rushed into the street and flagged down another horse-drawn cab. As I was being rushed to the Harbin Railroad Hospital emergency room, I sank into a stupor, knowing nothing but the intense pain that wracked my body.

On arriving at the hospital, an orderly wheeled out a gurney and rushed me inside. A middle-age Japanese surgeon clad in a white gown joined us in the examination room. He asked a few preliminary questions, placed his hand on my belly, and said to my parents and to me, "It's a ruptured appendix." He told Mother and Father that I required immediate surgery. This was more of a shock for Mother than Father, for she had never before visited a Western-style physician, much less being suddenly confronted by the prospect of such a violent course of action to be performed on her adored son. But Father, being more worldy-wise, signed the consent and had Mother do likewise.

I was wheeled into the operating room, wide-eyed and terrorized. I was told to sit on the edge of the stainless steel operating table, with my legs hanging over the side. Telling me to bend forward, the surgeon told me he would give me an anesthesia. He drew out a long needle—the longest I had ever seen—and quickly punctured the skin at the base of my spine, pushing the needle into the lumbar nerve. The explosion of pain momentarily surpassed the agony in my gut, but I quickly realized I was able to feel less and less of my body below the chest. I was sure I was being subjected to a most bizarre form of acupuncture!

Lying flat upon the operating table, I watched the proceedings through wide, fear-filled eyes. First a gowned nurse arrived and cleaned my belly with an antiseptic solution, then efficiently draped gowns over my groin and belly. I could not make out the arrangement, and did not, of course, know enough to figure out that a small area of my abdomen remained exposed for the surgeon's scalpel.

I felt myself opening under the blade of the surgeon's scalpel, but it was not an unpleasant feeling. Just pressure enhanced by what little I could see and the great deal I was able to imagine.

Then the worst feeling I have ever experienced swept over me. The surgeon reached into my abdominal cavity to find the ruptured organ and, in so doing, pushed my coiled intestines from side to side. My insides were literally churning. The nausea was complete and well beyond any sort of control I could exert. I retched and fought for breath, and I certainly attempted to slide out from beneath the surgeon's hand.

The nausea suddenly gave way to the impulses of my restored senses of hearing and sight. I was fully aware that a great pool of pus was being drained from my innards. I even got the impression, despite the surgeon's studied taciturnity, that he was satisfied that he had gotten to me in the nick of time. The overall sensation in that cold room was positive.

The incision was closed with sutures, and a rubber tube was left protruding from my abdomen to drain the infection. In due course, I was wheeled to a sleeping room and placed in bed. I was weak, but jubilant over the loss of the excruciating pain. I learned later that only forty-five minutes passed between my arrival at the emergency room and my being wheeled out of the operating room.

At the first glimmer of dawn lighting the room where I slept, I awakened to find the pain and feverishness almost gone. Clinging to my small hand lying atop the bedcovers was Mother's gnarled, arthritic hand. All night long she had sat beside me, gently dozing as sleep overtook her. Her eyes still closed, I did not want to rouse her from her much-needed rest, but how I longed to shake her hand and express my joy at the absence of pain.

Some hours later while making his morning rounds, the surgeon who had operated on me the night before stopped at my bedside. After a perfunctory examination he grimly announced that I could not have possibly survived if my parents had waited any longer to bring me to the hospital. Then, his right index finger jabbing the air for emphasis, this taciturn Japanese surgeon lectured Mother.

"It is obvious that the herb doctor made the wrong diagnosis," he said, almost angrily. "Though the acupuncture relieved the pain, it also masked the basic problem. In addition, the hot compresses he instructed you to place on the boy's abdomen promoted the rupture of the already inflamed appendix." Concluding in a somewhat lighter tone, he said, "Dong-kyu is very lucky to be alive." His lecture finished and his mission accomplished, he turned abruptly and strode from the room.

This was my first contact with Western-style medicine. It made a deep and lasting impression upon my grateful young mind—not just because of my intense relief from the pain which had held me in its relentless grasp for what seemed an eternity—but because somehow I realized that myth and mystery had no place in treating the ill. The knowledge and skill which must have come from intense study in the field of medicine as practiced by this Japanese surgeon was indelibly imprinted upon my mind. At this great distance in time from the actual incident I cannot say that such serious thoughts were coursing through my mind in these words, but I distinctly remember that ever after I had a profound respect for the Japanese surgeon and the medicine he practiced which had saved my life.

CHAPTER THREE

One of my favorite relatives was Uncle Kil-yong, the third of Father's four younger brothers. Kil-yong had enlisted in the Japanese Army years before. He had been selected for the military police and had risen to the rank of sergeant, a sure sign of his aptitude for the work and his extreme devotion to duty. Koreans simply did not advance in the Japanese armed forces unless they were superior in every way to their Japanese counterparts. Unfortunately, Kil-yong's Japanese superiors directed him to spend a great deal of his time locating and suppressing Korean underground freedom activists.

After serving for a number of years in Osaka, Japan, Kil-yong had visited us in Harbin in 1943. As an eleven-year-old boy I felt immense pride marching along beside him through the streets of Harbin. He was resplendent in his immaculate military uniform, which in my young eyes seemed to sparkle and glow in any kind of light. I was even more intrigued with the long, noncommissioned officer's sword hanging from his sturdy leather military belt. As it occasionally clanked and glittered, I not only felt safe and secure but superior to the other Korean boys I knew. But most of all I was proud to see all the Japanese soldiers we encountered saluting him as we passed. None realized that he was a lowly Korean, all of whom were subordinated to their Japanese conquerors.

Kil-yong's trip to Harbin arose from his growing unhappiness with his job in the Japanese military police. The visit was an opportunity to get away from the work for awhile, but mainly he wanted to discuss his options with father. He had not been aware of our family's

33

circumstances prior to his visit, so perhaps he was also motivated by a sense of loyalty and a desire to be of help. He then was able to arrange a transfer, undoubtedly with Father's assistance, to the Harbin Police Department with the rank of lieutenant. Whatever Uncle Kil-yong's motivations, I knew him as a kind and generous man. He became a substitute father for me and my sisters.

Now, on August 8, 1945, just four days after my surgery, I worried that Uncle Kil-yong had not appeared at the lunch hour. All through the afternoon I fretted over his absence, but at dinnertime in he walked, bearing a broiled chicken in borscht he had purchased at my favorite Russian restaurant. Good food of any sort was difficult to obtain at the time, for the war was going badly for the Japanese. Meat, sugar, and even rice were rationed. I ate so much of the borscht that I upset my stomach, so Kil-yong suggested we take a walk in the garden behind the hospital building. It was difficult for me to walk, but I was glad to get out of bed and make an effort to return my body to its normal vitality.

We were leisurely strolling through the garden when the quiet of the evening was pierced by the long, loud wail of an air-raid siren. Uncle laughed when I hid under a bush. Minutes passed, then large planes flew into sight overhead. Never before had I seen airplanes, and was doubly surprised to learn from Uncle that these were Russian aircraft. I was shocked to learn that the Soviet Union had declared war on Japan that very day.

Three days later, on August 11, all the Japanese physicians and nurses disappeared from the hospital. This abruptly terminated my convalescence in the Railroad Hospital, for there was no one to care for me or even the more seriously ill patients. Then, just four days after that, on August 15, 1945, the Pacific War was ended with Japan's unconditional surrender.

The day after the disappearance of the Japanese hospital staff, my parents arrived to take me home. Unfortunately, my incision had not yet healed, and the rubber tube the surgeon had put in to drain my abdominal cavity was still in place. It was constantly dripping a foul-smelling fluid. In the days that followed, Mother kept the incision clean with an antiseptic and alcohol. When I had to walk, I was bent over like an old grandfather because of the pain. It would be almost a year before I could straighten up.

*

Within a few days of my return to Mother's care, several large ships flying Russian flags docked at Harbin. Soon, many trucks filled with Russian soldiers began streaming through the city streets. The Red Army met little opposition when they invaded Manchuria, and there was no fighting at all around the Harbin area.

Though we were Koreans and a subject people of the Japanese, my family felt genuine fear from possible retaliation from the Manchurian people, who had been dismally treated by their Japanese overlords. During the final war years, there had been no end of discrimination against them in such vital areas as the availability of well-paying jobs and food rationing; as the food supplies available to civilians diminished, there was not always enough to go around to the Manchurians. As soon as the Japanese civil and military authorities evacuated the city, the Manchurians began taking the law into their own hands, as did numerous Korean residents. The Russians did not immediately clamp down on the near-anarchic conditions, possibly because a good deal of "housecleaning" was being done without risk to themselves. Since both Father and Uncle Kil-yong had worked for the Japanese, both felt the need to avoid

Donald Chung, M.D.

native Manchurians, Korean residents of Harbin and the new Soviet occupiers. They went into hiding at the home of Father's concubine.

*

Late one night about a week after I left the Railroad Hospital, I was pulled from my sleep by an insistent knocking at the door of our small four-room home. Mother was up in a flash, whispering orders that we four children burrow into our covers and remain still and quiet.

I was so overcome with curiosity and fear of the unknown, that I peeked out from beneath my blanket.

There, in the doorway, was a dirty, mean-looking Russian soldier, about fifty years old. He was pointing his long rifle at Mother's stomach, saying things neither Mother nor I could possibly understand. A moment later, two younger soldiers burst through the doorway, covering the entire living room with their machine guns. As the older man held Mother at gunpoint, the two younger men searched every corner of the single-story Russian-style house—living room, kitchen and the two bedrooms—until they came upon my older sister, Moon-hee, in the corner bedroom. It was quite evident that she was the object of the menacing intrusion. I vaguely recalled having seen these three soldiers loitering in the street during the day before their break-in. They must have seen Moon-hee and decided to come for her in the night.

Moon-hee was nineteen years old at the time. She had always been the brightest student in her classes, and was known as the sweetest girl in the complex of Russian-style houses and apartments that was our neighborhood. She was like a second mother to me; she had taken me to school every morning when I was in first grade, and had given me hot tub baths until I

36

was ten years old. She had been my tutor all the way through elementary school. She cheerfully ran the family whenever Mother was working away from the house.

I was too young and naive to know exactly what these strange, brutal men were doing, but I watched horrified as they beat and attacked Moon-hee, one after the other. I knew they were hurting my sister because of her moans and tearful cries of anguish. Were they going to kill her? One of the men crouched over her on her bed, ripped off her nightdress, and began moving his body back and forth on top of her, emitting sharp cries as though something might be hurting him. I watched this going on, transfixed, too shocked and frightened to cry out and too terrorized to act on my strong impulse to throw off my covers and attack the man with my fists. As he continued the strange motions, the others stood, glaring down at my sister and muttering in what I assumed to be Russian to the man on top of Moon-hee. Suddenly, the man attacking my sister emitted a strange sound between a howl and a grunt and thrust himself upward, handling my sister roughly, pinning her down so the other men could take their turns. The same thing went on twice more, the same motions, the same odd sort of grunts and low howls, thrusting of their body back and forth, viciously and frantically at times, until they, too, seemed to all at once collapse and draw back. All the while they were emitting a sort of screech.

As if nothing had happened, as though they had just completed a social call, the three men left the house. Only at some later date was I to realize that I had looked on at the callous, inhuman rape of my beloved sister.

Quickly Mother slammed the door shut behind them and collapsed in tears and whimpers. I was overjoyed to see that Moon-hee was not dead, though she was incapable of doing more than sob. Her eyes would remain red and swollen from continuous crying for many days, and she repeated over and over that she did not want to live any longer. The family was utterly devastated.

*

A few days later, still haunted by the shock and fear of the late-night intrusion into our home by the Russian ruffians who assaulted Moon-hee, we were visited by a tall, tough-looking Asian man wearing dark glasses. He had come, he said, to speak with Mother.

"I am a member of the Liberation Army of Korean Independence Fighters," he announced. "I work at the Russian Army Commandant's headquarters. Your husband, Chung Bong-chun, is wanted at headquarters as a collaborator because he was a clerk in the district attorney's office working for the Japanese. The police will be coming any time now to take him away. You should know that in many cases such as this the guilty culprit is sent to Siberia." He paused momentarily, letting the impact of his statement sink in, completely terrorizing Mother and the rest of us who had crowded around her to find out what this stranger wanted.

Then, with a condescending tilt of his head, he added, "It is possible for me to get his name removed from the list."

Hearing the man speak, Mother became increasingly pallid with new fear. Despite all the years of neglect and mental abuse at Father's hand, she pleaded with the man, "Please, sir, do what you can to spare my husband."

His response came swiftly. To insure his help, the man demanded that Moon-hee spend the night with him.

It seemed to us that Mother practically disintegrated as we watched helplessly as she was faced with the worst dilemma of her life. Although she had no

38

assurance of the truth of what the man had told her, either about the danger which faced her husband or of his ability to save him, she knew she had to choose between the husband who openly disavowed her or another violation of her beloved elder daughter.

But familial attachments run deeply in the beings of people like my mother, people whose very lives have always been decided by others, whose ways follow the patterns set by ancestors in ages past, whose meekness and compliance come as easily as breathing. Whose loyalty is inviolable. The choice was made as Mother's sad, fear-filled eyes motioned to Moon-hee to accompany the man and do his bidding.

All hope seemed drained from us as we were caught up in new waves of revulsion and fright. What was really happening to Moon-hee? Would she be returned to us or would she, like so many others caught up in wars and revolutions, disappear from the very ground she walked on. The hours dragged by, with few words spoken, our gloom increasing as the daylight faded and night came on. Did we eat? Did we sleep? Such memories have long since faded, but somehow we managed to survive the seemingly endless night.

Early the next morning a taxi stopped in front of our house and an emotionless Moon-hee emerged from it. Her spirit had died the night she was assaulted by the Russians so this time it appeared as though she was scarcely aware of what happened. Joyfully we greeted her but were dismayed by her utter insensibility. As she sought solace in seclusion, we granted her this trifling boon, hoping that in time the old Moon-hee would return to us.

Letting no time elapse, however, Mother roused her long enough to shave Moon-hee's scalp and gave her a shapeless uniform commonly worn by boys. Thereafter, for a long time, Moon-hee seemed safe in her new attire.

*

Late one night in early September Father came to the house carrying a small bag with just a few personal essentials.

"I am leaving Harbin tonight with Kil-yong." he said. "It is our hope and plan to reach Seoul," he continued. "From there I will contact you." He spoke these last words directly to mother, and it could have been my youthful fancy, but I thought I sensed a glimmer of compassion in his eyes for this good woman who had so courageously borne his children and raised them without his help.

There was no doubting, though, the presence of tears glistening in his eyes as he fondly embraced me and whispered "Good-bye" in my ear.

Several days later, a close family friend introduced Mother to a man claiming to be an interpreter working for the Red Army. The stranger told Mother that he was arranging for a train to carry people back to Korea. Mother instantly paid the man the substantial sum of money he was asking. He told her to pack right away and prepare to leave at a moment's notice.

Early the next afternoon Mother called for a taxi. She wanted to take a final tour of the city in which we had lived for the past eleven years. Mother sat in front with six-year-old Jung-hee, the only one of us born in Harbin. I sat in back with Moon-hee and Ok-bong. Along with Jung-hee, I had no recollection of having lived anywhere except Harbin. It was as much my city as it was hers.

After passing through the southwest section of the city, where most of the Korean immigrants lived, the taxi slowly climbed a steep hill, right in the center of Harbin, where stood the tallest buildings. We all got out of the taxi at the crest of the hill and gazed down for the last time on all the various sections of the city to which we had come in search of a better life. In a way, we had found it, but it was now fast slipping beyond our grasp and we were anxious to leave in an instant.

As the taxi passed the racetrack on the outskirts of the city, I vividly recalled the Sunday afternoon when Father had taken me to the races. Father was normally quite reserved, but he always became highly emotional at the races. As the horses neared the finish line, he jumped up and down, shouting at the top of his voice. He lost every race, but kept betting. By the time the last race ended, he had even wagered and lost the bus fare he had tucked away in an inner pocket of his stylish Western-style suit. I recall how sad and drained Father's face appeared during our three-hour walk from the track to Mother's house.

So on this, our last tour of Harbin, I shared the memory with Mother and my sisters. "The moon was full and bright in the dark summer sky," I began my recollection. "We were both tired and hungry. We barely spoke to each other, our intimate thoughts our own guarded secrets. I believe that was when Father decided to quit going to the races." All of us, including the taxi driver—and to our delight even Moon-hee laughed until our bellies ached.

We drove into the beautifully-built historical Russian section of Harbin and stopped at last by the Sungari River. As my small family stood on the river bank, the rays of the setting sun were reflected in a reddish-golden aura upon the water. Just as surely as the sun was dipping into the western horizon, I knew my destiny lay to the south—my homeland of Korea. Silence engulfed us, each lost in shared solitude and memories.

In that single instant all our summers came rushing in on me. We had watched boat races on this river or caught fish for sport as well as food. On a few

41

occasions, Father had taken us out for an evening cruise. Russian bandsmen from the old pre-Japanese invasion days, dressed in dark black uniforms resplendent with red stripes, gold braid, brass buttons and atop their heads jaunty black Russian-style caps, stood on the bank and played lovely music at each departure and return of the cruise ships. The twanging, tinkling music of the Russian steppes repeated in my memory just as it had in those now far-off days. I recalled the winters when I had enjoyed sledding down the river's long banks. Always a bit daring in this escapade, I wound up with bruises and scraped knees. It was here I had witnessed exciting ice festivals and ice-skating races on the sparkling frozen river.

For me, this sentimental tour of the city ended in the best possible way. We stopped off at the Russian restaurant at which we had always celebrated my birthdays. There, for the last time, I was treated to my borscht.

It was well after sunset when we returned home, emotionally wrung-out, sorry to have seen the last of this pleasant city but none-the-less eager to return to our native Korea. We knew that we would each be able to take only a few possessions on what we expected to be a hazardous journey, and that saddened us all the more, for most of what we would be leaving behind had been earned from Mother's incessant, difficult labors.

*

A few evenings after our sentimental journey through Harbin, Mother received word from the Red Army interpreter that we were to come immediately to the city railroad station.

It was hot and humid. The sky appeared to be a dark gray blanket through which peeped no stars and no moon. We left the house quietly, not looking back, each carrying as unobtrusively as possible the small bundle of possessions we had made up days earlier. Fearful of being stopped by Red Army patrols, we fairly crept along in painful silence through the heavy darkness keeping to the shadows. After walking for several seemingly interminable blocks Mother stopped a black car whose driver turned out to be a local Russian. He drove us directly to the station.

On foot again, we struggled through the enormous crowd of refugees that had been gathering for some hours. After some time, pushing and shoving her way through the throng, Mother located the interpreter. Just as the train began to get up steam and began slowly creaking along the tracks, the man assigned us to an already-overcrowded freight car. As we struggled aboard, I saw other frantic refugees clambering up the sides of the cars to the roof, perching perilously like birds of passage to every inch of space. With a shriek of the whistle, the locomotive began to increase its steam and slowly pull the train from the station into the now darkened city. Huddled all around us, compacted together alike bundles of straw, were people like ourselves, families fleeing the invading Red Army, hoping to find peace and security in our mutual homeland, Korea.

The journey was a chaotic, troubling adventure, far different from a trip I had taken to visit relatives in Korea two years earlier. Then, as I traveled with a schoolmate whose family was also from the vicinity of Chu-ul, the train had passed swiftly and efficiently from the Manchurian plain to the Korean highlands. But now there were no orderly comings and goings of trains in this immediate postwar period; schedules were nonexistent and encounters between trains were totally

43

unpredictable. Our train was shunted off the main line at many stations so that others could pass in the opposite direction or, as far as we knew until it was safe to continue. Mostly, we stopped for Red Army troop trains, which had absolute right of way. Russian soldiers, all armed to the teeth, frequently stopped our train in order to conduct searches and inspect passengers and their belongings. Each such inspection, particularly at night, brought goosebumps to my skin. I was terrified of the Russian soldiers, certain they would again attack my sister. However, they never bothered with any of us.

Though it was less than four hundred miles from Harbin to the Korean frontier, it took eight days for the overcrowded train to reach the Tumen River and enter Korean territory. At this point, we entered the mountainous Taebek Plateau. Once, the grade was so steep that the train's huge steel wheels spun on the track. All the passengers were ordered to get out and walk up the slope. As we walked, hundreds of jubilant Korean voices broke into traditional Korean folk songs. I was thrilled to the core of my being, for the Korean language and nearly all aspects of our unique Korean culture had been ruthlessly suppressed by our former Japanese overlords. After a lifetime of speaking only Japanese outside my home, here I was, back in my own homeland, singing my own songs in my own language. The cool, fresh air of our native highlands invigorated us during the long, slow walk up the hill beside the slow train.

From the top of the slope onward, the train traveled quickly and with few forced stops. Finally, ten days after leaving Harbin, my small family arrived at our destination, the town of Chu-ul, in northeastern Korea.

We were home.

CHAPTER FOUR

Mother's mother still lived in Taehyang, the small farming village about four miles southwest of Chu-ul in which I had been born thirteen years before. After alighting from the refugee train at Chu-ul, Mother, Moon-hee, Ok-bong, Jung-hee and I picked up our meager belongings and started walking to my grandparents' farm. On the way, we passed the mountainside cemetery where our ancestors were buried, which signified that we were home, at least in spirit. During the walk, Mother took particular delight in openly speaking to us aloud, in our Korean mother tongue. This was the first time she could recall speaking thusly in the village of her birth.

We arrived unannounced at my grandparents' home in the late evening, right at dinnertime. Grandmother burst into tears as she welcomed us. Mother's eldest brother, Kim Dong-sik and his family, who lived with Grandmother, gave up their dinner for us and prepared a new meal for themselves. We were thus woven directly into the fabric of the family. We were all exhausted from the arduous journey, and it had been ten days since we had tasted hot food, so the hot steamed rice and spicey soybean-paste soup were perfect restoratives.

Beginning the very next day, I encountered many of the relatives I had not met during my visit two years before. I had heard of many of these people over the years, but I never imagined that I would be living among them. The reality of an extended family was unique in my life, and took some adjustment on my part as I learned the dynamics of various relationships between and within generations. As I had been all my life, I was treated as a jewel by my relatives, for I was still the only boy of my

45

generation. Such treatment certainly eased the shock of transition. I also began learning Korean customs which had either been proscribed by the Japanese or impractical to follow in Harbin. I was "home", but I wasn't *at* home.

Within a week of our arrival, I was enrolled in the local junior high school, picking up where I had been forced to leave off because of appendicitis and the fortunes of war in Harbin. There, for the first time in my life, I added to my store of spoken Korean by learning the unique Korean *han-geul* alphabet. I was already the most-educated man in the history of my family. The only member of my family with more education was my second sister, Ok-bong, who had completed junior high school in Harbin. I was confirmed in my early surmise that I had no particular aptitude for scholarship.

Father and Uncle Kil-yong appeared within a month of our arrival. They told us that they had first fled to Seoul, as planned, but neither could find work there, so they had come home. Within days, Father and Mother decided to purchase an old house in the middle of Chu-ul and also rent a small stall in the town's open market, where they would peddle used clothing.

*

Soon after we moved, life began taking on a comprehensible rhythm far different from what I had known as a boy growing up in a large, cosmopolitan city in a foreign land. I was soon able to make friends among my peers, which was not entirely positive in that I and they were of an age when exploring one's adult prerogatives often led to clashes with adult authorities less understanding than we about the rigors of growing up.

One of my great advantages lay in the fact that Ok-bong found work at the local movie theater as a ticket-taker. I was thus able to wheedle my way into the theater without paying—a double bonus in that schoolboys were not allowed to go to the movies on weekdays. At other times, I joined my friends when they sneaked into the theater by way of a window high up on the theater's outside wall. We had to form human ladders and then pull the low men up behind us. This was fairly typical of our teenage pranks. I also had my first brief encounter with smoking, another form of teen rebellion even in semi-rural Korea.

On the other hand, several of my new "provincial" friends had unusual and unexpected tastes. Several had nurtured an appreciation of western classical music. I vividly recall sitting among them with my eyes closed, hearing forms of music I came to dearly love. Later, we discussed and interpreted this wonderful music. Our more wholesome activities included hiking in the mountains, fishing in nearby mountain streams and cooking our catches over open fires as we discussed the newfound and startling aspects of adult life, which daily confronted us or hovered just beyond our grasp—sex, politics, earning a living, future plans. For me, this was the golden age between the naivete of childhood and the cold realities of adulthood.

One of the joys of Chul-ul was its famous and popular hot springs, which were visited by people from throughout Korea whose afflictions might be remedied in the warm, sulfurous water. Often, when there was nothing we had to do, my new friends and I walked the ten miles into the mountains northwest of town to reach the main springs, which were set in a beautiful spot against the mountainous backdrop that dominated all vistas in the region. The area around the farthest springs was built up with gorgeous Russian-style summer homes and bathhouses. I was told that the Russians believed strongly in the medicinal powers of the hot

47

springs, so had been numerous and prominent among visitors to the area. My first such walk through this area soon after our move to Chu-ul took my breath away, for the fall season had brought the leaves to spectacular shades of yellow-gold and rust-red; I had never seen anything to match this awesome tunnel of living color set against a sparkling blue sky. Suddenly, the stark man-made plains city in which I had been raised seemed poor in comparison. Something deep within me resonated to the sights and sounds here; I felt truly at home.

*

It was fortunate that we had the hot springs nearby, for I had picked up a case of scabies on my hand during our train journey from Harbin. Until I could get the treatment, Mother had me sleeping with thick socks on my hands to prevent me from scratching, thus spreading the disease. The sulfurous water cleared up the parasitic skin condition and provided me with an excuse to visit the wondrously beautiful area several times a week over a period of weeks.

There was a severe shortage of food at this time, and we could only afford to eat rice once a day. Our country relatives helped us with offerings of beans and potatoes. We even ate the dried residue of yellow beans after the oil had been pressed out. Though such food was thought to be fit only as animal fodder, it had become a staple in the area even before the end of the war.

Our house was a single-story L-shaped thatch-roofed structure built chiefly of wood and clay. It was the simplest form of Korean house and contained a living/sleeping room, another sleeping room, and a kitchen. The toilet was set apart from the living area.

We did not have enough coal during our first winter in Chu-ul to keep the house warm, so we often wore several layers of clothing when we slept, all crowded into the two sleeping rooms atop our cold *on-dol*, the unique Korean raised floors with heat-carrying flues beneath.

Many snowy evenings Mother and Father returned from the open market, their cheeks red and fingers blue from the cold. On many such evenings, they reported that they had not made a single sale that day.

Despite such hardships as enduring the bitter cold and the lack of funds to keep the family in enough food and provide other small comforts, I saw joy etched among the increasing number of lines in Mother's face. For the first time in eleven years the family was once again together under the same roof. After all the years of emotional pain and back-breaking labors, Mother's husband had returned home. It was a difficult lesson to learn, and how much of it I took to heart at the time I cannot say at this late date. But as the years went by and as I, myself, became inured to poverty, the lesson came home to me, and I learned that when the spirit blooms, even abject poverty, illness, broken dreams, or political repression lose some of their power to stifle the individual's enthusiasm for life. For in that humble little home where family ties were the greatest possession in the whole world, I saw my mother's spirit bloom in Father's presence in our midst.

*

This period was relatively unmarred by the grave political happenings following hard upon the end of World War II.

After years of watching idly as the Western powers reduced the Empire of Japan to a burned-out shell, the Red Army had swept into Manchuria and driven on into Korea as the war was winding down. By prior agreement with the Western Allies, the Red Army accepted the surrender of Japanese armed forces in northern Korea, above the 38th Parallel. Japanese forces south of the arbitrarily-drawn line surrendered to the United States Army. Following the surrenders, both the Red Army and the United States Army stayed on in their respective sectors as occupiers.

When the Red Army marched into northern Korea, it was accompanied by a cadre of Korean Communists. Under the guns of the Soviet troops, a Communist-controlled provisional government was quickly established by the simple means of placing Korean communists in key positions of authority. The sealing of the 38th Parallel began almost immediately.

While the Soviet-backed Korean Communists established their power in the north, many political factions surfaced in the American-occupied southern zone. Unfortunately, the American military commander initially suppressed all forms of political expression, and many southerners who were anxious for political freedom were imprisoned.

In time, to counter the Communist-dominated government in the north, the American military authorities developed a policy which encouraged and condoned the ruthless tactics of the far-right Korean political factions. The most-popular moderate and liberal leaders were brutally assaulted and sometimes murdered by strong-arm squads controlled by the right-wing parties.

Thus, the brutal thirty-six-year colonial repression at the hands of the Japanese was being replaced in both parts of Korea by virtual dictatorships supported by the arms and might of outside forces—the United States and the Soviet Union.

We were too far removed geographically from the centers of the emerging conflict to be troubled or much affected by the political events transforming our nation. But unknown to us, we were soon to be in the eye of a renewed domestic conflict.

What we thought to be our newfound idyllic family life ended abruptly one freezing cold afternoon in January of 1946. While our parents were at work at the marketplace tending their used-clothing stall, my sisters and I remained at home on this particular day. Suddenly there came a knock on the door and upon opening it, we were shocked at the strange apparition standing there before us. Could this be another refugee from Harbin? I wondered, for the figure was dishevelled beyond recognition, covered with ragged dirty clothing, standing in worn-out shoes caked in filth, the head and face wrapped completely in a soiled and tattered blanket to fend off the freezing moisture in the air. As the blanket was lifted slightly so the person could speak, we saw the vaporous breath turn to ice as the creature panted. Mystified, we waited for the stranger's face to be bared.

It was Yim Ok-wha, Father's concubine!

Despite our dislike of her, we invited her in. Ok-Bong bundled up as best she could and ran to fetch Father while the rest of us tried to make Ok-wha comfortable and warm with hot tea.

Soon Father arrived, at which time Ok-wha opened a shabby piece of luggage she was carrying and distributed gifts to each of us, a custom she had followed regularly while in Harbin. My gift was a pair of new white rubber shoes.

As Ok-wha hungrily sipped her tea, she began to tell us her story. It seems she had left Harbin to return to her hometown of Kunsan on the southern tip of the Korean Peninsula. She stayed there only a few months because, she stated "I decided to come to Chu-ul to be near your father." Little by little the story of her hardships emerged.

51

"It took me two weeks to cross South Korea by train, but the rail line ended many miles from the 38th Parallel. When I learned the frontier between the south and north zones was sealed, I set out across it on foot."

Because of her utter exhaustion, there were many pauses in the telling, but we sat quietly, waiting for each new episode to unfold.

"In many places the border is a wasteland and it is relatively easy to evade armed security patrols. Occasionally meeting up with other refugees, I learned that South Korean soldiers would shoot anyone going north, and that the Russians and North Koreans would shoot anyone at all. Fortunately, I never saw any soldiers."

She had struggled on foot across frozen mountain trails. Many times she almost gave up, but spurred on by her will she somehow managed to keep going. Often she was delirious from the extreme cold, sheer exhaustion, and hunger.

"When I spotted a band of refugees traveling my way, we joined up to share whatever information we had, but mostly so that when night came on, we could huddle together, sharing our bodies' warmth with each other, for we had all seen the frozen bodies of people like so many discarded signposts along the way and didn't want to join their number."

Gratefully accepting more hot tea and seeming to be a bit more comfortable, she told us she finally crossed the frontier.

"After that, knowing I was now safely in the north, I begged rides in anything from trucks to farm carts. Always the cold was my worst enemy. To reach my goal hastened me on. I was always fortunate to find food enough to keep me alive and a safe place to sleep."

I listened to this extraordinary revelation with mixed feelings. We children hated Yim Ok-wha. Her very existence was an affront to our belief of how family life should be conducted. She had deprived us of our father. Ok-bong, who was more outspoken than the rest of us, was known to have gone to her house in Harbin on several occasions to loudly berate her for stealing our father. Still, her tale was so touching that we were all on the verge of tears.

Of course we took her in, but it wasn't long before Ok-Wha learned that her longed-for goal was a mirage. Only a few days later our visitor was gone. I learned about it when I returned home from school. She had left a note on her pillow. It stated simply, "I give up. I return your father to you."

Father, possibly the only one who could explain her decision, never mentioned what led to her departure. However, several concomitant events revealed what might have had something to do with it. At just about this time, the Communist Women's League was formed. One of its first tasks was the "Clean-up Movement of All Concubines." And it was at this time that we learned that Father had met a new woman shortly after he returned to Chu-ul from Seoul. The new woman was married, but had no children. Her husband abandoned her when he found out that she was involved with Father. With all of these circumstances coming at the same time, Father became increasingly open about his new relationship outside the family. Once again, as before, he hardly spent any of his nights at home with us.

So emotionally we were thrust back into the Harbin dilemma, but with our increasing maturity, my sisters and I were now more able to express among ourselves our contempt for him.

*

Donald Chung, M.D.

The early spring of 1946 saw the beginnings of a land-reform program in North Korea. Since seventy-four percent of the North's population was engaged in agricultural activities at the time, this was seen as an important step by the new government, which was based in Pyongyang.

Most northern farmers were just tenant farmers with no land of their own, while others either owned small plots or combined tenant tracts with their own in order to eke out a living.

In March, 1946, the newly-created Peasant Federation demanded agricultural reform and proclaimed an Ordinance on Land Reform. All plots of ten acres or more that had been formerly possessed by "Japanese imperialists, national traitors, Korean landlords and churches" were confiscated without compensation and distributed to landless peasants or peasants owning plots smaller than ten acres.

I was drawn into the land reform program with my eighth-grade classmates when we were called on to help officials charged with redistributing the land around Chu-ul. One of my classmates, a middle-aged farmer, and I walked for two hours into the mountains and took up our assigned station at a small farmhouse. We used the simple mathematics we had learned in school to divide the available farmland according to the number of peasants in each farm family.

As Communist control reached into all levels of northern society, a number of high school students from Chu-ul were selected to receive special political indoctrination in the Soviet Union. Only students from the farm or labor classes qualified; I was not eligible because Father and Mother had become small-time entrepreneurs. When these students returned from their courses, they quickly achieved positions of leadership in the student body. They conducted lectures on the superiority of Russian industry and explained how Soviet society continued to improve under Communist rule.

The secret police force was well established in North Korea—as we now referred to our truncated nation—by mid-1946. The local secret police headquarters was housed in the former Japanese police station in Chu-ul. A crackdown against anti-Communist activities was begun and, in time, it was to limit many of the personal freedoms we had always taken for granted.

Uncle Kil-yong had acquired a small radio. Each night, he lay beneath a thick blanket which he hoped would hide the radio and muffle the sound of the nightly news from Seoul.

One night, a secret policeman broke into the house and confronted Kil-yong. "As I stood outside," the intruder declared, "I heard you listening to the South Korean news for the past half-hour." The policeman was an old family friend who knew that Kil-yong had served in the Japanese Army and as a policeman in Harbin. Kil-yong was unable to suppress his rage at this former friend's betrayal and threatened him with a kitchen knife. The man drew a gun, handcuffed Kil-yong and pushed him off into the night toward the police station.

A week after his arrest, Kil-yong stood trial in a People's Court. We arrived as the prosecutor was charging that Kil-yong had collaborated with the Japanese against the Korean people, had listened to proscribed broadcasts from South Korea, and had threatened the life of a police officer with a deadly weapon.

Kil-yong stood alone. There was no protest, and no attorney for the defense. A jury of farmers and laborers heard the prosecutor's case and immediately sentenced Kil-yong to five years at hard labor. A few days later, my favorite uncle was sent to work in a coal mine in the northern part of our own North Hamgyong

Donald Chung, M.D.

Province. The family was deeply shocked, but there was no authority to which we could appeal for justice in Kilyong's behalf. He was simply gone.

CHAPTER FIVE

One day in June, 1946, there appeared on the bulletin board at Chu-ul Junior High School a notice explaining that a new medical-technical school was to be opened in September in nearby Chongjin, the capital of North Hamgyong Province. The objective of the school was to provide a three-year course aimed at producing independent medical practitioners who could provide medical care in areas where there were too few or no fully-qualified physicians. The notice stated that a recruiting drive for the new school's first class was underway.

I had come away from the crucial experience of my appendectomy with a deep admiration for the Japanese surgeon who had relieved that dreadful pain and, in all probability, had saved my life. I even harbored dreams of one day becoming a Western-type doctor myself, though I knew the remoteness of that dream because I considered myself a mediocre student and because Western-style medical training was virtually inaccessible to someone of my background. So it was with mounting excitement that I stood reading the news of the opening of the medical-technical school only twenty miles—merely an hour's ride by train—from my home. The vague dream suddenly crystalized and came within my grasp.

That evening at dinner, I made my formal announcement, "I want to be a Western-style doctor." I explained about the notice at school and, to my delight, everyone was thrilled with the idea and I received warm, positive encouragement.

I applied the very next day to take the tests required by the new school. My application was approved

57

within a matter of days, and a date was set for my interview and written examination. I never found out why I was given the opportunity, nor even what criteria were used in selecting from among what must have been a great many applicants. Still, the acceptance of my initial application was but one small step on the way to fulfilling my dream. I often wonder if I would have gone beyond even this small step had I known the truly monumental hurdles that lay before me.

*

I left Chu-ul a day early on my first trip to the area's largest city. I had barely glimpsed Chongjin as the freight car bearing us from Harbin rumbled through it. All our sights had been set on Chu-ul and we had little interest in any points in-between.

Mother packed steamed rice and dried fish for my lunch and accompanied me to the bus station. Though the cord that bound us would never be truly severed, still it was beginning to lengthen a bit. As I was, for the first time, venturing into the world beyond our family circle, Mother would remain bound in place, watching ever through the distance that separated us in body, though never in spirit.

Just as I stepped forward to board the rickety vehicle, Mother encircled me in her arms and for a moment or two held me close. Then, with a look born of her limitless love, she said,"My son, just be yourself and you will pass the examination. Have no fear."

Confidently then, encouraged by both her embrace and her words, I stepped up into the bus, took a seat in the rear, and kept my eyes on Mother—my steadfast anchor and trustworthy compass—as the bus chugged on its way. I watched her standing motionless beside the roadway for a long distance, until a curve in the road hid her from my view.

Because of the severe post-war gasoline shortage, the buses of the period ran on power generated by wood fuel. Each bus had a huge cast-iron boiler built in the back of the passenger compartment, and steam was generated by burning chopped wood to boil water.

The narrow, unimproved roadway wound along mountainsides overlooking steep, narrow valleys. At times, the wheezing bus barely crawled up a steep incline, but it kept puttering along, passing villages, small towns and farm plots green with growing produce. Finally, we reached the broad, endless streets of Chongjin in midafternoon. Obeying Mother's strict orders, I went straight to the house of Mother's sister, where I would spend the night.

I rose early the next morning, excited and unsure of myself, and walked to the school. The city of Chongjin sprawled along the seashore. Tall chimneys belching smoke into the morning sky marked the complex of great steel mills at the southern end of the city, while the largest port complex in North Korea dominated the northern end of the sprawl.

The medical-technical school was isolated in the middle of large open fields about five miles west of the city's downtown area. The white brick building had been a Red Cross hospital during the Japanese rule. The ground floor was divided into a working out-patient clinic, pharmacy, lab and operating rooms, while the second floor accommodated a hundred beds for in-patients. Less than half the facilities were being used because of a severe nationwide shortage of qualified physicians. All of the Japanese doctors who had lived in North Korea had fled at the end of the war, and there had simply not been enough native Koreans trained during the thirty-six-year Japanese occupation. The newly-founded medical-technical school had its office and several classrooms in a wooden annex next to the main building.

I did not like what I saw when I pushed open the door to the auditorium, in which the written test was to be administered. There were two hundred applicants in the room, all tensely waiting to compete for the sixty available slots. I saw that some of the young men and women in the large room were old enough to have been college graduates. In fact, everyone seemed to be older than me, even a classmate from Chu-ul Junior High School, who was indeed several years older than I was. His name was Kim Ki-jin, a tall, slender son of the herb doctor who served as the junior high school doctor.

It was obvious that a great many people farther advanced than me shared my feelings about the medical profession. That so many were willing to enter it at any level, even reverting to the role of high-school-level students in order to realize their dreams, did not auger well for me. The whole atmosphere made me nervous. I was certain that I did not have much of a chance.

I felt good about the written test, which consisted mainly of subjects I had been studying in junior high school. Though I did not consider myself a high achiever—I was lazy-minded—I was one of the better students in my class. The interview session was comprehensive, but I somehow managed to maintain a calm exterior throughout, and I was certain that my single-minded determination and dedication made a good impression with the panel of interviewers. I returned to my aunt's home exhausted but confident in my showing.

There followed three weeks of uncertainty and suspense. How I got through those days I no longer remember, but I do know I put on a brave face and carried on my daily duties with a calm exterior but a seething sense of urgency inside. At the end of that time I received the notification at home that I was to be admitted to the school in September, at the start of the new semester. Also to be admitted was Kim Ki-jin, my classmate in Chu-ul.

Our home was now filled with happiness and joy, mingled with wonder at what would happen next. But it was Mother's pride that outshown even my own sense of accomplishment. Though the years have been kind in bestowing upon me recognition, nothing compares to the feelings of intense self-esteem her reaction caused in me.

Looking at me with a devotion especially reserved for the first-born son, her simple undramatic words belied her inner feelings. "Son, you will be the first in the history of our family to become a doctor. I know that you will be a 'big man'." This last phrase was a colloquial one meaning someone of importance and eminence.

*

Classes started on September 1, 1946. My freshman class was made up of sixty students. On that first day, we assembled in the auditorium so the dean could introduce us to all the teachers. We students found ourselves in the hands of some of the most prestigious names in medicine in our nation. Most of the faculty members were graduates of Kyongsong Imperial University School of Medicine or Seoul's Severence Medical School, which had been established during the Japanese occupation. Some of the professors were refugees from Manchuria, like me. Many faculty members had undertaken post-graduate work or conducted research in Japan or Germany.

Our textbooks were written in Japanese or German, and, right from the start, lectures were delivered in Japanese and German, with some limited English medical jargon thrown in.

Donald Chung, M.D.

One teacher, Father Fisher, was a Catholic missionary priest from Germany. We called him *"Uh Shinbu,"* which means "Father Fish" in Korean. He was over six feet tall and weighed more than two hundred and fifty pounds. He always wore gold rimless spectacles. He taught many of the subjects of our non-medical school curriculum—German, Latin, music and others. Fortunately, Uh Shinbu spoke Korean with native fluency—much better than I, whose first language was Japanese and who had been speaking Korean outside the home for hardly more than a year. In Uh Shinbu's music theory class, we all sang songs like *The Blue Danube* and *The Lorelei* while the priest accompanied us on the organ and led with his fine tenor voice. In comparison to the medical classes, which tended to be ponderous, Uh Shinbu's music classes were great fun.

*

I had decided to commute to Chongjin because I did not feel ready to live away from home. This decision turned out to be especially hard on Mother, who was up each morning at four o'clock to prepare my breakfast and lunch and see that I was on my way to catch the five o'clock train to Chongjin. There were many other students on hand to catch the same train each morning, but nearly all of them alighted at Kyongsong or Nanam; only a very few of us rode all the way into the big city. Though it was something like twenty miles from Chu-ul to Chongjin, the ride took an hour because the ancient steam locomotives could barely wheeze over the high coastal mountains from town to town. Once at the railroad station, I still faced a forty-five minute walk to school, leaving me about thirty minutes before classes began.

I was just getting on toward my fifteenth birthday, and it was on the long train rides that I began to feel the first tugs of puberty. There was another student, a girl, who sometimes sat beside me. When she did, my heart would pound in my chest and I was unable to suppress the crimson blush that I could feel spreading over my entire face. Lights came on automatically whenever the train entered one of the numerous tunnels along the way, but they were very dim. That made me even more fidgety, and I would start breathing hard. There was no way for me to control all these symptoms.

Though the train was supposed to be running on a regular schedule, it was often delayed. On days that I overslept, I had no choice but to trudge to the main highway on the north side of Chu-ul and try to sneak a ride on one of the big trucks that constantly passed by. When a truck that had room on the back came by, I would run out onto the dark road, catch hold of the tailgate with both hands, and hook my leg over the barrier. Then, with all my strength, I would roll my entire body onto the bed of the moving truck. If my luck held out, I would enjoy a free and quiet ride to school.

Too many students on one truck or a recalcitrant driver could change the story. At such times, the driver would send his assistant to the back of the truck to chase us off. If we students chose to ignore the order to depart, the assistant might grab our school caps and throw them into the street, or use force to eject us, often while the truck was moving. So there were days when I had to risk my well-being hooking rides on several different trucks in order to get to school on time.

Classroom work usually ended by three o'clock, and I left at four-thirty to catch the five o'clock train home. Walking home from the station in the twilight, I could see the smoke from our chimney from a long way off. Dinner for the family would usually be on the table when I walked through the door.

*

I struggled with the balky trains and unfriendly truck drivers for six months, past my fifteenth birthday. By then, it was obvious that I would have to leave home and find a place in Chongjin. Mother came into the city with me one weekend and we searched through the neighborhoods around the school to find a small room for me to rent. In time, we came to what amounted to a small farming village within the confines of the city. Its fifteen or so homes were just across the fields from the school, so it would be an ideal location if any of the families had space for me. Luck was with us. A young couple with one small child had one of its two on-dol sleeping rooms free and agreed to take me in for a rental fee we could afford.

Mother cleaned the room from top to bottom, bought some pots and pans, and showed me how to cook for myself—an art as mysterious to me as any I was learning in my medical classes. Despite Mother's patient teaching, however, the technique for properly steaming rice on the coal stove eluded me for some time. I never seemed to get the proportion of water to rice just right. Either the result was too sticky because I put in too much water, or it was hard and dry because I did not put in enough. Worse, I sometimes burned the rice, and that would smell up the entire house and render the pot almost impossible to clean. I was on my own for the first time, away from the family and living by myself. Somehow the glory of my situation eluded me, for I had traded the long, sometimes dangerous journeys from Chu-ul for the opportunity to starve myself. Fortunately, on rare occasions, my landlords invited me to share dinner with them.

Mother came to Chongjin every weekend to hand-wash my laundry and purchase my food supply for the next week. She knew how hard it was for me to prepare rice on the unpredictable coal stove, so she bought me an electric hotplate and even began bringing rice which she had pre-washed and dried at home. In time, her patient instructions found the mark: one cupful of rice combined with water up to the mark she incised on the side of the cooking pot. From then on, cooking rice was no problem—except when I switched on the hotplate and fell asleep.

Chongjin was a major port, so the supply of seafood was large and varied. I soon learned how to cook mackerel, cuttlefish or crab to go along with the steamed rice. In fact, and much to everyone's amazement, I was a fairly good cook by the end of the semester.

*

A new freshman class was admitted to Chongjin Medical-Technical School in September, 1947, and I advanced to the sophomore class. All of the new students were high-school graduates and, thus, a more homogeneous group than my class. There were more girls, too; nearly one-third of the new admissions were girls.

At this point, my classmate and hometown friend, Kim Ki-jin, suggested that we room together as a way of sharing living expenses and having a study partner on hand. The new living arrangement worked well. We took turns with the cooking and shared in all the everyday chores. Being able to study together benefited us both. Ki-jin was also several years older than me, and was socially adept. He taught me a great deal, mostly by example, about the ways of the world and how to get along with people. I was still a shy loner, but I felt myself growing up under Ki-jin's helpful guidance. Moving in with him was one of the best things that happened to me during this phase of my life, for I found a true friend in Ki-jin.

At this time, the medical-technical school was offering a three-year course leading to a diploma. It was expected that the school's graduates would be assigned by provincial or central government authorities to man medical dispensaries in small villages and towns. The school worked under severe limitations. There was no library, and the number of textbooks was so severely limited that we had to share them on a rotating basis. We all worked extremely hard to get the most we could from the textbooks in the limited time we were able to use them. Lecture notes became, and remained, our chief source of medical knowledge. Competition was keen. During the first semester of our sophomore year, bacteriology, anatomy and physiology were added to the curriculum.

As the classroom work improved and became more intense, the school itself became better organized— a better place to live. Student clubs were formed, and planned activities were offered in sports, music, drama and dancing.

CHAPTER SIX

In December, 1947, just before our winter vacation, the student body of Chongjin Medical-Technical School was treated to a special musical program in the school auditorium.

A small chorus of students sang many of the best-known popular songs of the day along with a selection of Korean folk songs. There was also a short operatic drama, produced by members of the student body. The high spot of the program for me, however, came during the interlude between these main acts.

One of the freshman girls, whom I did not know, wearing the traditional two-piece white silk Korean dress with monk's cowl, danced the *Sung-mu*, the Buddhist monk's dance. The theme of this dance is the fundamental human struggle between the flesh and the spirit.

I was seated in the third row, very close to the stage, and from the moment she appeared, the rest of the audience seemed to disappear, and I felt she danced for me alone. Her shimmering long black hair, falling almost to her waist, framed her milk-white face. I could even detect a spattering of freckles across the bridge of her nose sprinkling out across both cheeks. Her eyebrows were two perfect dark crescents, which, along with slight touches of rouge on her cheeks, accented the whiteness of her skin. Her waist was slender and her fingers were long and delicate. Instantly I was intoxicated by this charming creature. Was it the suggestiveness of the dance, its theme inbred from infancy as part of our Korean culture, that caused the inner turmoil surging through me? Whatever it was, I was exultantly ravaged.

She stood at the center of the stage, motionless as a statue. As soon as the twelve-string Korean lute sounded, she began her dance. First her fingers, then her hands, then her shoulders, waist and, finally, her legs moved in a smooth rhythmical flow. The dance lasted less than ten minutes and at its end I was roused from my reverie by the cheering audience rising as one in a standing ovation. Still mesmerized by her performance, becoming once again a part of the crowd, I realized she had all unknowingly stolen my heart.

It snowed through that long night. I know because I could not sleep. The image of the dancing girl—whose name, I had learned, was Chun Hae-jean—kept coming between me and rest. Whether I shut my eyes or kept them open, the image of her dancing form remained before me. It was the first time in my life I had dreamed about a girl.

Next day, after a half-day of classes, all the students would be leaving for their winter vacations. There would be no opportunity to meet Hae-jean before classes resumed in a few weeks. I must do something before she left for home, but still quite shy, I knew in my heart that there was no way I could muster the courage to talk with her about my feelings. I was miserable all night. I was overpoweringly thirsty, and my mouth was dry. I kept getting out of bed to fetch drinks of water or to pace the room. As midnight, one o'clock, and then two o'clock passed, I felt my heart pounding harder and faster. I could think of no way to settle down, so I woke Ki-jin and asked him what I should do.

My friend turned his face toward me and, still half asleep, asked, "Why don't you write her a love letter and drop it into her mailbox as soon as school opens in the morning? If you're lucky, she might even pick it up before she leaves for home."

This sounded like an excellent way out of my dilemma. I sat down and, for the first time in my life, attempted to compose a love letter. I wrote and rewrote, discarded and rewrote again. It took me more than three hours to complete the task.

"Dear Hae-jean. May I introduce myself to you? My name is Dong-kyu. I am in the sophomore class. Your superb artistic performance on the stage yesterday impressed me very much. I could not take my eyes off the graceful lines your body made in the dance. You touched my feelings deeply. You were beautiful in the white silk dress. It has been very cold and snowing outside, and I have not been able to sleep for even a minute. Your beautiful dancing image is constantly in front of my eyes. It is already five in the morning; the snow has let up at last, but I am very tired. Now my heart is calmer and I am able to write to you. My dear Hae-jean, I have never felt this way before in my whole life. I am dying to meet you as soon as possible even though I doubt very much that I would be able to talk to you this way if you were standing in front of me. My big worry now is that you might leave school for the long winter vacation without checking your mailbox in the hallway.

From someone who is in love with you."

I read and reread the letter until the school building opened at seven o'clock. It excited me and made me happy just to think about Hae-jean picking up my letter.

At five minutes to seven, I walked to the school. It was very quiet, and no one was around. I found her mailbox in the hallway and carefully pushed the letter into it so that a corner remained visible from the outside. Then I went back to my room and fell into a sound sleep for a half-hour. I was utterly drained from the restless emotions of the long night.

At eight o'clock, when I went back to the school, there were many students milling about in the hallway. I wandered back and forth near Hae-jean's mailbox—before class, between classes, and after the last class was finally let out. The corner of the letter remained in evidence and Hae-jean was nowhere to be seen. Most of the students had already left to begin their vacations. I was overcome with sadness, for all the hope that had been building up in my heart was dashed. I was so depressed that I nearly cried from my disappointment.

I packed and caught the next bus home. When I reached the house, I looked so exhausted and dejected that Mother began to worry aloud: "Are you in some sort of trouble? Are you sick? Are you in pain?" In truth I had a terrible pain in my heart, but I was hardly about to share my awesome feelings with anyone in the family. I was too shy. I had never felt remotely like this before, and I had no idea what I might do to erase my emotional turmoil. I was certain that my world was coming to a sad end.

I was listless and quiet throughout the interminable weeks of vacation. Mother worried so about my depression that she made arrangements with her younger sister, who still lived in Chongjin, to take me in when school reconvened. Of course, Mother felt that loneliness was at the root of my uncharacteristic behavior.

The day before the new semester began, Mother and I traveled to Chongjin and moved all my belongings to my aunt's home, a two-story, four-bedroom house in the northwest part of town, right up against a mountainside, and within walking distance of my school.

Auntie's family was kind and friendly, and life in their home was casual and congenial. Everyone sat down to eat together. We all talked freely over the meal about our day's experiences, general news or whatever came to mind. This was a great departure from the formality of my family's meals, when Father, Mother, and my grandparents ate quietly at one table while we children sat at a second table in the corner of the kitchen. Conversation during meals was forbidden unless it was to register appreciation for the food.

I did not feel I could be as happy living at Auntie's house as I had been living with Ki-jin, but I was fortunate to be part of a way of life I had not experienced to that point.

*

I got up extra early on the first day of the new semester and used the extra time to stand in front of a mirror. I could barely get my breakfast down, I was so nervous and excited. As I left Auntie's house, I could see the white-painted hospital and school buildings far across the snow-covered grain fields. Though I had seen this scene uncountable times over the past fifteen months, it had never looked so beautiful. Because it was winter and the fields were fallow, I was able to take a short-cut directly across the snowy wastes.

As I left the house and was about to step off the road and into the first field, I saw that a woman in front of me was also walking toward the school. Her back was to me, but she reminded me so much of Hae-jean that I incessantly blinked my eyes in order to get a better look. I also speeded my pace. The closer I got, the more certain I was that it was Hae-jean. I walked even faster, and even ran for short stretches. However, whenever the woman turned to look back, I slowed my pace and fell farther behind. Finally, when I came close enough to see that I had been dogging the heels of a middle-aged lady, I nearly collapsed from the effort, the embarrassment and the sheer weight of despondency. The woman compounded my bad feelings by cheerfully calling out, "Good morning! You must be in a hurry." All my energy drained from me. Then, to vent my anger and disappointment, I closed my eyes and ran as hard as I could all the rest of the way to school.

I planned to check Hae-jean's mailbox as soon as I stepped into the hallway, but there were many students milling about and I was too timid. As soon as the hallway cleared, however, I strode manfully to her mailbox. The letter was gone. My enthusiasm bubbled up. She had picked up the letter! Had she read it? My hopes of meeting Hae-jean came to life again. I could hardly concentrate as my morning classes ground forward. I wondered what would happen next.

I was eating the lunch Auntie had prepared for me, when I sensed someone coming up behind me. There was a tap on my right shoulder. I stiffened as I heard a female voice say, "You must be Dong-kyu."

The girl about whom I had been dreaming my life away was standing right next to me. She had talked to me! I could not believe that this was really happening.

She continued to speak and she behaved naturally, without a hint of shyness. I listened intently and let her do most of the talking, for I was certain that I would ruin everything if given the least opportunity. Besides, I had no idea what to say.

At length, she asked for my address. When I told her, her face lit up. "Why, that's only a block from my house! Why don't we walk home together?"

Things were moving smoothly, better than I could have wished. I began to wonder why I had made it seem so difficult.

Later, on the way home, I learned that she was seventeen, two years older than I, and that she was also staying with relatives in Chongjin. I could scarcely believe it when she said she was from Chu-ul. Incredibly,

72

she had also been raised in Manchuria. Her family had returned to Korea a year after mine.

The three-story house in which she was staying was on the same street as Auntie's home. She pointed out her room in the middle of the third floor, facing the street. We made no promises to meet again as we separated that afternoon, but, after dinner, I returned to her house and stared at her bedroom window in the hope of catching even the merest glimpse of her or even her shadow. I stood in the cold for two hours, but I saw nothing.

*

During the weeks that followed, we often talked with each other for a few minutes now and again at school. Then, one Saturday afternoon, Hae-jean came into Auntie's backyard, where I was sitting in a chair in the sun, and asked me if I would like to go to a movie with her. She explained that she had already purchased the tickets, which she was clutching in her hand. We walked side-by-side, very close together, all the way to the theater. Because students were not allowed to attend any but educational films, she led me to the rear seats on the topmost level, where no one else was sitting.

Later, I could not recall anything I saw in the theater. The screen may as well have been blank. I was too excited and nervous from sitting in the dark next to Hae-jean to take any of it in. I was pulled from the abyss into which I was cheerfully settling when she whispered, "Dong-kyu! We have to leave a little before the end of the movie. We can't be seen!"

One Friday afternoon, in the early spring, we hitched a ride on a truck bound for Chu-ul. The sky was clear and blue, but it was still quite chilly. We sat in the back of the truck, behind the driver's seat. Neither of us

73

spoke much, but we could barely keep our eyes off one another. When we needed to speak, we had to shout above the noise of the wind and the truck. I was in ecstasy.

Hae-jean left Chu-ul at the beginning of summer vacation, so I did not see her at all that summer. She did not return to school in September either. She never told me why she left, never even wrote to say she was leaving. Two years later, I was walking across Chongjin Bridge and saw her in the distance. She looked like a mature woman. She was wearing a maternity dress! I was sad to see that her face was puffy, and to note how different she looked from that exhilarating day we hitched home on the open truck. I could not summon the courage to step up to her and talk.

I never saw Chun Hae-jean again. But the vision of the girl in white performing the ancient Korean dance whirled in my mind long thereafter. She remained in my memory as the first romantic interlude of my innocent adolescence.

CHAPTER SEVEN

Chongjin Medical-Technical School, which had been established September, 1946, to provide a three-year program to train medical practitioners, was re-accredited at the beginning of September, 1948, as a full-fledged medical college. By that time, North Korea boasted fifteen universities and colleges, including three medical colleges—one at Kim Il-sung University, in Pyongyang, the capital of North Korea; one in Hamhung, the capital of South Hamgyong Province, in southeastern North Korea; and the new one in Chongjin, also in northeastern North Korea.

A special qualifying examination was required of those members of the student body medical-technical school who desired to enter the new medical college. Naturally, I took the test, and passed. Some of my older classmates who had previously graduated from high school or had even more schooling were advanced to the sophomore class. However, I was admitted to the new college freshman class—which nevertheless saved me from attending a final year of medical-technical school. This meant that I was by far the youngest member of my college class.

Chongjin Medical College offered a five-year program which combined pre-med courses with the normal medical school curriculum. In addition to my old medical-technical school classmates who placed in the new freshman class, fifty new high school graduates were added to the freshman student body. My former classmates who had not passed the entrance examination or who were not willing to spend five years studying to be regular Western-style medical doctors were transferred to the medical-technical school at

75

Songjin, a port city about fifty miles south of Chongjin. One of these was my former roommate, mentor and close friend, Kim Ki-jin.

Across the fields, about a mile south of Chongjin Hospital, was a rectangular three-story red-brick former high school building with a large athletic field just to the south of it. This was to be the new college campus, though the hospital remained the medical college's training center.

The school became better in every respect— organization, equipment and staff—almost overnight. Each department was chaired by one full professor who was assisted by several clinical faculty members, usually lecturers who maintained their practices in the cities and towns outside of Chongjin. The medical college's first president was Dr. Yang Jin-hong, the bacteriology professor. He was a short, fat, active man who had graduated from Seoul's Kyongsong Medical School. Following advanced work in Germany, he had taken up practicing in Chongjin and, over the years, had become quite successful.

All of the male students were required to wear a navy-blue uniform consisting of a double-breasted coat and a "Lenin" cap. The female students wore the same type coat over a navy-blue skirt and the Lenin cap. This, in fact, was the uniform worn by all the students attending North Korea's fifteen colleges and universities. The only difference was that each school's emblem was worn as a cap badge.

Each student was further required to carry a black cloth-bound three-inch-by-four-inch identification booklet. Most of us simply suspended our booklets around our necks with string. The first page identified the student by name, birth date, present address, date of admission, dates of subsequent advancement to higher classes, and the dean's signature. A photograph was pasted into the upper right corner of the first page. From the second page on were the records of our academic achievements: Subjects we had taken and were currently taking, the name of the course professor, our grades, dates of examinations, and the professors' signatures. Grades were based on a five point system; "5" was an "A" and the lowest "passing" grade was a "3".

Our first-year curriculum included inorganic chemistry, organic chemistry, physics, Latin, biology, parasitology and anatomy. Each course was administered and taught by a full-time resident professor except for biology, which was in the hands of a member of the clinical faculty who taught part-time.

Examinations were given at the end of each semester, in January and June. They were mostly oral exams, one-on-one with the resident professor. In most cases, the professor prepared several cards, each with a different set of questions, and spread them across a table. As soon as a student entered the professor's office, he or she selected a card. We were then called upon to answer specific questions or to discuss in detail the topics listed on the card we had selected. At the conclusion of the test, the professor would write the score and his signature in our black ID books. My first year of college was largely a repetition of the work I had already done at the medical-technical school, so I was able to attain a "5" in each course except inorganic chemistry, where I came in with a "3".

*

A new dormitory for the female students was built behind the college building, and Dr. Yang, the college president, donated his three-story private clinic in downtown Chongjin for use as male-student housing. I moved into Dr. Yang's clinic with a new roommate, Yi

Donald Chung, M.D.

Jung-gi, a graduate of Hamhung High School and formerly my classmate at the medical-technical school. Jung-gi was one of those who had been advanced to the college sophomore class in September, 1948. He was several years older than me and, like me, an only son. He treated me like a younger brother.

Jung-gi was intelligent, handsome and tall, perhaps five-feet-nine-inches and one hundred eighty pounds. He was extremely talented in sports. In fact, he was a star player on the school volleyball and soccer teams. He could jump high and really smash the volleyball down hard and accurately. He played center forward on the soccer team. To top everything off, he was the college's premier high jumper and our top man in the 100- and 200-meter dashes.

Unfortunately, our school teams did not excel. I well remember our teams practicing extra hard traveling to Pyongyang to participate in the Pan-Korean College Games, and then coming back without any trophies. Jung-gi was dating a girl from my class who played on the girl's team. He once asked me to attend a game in which our girl's team was competing against a team from one of the other provinces. Both teams were highly competitive and the score remained close throughout the game, favoring first one team and then the other. At the very last minute, Jung-gi's girlfriend scored a basket. Unfortunately, it was at the wrong end of the court. Rather than winning the tied game, she provided the opposing team with a two-point victory.

Jung-gi also had a married sister about ten years older than him who lived in downtown Chongjin, near the harbor. Her husband was a photographer and she was chairperson of the parent-teachers' association at our school. I spent many weekends with Jung-gi at his sister's home, where I was treated as a member of the family and where we poor, malnourished medical students were always treated to a real feast.

*

My own family life was more or less on "hold" at this time. I was very busy at school, and would have preferred to go home only on holidays or school vacations. My life in Chongjin was very full, I was used to being on my own, and I am sure I simply did not want to face the tension and the subtle degradation of Mother at Father's hands. However, I went home most weekends out of a sense of duty to Mother.

By 1948, Father was chairman of the local chapter of the People's Democratic Party, which kept him busy and away from home a great deal. In 1949, he went to work as a Party clerk in Pyongyang, so was home only infrequently.

Family life, however, reached out and touched me one day as I was watching soccer practice in the school yards one afternoon early in the 1949 school year, when my eldest sister, Moon-hee, paid me an unexpected visit.

Moon-hee was then about twenty-three. With all of her bitter experiences at the hands of those who brutally used her body and all the duties and responsibilities she assumed as head of the household while Mother worked, she was still the same sweet innocent sister I had always known.

She was very pretty, with dark shining hair that she carefully parted down the middle and pulled back into a bun on the nape of her neck, her well-proportioned features and sparkling eyes were set off by the delicate arch of her black eyebrows. There was always an air of tranquility and modesty about her sensitive face. Her natural beauty was enhanced by the absence of any trace of make-up.

On this visit, she was dressed in the traditional high-waisted white skirt topped with a short blouse. Sitting there on the edge of the playing field, shaded by the softly billowing branches of a verdant pine, we talked about my life at school, how I was progressing, my courses, my satisfaction with my record. As we talked, Moon-hee unwrapped some treats she had brought from home for her only brother—rice cake and honey. It was our custom to dip a piece of cake into the honey before eating it, so Moon-hee did this and fed me in between sentences.

After exhausting my small store of news, Moon-hee took my hands in hers and began to explain the reason for her visit. Actually, she had stopped off on her way to Hwanghae Province, in the far southwest of North Korea. There she had obtained a job which astounded me. Moon-hee, my dainty, delicate sister, was to be a guard at a female prison! All the memories came rushing back of Moon-hee's tender mothering during Mother's working hours, her tutoring assistance with my early schoolwork, her presence whenever I needed her. Then the terrifying nightmare replayed in my mind of the brutal raping she had endured in Harbin, and the sexual submission to a stranger to save Father from probable exile in Siberia.

Even after leaving Harbin, trouble followed her. During my school years in Chongjin, she had suffered through two brief marriages. I was never told why these marriages failed, and I never asked, but I instinctively felt that the horrors of Harbin had somehow, in an underlying, deep psychological way, contributed to the cause. I knew that I, a passive observer of that terror-filled night, would never be able to completely erase the scene from my subconsciousness. Such imbedded experiences as well as the awareness of the unhappy married life of her parents undoubtedly, I was sure, reflected in some degree on the marital failures she experienced at a time before she could have assimilated such happenings in a way as to preclude them from affecting her ability to form new, meaningful associations involving the sexual encounter. These thoughts remained unspoken as we talked on for several hours, touching only on the periphery of our now separate lives.

Our eyes seemed to bore into each other's, acting out some primal need to imprint upon our hearts and minds every miniscule detail of our mutual devotion. A silent sadness overwhelmed us. Looking back through the mirrored years, I cannot recall a single instance so filled with sorrow.

Finally the time came for her to leave. We embraced as tears streamed from our eyes, tears we could not stop for many minutes as we clung together. Finally she broke free, still holding my hands in hers, until she backed completely away. Her last words remain imprinted on my mind as words graven in stone. "Study hard, Brother. I know you will become a fine doctor and a big man." Then turning quickly, she walked away, casting glances over her shoulder at me until she was out of sight.

The shadows had lengthened, and the playing field was empty. The murmurs of the wind sighing through the pine branches seemed a melancholy accompaniment to the drama just concluded.

I wonder if I would have stood by, watching my beloved sister walk out of my life, had I known that thirty-five years would pass before I saw Moon-hee again.

PART II
Wars of Liberation
(September, 1949 - December, 1950)

CHAPTER EIGHT

In December, 1943, in the midst of World War II, President Franklin Roosevelt, Prime Minister Winston Churchill and Generalissimo Chiang Kai-shek, meeting at the Cairo Conference, agreed that Korea would "in due course" become free and independent. This decision was reaffirmed at the Potsdam Conference of July, 1945, by the same three great powers, and it was also endorsed by the other major power that was by then also conferring on Asian problems—the Soviet Union.

The Soviet Union declared war on Japan on August 9, 1945, two days after the bombing of Hiroshima, by which time Japan's defeat was a certainty. This was four days after my appendectomy, and the day on which I saw Soviet warplanes in the skies over Harbin for the first time. On the same day, the Soviet Union announced its adherence to the Potsdam statement, and, also, to the Cairo declaration. Thus, the Soviet Union secured for itself a legitimate pretext for gaining a foothold on the Korean peninsula.

When Japan announced, on August 8, 1945, that she was willing to surrender unconditionally, the United States government decided, for mainly military considerations, that Soviet troops would be free to accept the Japanese surrender north of the 38th Parallel while U.S. troops would accept the surrender south of the Parallel. There were elements of the Red Army in Korea by August 12, nearly a month before the first U.S. units arrived in South Korea from Okinawa. By August 26, Russian troops were taking up positions along the 38th Parallel.

The 38th Parallel had never been intended to serve as a military boundary nor, for that matter, as a political one. The occupation of Korea had been neither contemplated nor discussed at the Allied great power meetings from 1943 onward. There was no thought, the new American president, Harry Truman, had said, of a permanent division of Korea. But, to the Soviets following their own logic and rules of practicality, a line was an acknowledgment of a boundary, and therefore, real. Moreover, they could string their "iron curtain" along the line, seal it off, and close it to traffic and commerce. In this way, occupation by one nation, Japan, was replaced by occupation by two nations, the United States and the Soviet Union. The nation of Korea—which had always been one nation populated by one people speaking one language—was effectively divided into two *de facto* nations.

For almost two years following the Japanese surrender, a Soviet-American Commission tried, in theory at least, to develop details for a provisional government for all of Korea to be established under the guidance of a four-power trusteeship for a maximum of five years. This was in accordance with the terms worked out at the Moscow conference of the foreign ministers of the four Allied powers on December 16, 1945. But the growing conflict between the Soviet Union and the United States was by then leading to a hardening of attitudes on both sides. These newly-forming attitudes militated against the Commission's task and doomed its efforts to nearly total ineffectiveness.

The Commission held fifteen formal sessions between January 16 and February 5, 1946. It was this brief, but bitter, experience that led the United States to place the "Korean Problem" before the United Nations on September 17, 1947. Despite the opposition of the Soviet Union and the Communist Bloc nations, on November 14, 1947, the UN called for the nationwide election of a national assembly. The UN Commission, established to observe the elections, was welcomed in the South early in 1948, but the Soviets refused to allow it entry into the North and even refused to discuss the matter of elections under any conditions. As a result, on May 10, 1948, the first elections in the history of Korea were held, under UN supervision, south of the 38th Parallel only. The National Assembly, which convened on May 31 to draw up the first constitution of the Republic of Korea, seated 198 members. The constitution, which established a presidential system of government, was formally promulgated on July 17. The first president of the Republic of Korea, Syngman Rhee, was inaugurated on August 15, 1948, a date chosen to commemorate Korean independence from Japan three years earlier. On the same day, sovereign authority was formally transferred from the United States Military Government to the Republic of Korea.

While South Korea was moving rapidly toward an outwardly democratic and independent form of government, Kim Il-sung, a well-known anti-Japanese Korean nationalist, arrived home in the North with his followers and Red Army troops in September, 1945. On October 3, Kim was introduced at a citizens' rally in his native Pyongyang as a nationalist hero. The introduction was made by Cho Man-sik, the first head of the Council of People's Commissars, a renowned oldtime anti-Japanese guerrilla fighter who had entered China decades earlier vowing never to return home until Korea had been cleansed of its Japanese overlords. On October 10, the "Conference of the North Korean Five Provinces Party Representatives and Enthusiasts" was summoned to Pyongyang to organize the "North Korean Central Bureau of the Korean Communist Party," which proclaimed itself "the first Korean Communist Party organization established on the principles of Marxism-Leninism and guided by true Communists."

The establishment of the Central Bureau and the election of Kim Il-sung as its First Secretary were Kim's initial steps toward consolidating absolute power in his hands. He thus effectively replaced Cho Man-sik as leader of the nation. On February 8, 1946, Kim organized the "North Korean People's Committee," which was simply a disguised regime. The process of legitimizing the new social, economic and political order in the North began in November, 1946, when delegates were elected to local governing bodies. In February, 1947, these delegates held a convention of the People's Committee and endorsed a wide-ranging body of land-reform laws which had been issued since the formation of the North Korean People's Committee.

Immediately after the adoption of the resolution on Korea by the United Nations General Assembly on November 14, 1947, the Soviet Union, in a concentrated effort to establish a Communist regime in the North, formed a special committee charged with drafting a constitution. The draft version of the Communist Constitution, which the Communists claimed as representing sovereignty of all Korea, was adopted by the Cadre Conference on the North Korean People's Committee on March 2, 1948. On May 1, before the May 10 general elections in the South, the People's Committee approved the draft constitution and announced the establishment of a Communist regime for governing of the entire Korean nation.

*

During the summer of 1948, a small group of students from Chongjin Medical-Technical School was sent out in the evenings by the school democratic Youth League to campaign in the streets for the Workers' Party candidate for the Supreme People's Assembly. A small wooden platform would be set up on a street corner, and the portrait of the single candidate, together with those of Kim Il-sung and Joseph Stalin, was hung high on the wall behind.

Each meeting started with a hymn to General Kim Il-sung. The hymn was sung with all the reference usually accorded a national anthem. The song we sang in the quiet evenings went something like this:

Snow-bound Manchurian plain, tell me,
Long-long forest night, let me ask you?
Who is the unwavering partisan?
Who is the peerless patriot?
Ah, ah, his name is one we long to hear—our general.
Ah, ah, his name is brilliant—General Kim Il-sung.

We also sang *The Internationale* and some of the newer patriotic songs. After we had sung, our group leader would recite the candidate's qualifications and ask the audience to vote for him. The most important among the qualifications were that he be from the working class and had been recommended by the Workers' Party.

Because I was quite short, and despite my poor singing voice, I was always in the front row of students during the singing. The faces of the onlookers gathered in front of me were invariably expressionless. There was no debate of any kind; there were no alternative choices. This was the first time I had ever taken part in a so-called election. I could not understand why we had to campaign when there was only a single candidate.

*

The Soviet-style election was held at last on August 25, 1948; all of the candidates nominated by the Workers' Party, including the man for whom we had sung

89

on Chongjin streetcorners, were elected to become members of the Supreme People's Assembly. On September 9, the Democratic People's Republic of Korea was proclaimed an independent nation. On the same day, Kim Il-sung, who up to then had been chairman of the North Korean People's Committee, was named Premier of the newly-formed government.

A few weeks after the election, in a letter to Soviet Premier Joseph Stalin, General Kim Il-sung requested the opening of formal diplomatic relations between his country and the Soviet Union, including the exchange of ambassadors. In his reply of October 12, 1948, Stalin announced that the Soviet Union was "ready" to establish diplomatic relations. On October 18, the Soviet Union appointed General Shtikov, commander of the Soviet occupation forces in North Korea, to be the first Soviet ambassador to Pyongyang.

In the early years of our liberation from Japanese domination—1945 through 1950—the North Korean regime successfully insinuated Russian cultural norms into Korean school programs under the slogan "Learn from the Soviet Union." The immediate objective of the regime during this early period of social reconstruction was to transform through re-education and reorientation a backward and previously subjugated society into a highly regimented and energetic society capable of employing all its people and meeting all its own needs, from industrial and food production to the universal availability of quality medical care for all its citizens.

CHAPTER NINE

At the beginning of my sophomore year in medical school, in September, 1949, Lieutenant Kang of the People's Army became the college Military training Instructor. Russian language and Marxism-Leninism were added to the curriculum, and a full-time non-student supervisor was assigned by Communist Party headquarters to be chairman of the college Democratic Youth League.

The North Korean Communist Party had made youth its first priority. Already by June 22, 1946, the Central Committee of the Democratic National Unification Front was organized in Pyongyang from among representatives of three political parties and fifteen social organizations. A full-time chairman assigned to each college supervised and organized student activities both on- and off-campus. Every student had to join the League upon admission to college.

The League was closely controlled from the national, provincial, and city headquarters. Most, if not all, of the officers of the school and League-organized class units had their roots in working-class families, and they were well indoctrinated with Marxist-Leninist ideology. It was said that the officers were mostly members of the Workers' Party, but evidence of this membership was never revealed to students who were not themselves party members.

Each of our class units met twice a week. It was during those meetings that those of us whose grades had slipped, or who had done something of which the League did not approve, received harsh reprimands and were forced to stand before all the students in the class for "self-criticism." Many of our comrades in the class were merciless in their criticism of fellow students and in suggesting improvements.

I was a lukewarm personality, so somehow evaded any calls for self-criticism. However, my roommate Yi Jung-gi, always seemed to be the focus of some League retribution. I suppose a good deal of his problem was simply that he was extremely good-looking and self-possessed and excelled in all the things to which he put his active mind. He also came into contact with anti-Communists, and one of his best friends during our medical-technical school days—in fact, the student-body president—was reportedly caught by the secret police while undertaking some sort of anti-Communist activity. Jung-gi was never forgiven that connection with undesirable elements.

My class was also divided into groups of three-to-five students. If one of the members of a group was absent, the rest of the group had to check on him to find out why he had missed school. Unexcused absences were brought up at the twice-weekly class-unit meetings, and had to be explained by the absentee in detail, sometimes in humiliating detail. The members of the smaller groups also helped one another by undertaking group discussions of mostly ideological subjects.

Our work and study schedule was supervised by the Democratic Youth League even during vacations. When I attended the required League meeting at home in Chu-ul on the first day of the 1949 summer vacation, I joined a body of about two dozen students from many of the nation's colleges. The meeting and summer programs were chaired by a Kim Il-sung University student who was from Chu-ul. Kim Il-sung was North Korea's senior university, and the only one with a liberal arts college. It was a co-educational school located in Pyongyang and was considered to be the North Korean equivalent of

Moscow or Peking University. To be admitted to Kim Il-sung University was—and is—one of the highest honors a North Korean youth can attain.

The medical school League chapter called an emergency meeting on Christmas eve, 1949. Every student was required to attend. Despite threats, however, several Christian students stayed away. I never saw any of those students again. I had learned in class that the constitution of North Korea confirmed freedom of religion, so it was a bit difficult to understand why religious activity was both openly and indirectly repressed. Students from religious families were discriminated against and, throughout our society, those who did not profess any religious beliefs were generally given better opportunities than religious believers.

No matter how believers felt, they simply had to give up expressions of their religions if they were to have an opportunity to earn the bread to feed their children or continue in school.

Once in school, there was no way to escape the Democratic Youth League. The League's tasks at the medical school were clear; to inculcate the students with Communism and to inject Communist teachings and preachings into all aspects of our lives. The League maintained discipline, mobilized student labor for construction projects, and continuously involved itself in guiding our thoughts and actions.

*

Lieutenant Kang, our military training instructor, arrived in September, 1949, at the start of my sophomore year. He came directly from the ranks of the People's Army. He was about thirty years old, tall and husky. His normally expressionless face was tanned, and his voice was hoarse and low-pitched. He never spoke of where he had received his own military training.

All students, male and female, were required to take military instruction. The first few classes were held indoors to learn about the People's Army's organization, how to read maps, to learn tactics and the handling and care of rifles. There were few real weapons available, and those were Japanese and Chinese models used in World War II. We carried wooden dummy rifles during field-training exercises.

Military training classes were held every day, rain or shine. If it rained, we simply did our crawling and marching through the mud. We were sometimes called out for night sessions of simulated combat, usually with mud daubed on our faces to make us invisible in the moonlight.

I found it very difficult to understand why medical students should be subjected to the rigors of military training, particularly when it was all being done at the expense of time in which we could have been studying medical subjects. World War II had ended only four years earlier, the nation was at peace, and there was no way I could have guessed that war was going to break out between the halves of the divided Korean nation. Despite my misapprehension, I worked and studied as hard in the military training class as I did in my others. In the examinations of June, 1950, I earned a "4" in the course.

The study of Marxist-Leninist principles was also required as part of the regular curriculum at all levels. The "correct" ideological orientation of students had a high priority. Our main text for this course was a history of the Russian Communist Party, which was supplemented with many pamphlets published by the Workers' Party. Each chapter of the history text was taken up and discussed in detail by our professors, and we were expected to know all the details by memory. More important, we were expected to *apply* the principles derived from those early experiences of the Russian Communist Party to our daily activities. On my June 23, 1950, final examination, I earned another "4".

Regardless of how high their scores were in the scientific courses, those students who did poorly in the military training and Marxism-Leninism courses were the focus of serious criticism during the twice-weekly Democratic Youth League meetings. Through the League meetings, the military training and the Marxist-Leninist indoctrination, we were to become well equipped with Communist ideology. We were further taught to hate imperialism, mainly the brand promulgated by the United States and the Syngman Rhee government of South Korea.

All this came before my memories of an earlier hate campaign had been allowed to fade. During my school years in Harbin, I had been instructed by my Japanese masters to hate the American and British imperialists. In fact, every morning I spent in school during World War II, I had jabbed my wooden bayonet into straw dummies whose faces were caricatures of Franklin Roosevelt's and Winston Churchill's. Nothing much had changed.

*

Shortly after the beginning of my sophomore year, two new professors were appointed to the faculty of Chongjin Medical College. They had been selected from among a number of pro-Communist South Korean professors and intellectuals who had fled to North Korea, and they had been assigned to my school by the authorities in Pyongyang.

Hwang Su-bong was a biochemistry professor, a bespectacled slightly obese and balding man of medium

95

height. He had graduated from Kyongsong Imperial University Medical School, in Seoul, during the Japanese occupation. A bachelor, he lived in the student dormitory. He was a brilliant thirty-five-year-old who fluently spoke many languages, including English and German. He no sooner arrived at Chongjin Medical School than he undertook the study of Russian. Every time I saw him walking down a corridor or in the dining hall, he had his nose buried in a Russian language textbook. He told me that he had gone through the book over one hundred times in just three months. When he thought he had mastered the language text, he began reading Russian-language biochemistry texts. And he was soon incorporating more Russian terminology into his classroom lectures than any other professor on the faculty. He was both a gifted teacher in his field and a talented musician who practiced on his cello in his laboratory for at least an hour every evening after dinner. We never saw Dr. Hwang dressed in a suit and tie; he habitually wore his white laboratory jacket with a natty white silk scarf tied around his neck.

The other new professor from the south taught histology. He was a less talkative man than Dr. Hwang, and older, probably in his fifties. He was extremely devoted to his work, and was in his laboratory every day conducting experiments.

Both new professors were devoted Communists, and both became members of the Chongjin branch of the Workers' Party soon after their arrival.

*

Early in the spring of 1950, the student body was convened for a special lecture in the school auditorium immediately following our lunch break. We had no idea who would be delivering the lecture nor what the subject was to be.

The auditorium was soon filled, and every member of the faculty was in attendance, including the chairman of the school Democratic Youth League and Lieutenant Kang.

It was a sunny afternoon, but there was still a bite of winter in the air. Only the shuffling and rustling of people taking their seats broke the silence, as the assembled group sat quietly, awaiting the start of the program. As I glanced about, I was struck by the sea of expressionless faces. That this was not to be a festive gathering seemed to be acknowledged by the serious aspect of all those in attendance. Outside, a strong north wind reinforced the winter chill, rising forcefully enough to whistle ominously through the hall.

In time, Dr. Hwang, the new biochemistry professor, entered the auditorium accompanied by a gray-haired Caucasian gentleman who appeared to be in his early sixties. Professor Hwang stood at the podium and introduced his guest as a visiting professor from Russia. The Russian then replaced Dr. Hwang behind the podium and, using a large blackboard, launched into his talk. Professor Hwang, who had only been in North Korea for three or four months at this time, translated the entire lecture clearly and with authority.

The Russian lectured for about forty-five minutes on the classification and treatment of various types of war wounds. None of the students asked any questions at the conclusion of the prepared delivery. Either the topic was so unexpected that no one was prepared to ask questions, or no one knew enough Russian yet to risk a question in public.

After the visitor and teaching faculty left the auditorium, the chairman of the democratic Youth League strode hurriedly to the podium to make a special announcement. The People's Army Medical Training Center in Pyongyang had issued a call for new officer recruits. Any of us who were interested in enrolling were asked to raise our hands.

Silence, except for the occasional whistling of the wind, filled the auditorium. A chill crept into the air. Finally, six or seven members of the junior class raised their hands. Nearly all were Youth League leaders, and several days later they left for Pyongyang.

In a few months one member of the first batch of volunteers returned for a visit after completing the army medical training course. He was decked out in his new uniform—lieutenant's epaulets, high boots, and all. He told us that he had received a few weeks' training, then the class members had been commissioned lieutenants and captains and inducted directly into the People's Army Medical Corps. Most of the class had been assigned to units stationed near the 38th Parallel, but this young man had been assigned to the army hospital in South Hamgyong Province. It was only many years later that he admitted to me why he had subsequently been sent to Chongjin—to care for his commanding officer's mother, who was ill at the time.

*

Between April and June, 1950, I began to see more and more troop trains at the railroad stations whenever I took the train home to Chu-ul on weekends. All of these trains were heading south. The soldiers on the trains looked different from ordinary North Koreans. They appeared stronger, more-solidly built, and they were all deeply suntanned. They kept very much to themselves even when there were civilians around them who were waiting for trains. I also noted that there were a great many horses aboard the numerous freight trains that were also heading south in ever-greater numbers. I had no idea what was going on, and only much later did I learn that the robust, tanned soldiers were Koreans who had served in the Chinese People's Liberation Army, some for many, many years, against the Japanese before and during World war II, and then against the Nationalist Chinese, who were finally driven from mainland China in 1949.

It became clear in a matter of months that while we college students were being armed with Marxist-Leninist doctrine and intensive military training on our isolated campus, the North Korean government had been rapidly and steadily expanding its national military establishment.

CHAPTER TEN

As early as 1947, the Soviets felt there was an imbalance of power in Korea in the North's favor. On August 26, 1947, at the second of the U.S.-Soviet Joint Commission meetings, the chief Soviet delegate, Colonel General Terenti Shtikov, unexpectedly proposed that all foreign troops—both Soviet and American—be withdrawn from Korea in early 1948. Shtikov was said to be confident that, should the opportunity arise, the North Korean People's Army would have no difficulty overrunning the Republic of Korea.

The United States delegates rejected deliberations on this proposal on the grounds that the issue of withdrawal of foreign troops should be regarded as a part of the Korean question which ought to be dealt with at the United Nations sometime in the future.

In early March, 1948, a Soviet-Chinese North Korean joint military counsel, which was later to coordinate the work of both the Soviet military advisors and the Chinese People's Liberation Army "volunteers" during the Korean War, had established its headquarters in Pyongyang "to coordinate certain military activities of the three Communist parties."

On September 12, 1948, the Supreme People's Assembly issued an appeal to the Soviet and U.S. governments asking for immediate withdrawal of all occupation forces from Korea as a prerequisite for the achievement of unification and the establishment of a "democratic and peace oriented unified government" to oversee Korea's economic, political, and cultural prosperity.

In early December 1948, while Russian troops were withdrawing from North Korea following a three-

101

year occupation, a special strategic conference chaired by Soviet Defense Minister Nikolai A. Bulganin was convened at the Kremlin. At that time, Kyrio Kalinov, who was one of the working-level officers of the conference, was given detailed information on the so-called "Bulganin Plan." Kalinov left Moscow at the end of 1948 as a Soviet Army artillery lieutenant colonel and arrived in Pyongyang in early 1949. He then worked as a member of the special military mission of the Soviet Union charged with educating and training of the North Korean People's Army. (Some time later, Kalinov was transferred to East Germany, and, from there, sought refuge in West Germany.)

The so-called "Bulganin Plan" was aimed at communizing the Korean peninsula militarily within eighteen months. The major points, as detailed by Kalinov after his defection, were:

1. Strengthen the North Korean People's Army to a level that would make it possible for them to invade South Korea.
2. The appointment of Colonel General Terenti Shtikov, who was serving as commander of Soviet troops in North Korea at the time of their withdrawal, as Ambassador of the Soviet Union in charge of the Soviet military mission to the North Korean People's Army.
3. The dispatch of a special military mission consisting of forty members, including Major General Chatokov, a tank-warfare expert, and Major General Chazarov, an expert on intelligence tactics.
4. The reorganization of the People's Army's six assault infantry divisions around cores of Korean nationals serving with the Communist Chinese People's Liberation Army, plus the commissioning of

eight brand new front-line divisions and eight reserve divisions.

5. The Soviet Union was to supply five hundred new model T-34 tanks of the 32-ton class as the basis for the commissioning of two brand-new cavalry divisions.

6. Because of anticipated international difficulties, an air force was not to be established for the time being.

According to Kalinov, most of the war plan, with the exception of some minor changes in the number of tanks and the establishment of the air force, had been accomplished as scheduled by June, 1950, exactly eighteen months after the Moscow military conference.

Beginning early in 1950, the North Korean People's Army undertook repeated offensive training exercises at the divisional level. Prior to the outbreak of the Korean War, North Korean military forces had been estimated at 198,380 men, including 182,680 army, 4,700 navy, 2,000 air force, and 9,000 marines. They were equipped with about 500 T-34 tanks and armored vehicles about 200 YAK-9 fighter and reconnaissance planes, and about thirty naval patrol vessels. These soldiers were not only well trained by the Russian military mission and well equipped with modern Russian weapons, they were also well armed with the precepts of Marxism-Leninism in general, and in particular, with the inspiration of Stalin's work. This was the People's Army that was taking up its position just north of the 38th Parallel in the spring of 1950, fully ready for possible war.

In the meantime, in the early summer of 1949, the United States had begun what was to be much more than a troop withdrawal from Korea; the United States was withdrawing its troops from all of mainland Asia. In South Korea there remained only a small contingent of less than five hundred officers and enlisted men—known as the

Korea Military Advisory Group (KMAG)—whose mission was to help mold the Republic of Korea (ROK) military branches into a modern fighting force. On the whole, the KMAG advisors were satisfied with the ROK Army they had helped to develop, and they were confident of its ability to withstand any threat the North Koreans might pose.

While the "Bulganin Plan" was rapidly coming to fruition, American policy was clearly enunciated by U.S. Secretary of State Dean Acheson, in a speech of January 12, 1950, before the National Press Club in Washington, D.C. According to Acheson, the United States' defense perimeter in the Pacific ran from the Aleutians to Japan and the Ryukyu Islands, then south to the Philippines. As for the rest of the Pacific world, such as Korea, Acheson stated that should an attack occur the initial reliance "must be on the people attacked to resist it and then upon the commitment of the entire civilized world under the charter of the United Nations." It seemed clear that what Acheson meant was that Korea was not within an area where the United States would automatically react to aggression. This statement evoked despair and anguish in Seoul, and probably delight in Moscow and Pyongyang.

On May 19, 1950, South Korean Defense Minister Shin Sung-mo, told the press that intelligence reports reaching his desk indicated that the North Koreans were moving in force toward the 38th Parallel. He added that these moves further indicated a strong possibility of imminent invasion. American military authorities in Washington, D.C., however, agreed with intelligence summaries issued by General Douglas MacArthur's Far East headquarters, based in Tokyo, an evaluation that argued strongly against the notion of imminent invasion.

On May 30, general elections were held in South Korea which resulted in strong gains for independent candidates at the expense of President Rhee's supporters.

By June, South Korean ground strength totaled 98,000 men. Only 65,000 of these were combat troops spread out through eight divisions. These units were equipped with small arms and bolstered with only small anti-tank weapons and light artillery. The ROK Army had no tanks and its training by KMAG advisors had proceeded only through company-size exercises. There was no South Korean air force to speak of.

By mid-March of 1950, all North Korean residents within five kilometers of the 38th Parallel were forced to evacuate. By June, all railroads were declared to be on an emergency status. Except for a limited number of special public officials, all civilian rail travel was prohibited. A resident of Kosong at that time observed from June 8 on that there was a succession of trains moving southward toward the 38th Parallel, each carrying soldiers, tanks, artillery, vehicles, and carts. The highways in the area were also crowded with military automobiles and trucks.

On June 7, 1950, General Kim Il-sung proposed the holding of All-Korea elections, and again, on June 15, he proposed convening a Supreme People's Assembly in Seoul. This was done to mask the North Korean invasion plans. According to Chu Yong-bok, a People's Army major who was later captured by U.S. forces, a secret military leader's conference was held on Sunday June 11, at the National Security Department in Pyongyang. The meeting was opened by a statement from Major General Kim Kwang-hyop, director of operations of the General Command, who said, in part, that the North Korean People's Army was "going to conduct task force operations, mobilizing all combat divisions and all the firepower at this time. . . . The exercise may last approximately two weeks. . . . This secret should be kept

from friends, family, and even from wives." The formation
of the new I and II Corps was announced; Major General
Kim Kwang-hyop himself was to become the commander
of the new II Corps.

At sunrise on the morning of June 12, the II Corps
Headquarters personnel left Pyongyang on trucks and in
jeeps. They arrived in Hwachun the same evening and
set up tents.

Major Chu Yong-bok, of the II Corps Engineering
section, was also a Russian interpreter. He was recalled
to Pyongyang on June 12; at that time he was at Kumhwa
in transit to Hwachun. On June 19, the Russian advisor at
the National Security Department asked him to translate
a seven- or eight-page document which turned out to be
an operational directive written in Russian and issued to
People's Army engineering units. It ordered the invasion
of South Korea. As Major Chu remembers, the directive
included the following: each engineering battalion in an
infantry division was to clean up all routes by eliminating
all enemy mines and other obstacles by June 23; marching
routes and river crossings were to be secured in advance.
Routes of march, points of assembly, bridges and fords,
and supply points for each detachment were listed in
detail.

On June 22, the Supreme Commander of the
People's Armed Forces, General Kim Il-sung, issued
Combat Order No. 1, which ordered that specific targets
be established for each division and that attack
preparations be completed by noon on June 23. The date
of the opening assault was not given. However, the code
signals that would set off the attack were given:

Open attack: "Storm" by wire; "224" by
wireless.

Open fire: "Storm" by wire; "333" by wireless;
"red" by light.

The People's Army completed the movement of all its divisions to the 38th Parallel on June 23 under the guise of large task-force operational planning.

To the south, General Chae Pyong-dok, Chief of Staff of the Republic of Korea Army, issued an operational order on June 22 lifting the emergency warning of June 11 as of 2400 hours of June 23. He gave as a reason that there had been no specific danger noted behind North Korea's false call for peace and unity.

On Saturday, June 24, the KMAG office was empty except for one captain on duty. Even KMAG's interim commander had flown to Japan to spend the weekend. With the lifting of the emergency warning, leaves and passes, which had been suspended for the entire ROK Army, were granted, leaving only about one-third of all ROK Army troops in their barracks throughout South Korea.

At seven o'clock that same Saturday evening, it had just begun to rain when a party dedicating the new ROK Army Headquarters Officer's Club was getting underway in Seoul. About fifty high-ranking ROK Army officers and their KMAG counterparts were dancing to the band, laughing and drinking together. After the party was over, many of the South Korean and KMAG officers moved on to the nightclub in Myongdong, in the middle of Seoul, to keep the party going. The South Korean military leaders were relaxed, even befuddled, through partying and drink from the evening of June 24 into the early-morning hours of the 25th.

At the same time, a 90,000 Communist army was moving south.

It was just turning to dawn; the outlines of mountains and trees were becoming visible. The "Storm" was transmitted to every division.

It was 4:00 o'clock in the morning, June 25, 1950.

CHAPTER ELEVEN

Radio Pyongyang announced on the morning of June 25, 1950, "If the South Korean puppet government does not suspend its military activities near the 38th Parallel, the government of the democratic People's Republic of Korea will join the security corps of the Department of Home Affairs to take decisive measures for the smashing of the enemy. South Korean authorities will be held responsible for any results of this military venture."

At 9:30 that same morning, General Premier Kim Il-sung came on the air himself with a "Message to the People of Korea." Kim said, "The South Korean puppet clique has rejected all methods for peaceful reunification proposed by the Democratic People's Republic of Korea and has dared to commit armed aggression against the Haeju district north of the 38th Parallel. The Democratic People's Republic of Korea has ordered a counterattack to repel the invading troops. The South Korean puppet clique will be held responsible for whatever results may be brought about by this development."

War was declared by North Korea at eleven o'clock that Sunday morning.

*

There were no radios or newspapers available in the Chongjin Medical College dormitories, so those of us who lived there heard nothing of the approaching war, nor even of the initial invasion of the South. In fact, I did not learn of the declaration of war until the next morning, Monday, June 26, 1950.

It was a clear, hot summer morning with a slight wind blowing out of the north. At 9:30, after the first period, the students and faculty of Chongjin Medical College were called to assemble immediately at the south end of the soccer field to hear a very important message from "our hero," General Premier Kim Il-sung. About two hundred students gathered, as ordered, at the end of the soccer field. After singing patriotic songs for a brief interval, we were ordered to be silent.

This is the message that was broadcast through the field loudspeakers:

"Dear brothers and sisters! Great danger threatens our motherland and its people. What is needed to liquidate this menace? In this war, which is being waged against the Syngman Rhee clique, the Korean People must defend the Korean People's Democratic Republic and its constitution; they must liquidate the unpatriotic fascist puppet regime of Syngman Rhee which has been established in the southern part of the republic; we must liberate the southern part of our motherland from the domination of the Syngman Rhee clique; and we must restore the people's committees there—the real organs of power. Under the banner of the Korean People's Democratic Republic, we must complete the unification of the motherland and create a single, independent, democratic state. The war which we are forced to wage is a just war for the unification and independence of the motherland and for freedom and democracy. . . ."

As soon as Kim's speech ended, a dozen North Korean People's Army Air Force fighters swooped low in the skies over Chongjin—part of a carefully-staged sequence aimed at both provoking anger and hatred toward South Korea and building pride and confidence in our own forces and the cause they represented.

Between shouts of anger accompanied by angry faces and upraised clenched fists, we sang more patriotic songs. I was as much affected by the announcement—by the whole sequence of events—as the most-ardent Communists in the student body. I discovered whole new depths of pride and feeling for my homeland—if not for its government, about which I was as yet undecided. I felt very sad about the new turn of events, but I did not express my feelings to anyone because I was simply too shocked by the news to think clearly.

It never dawned on us that North Korea might be the aggressor in this new war. The claims put forth at this time by our government were that: the war was provoked by the "Unification by Advancing North" policy promulgated by the Syngman Rhee government; the People's Army counterattacked in order to liberate South Korea from capitalist-imperialist clutches; and the People's Army was going to win the "just" war because the Soviet Union and all other peace-loving nations in the world supported our war effort.

After the war had already begun, we heard details over the school radios of the advance to victory by the counterattacking People's Army. According to the reports, the People's Army occupied Tongdu-chon on the morning of June 25, then reached Uijongbu that same evening; by noon on June 27, our army had taken nearly twenty miles of the Uijongbu-Seoul Highway. On the fourth day of the "counterattack", the People's Army seized Seoul, the enemy capital. By then, our forces claimed to have inflicted 40,000 casualties upon the ROK Army—against insignificant losses among our military personnel.

A United States Army infantry force composed of 540 soldiers of the 21st Infantry Regiment—the first U.S. combat force to reach Korea—took up positions just north of Osan on July 5. Unprepared to face the onrushing People's Army tanks, this American force was obliged to leave all its equipment on the field and retreat. The defeat

111

Donald Chung, M.D.

of "invincible" United States Army troops gave the People's Army a proud sense of accomplishment. By July 20, Taejon, one of South Korea's major industrial cities, had to be abandoned by United Nations forces, and, in the wake of this disaster, our forces captured the commanding general of the United States 24th Infantry Division.

In a mere twenty-seven days, the People's Army marched 141 miles from the 38th Parallel to Taejon, an average of 5.2 miles per day. In so doing, it appeared that our forces had destroyed the ROK Army and defeated a large part of the United States forces based in East Asia.

*

The junior class was called to an emergency meeting of the Democratic Youth League one afternoon in mid-July. By the end of the meeting, the entire class of thirty or forty students had been drafted as medical officers into the People's Army and ordered to report to the Chongjin central railroad station at three o'clock the next afternoon.

My dormitory roommate, Yi Jung-gi, was a member of the junior class, so he was going, too. His sister managed to organize a farewell party on short notice at the small Chinese restaurant Jung-gi and I used to attend after soccer games. Ours was a very small group—just Jung-gi's sister and brother-in-law, their young daughter, and me. Jung-gi drank so much of the strong Chinese rice wine that we had little opportunity to talk. But talk was unnecessary for us to express the depth of emotions we shared. We each felt simultaneously the other's devotion to our native soil and our people. Though we did not know we were being mercilessly seduced in the Communist cause, our loyalty remained to our homeland. It is no wonder Jung-gi

112

overestimated his capacity for the strong drink, for after the party Jung-gi's brother-in-law and I carried the new inductee back to our dormitory room.

Jung-gi and I had been close friends since we met in 1946, and it had become obvious to me that he had little use and held little allegiance for the Communist system that utterly dominated our nation and our own daily lives. I expect I was somewhat influenced by him, and by the humiliatingly close scrutiny to which he had been subjected following the arrest and disappearance in 1946 by the security police of one of his closest friends for "anti-Communist" activities.

Following Jung-gi's last lunch in Chongjin, which was served by his sister, my friend packed a few personal belongings. His eyes were completely bloodshot and his face was puffy from drinking far too much rice wine the night before. In contrast to the characteristic alacrity with which he undertook all his activities, he moved with exaggerated slowness as he prepared to leave our room for the last time. He was sad and obviously upset to be leaving his sister, who had been like a mother to him since their mother's death some years earlier. Finally, however, we stepped out together on our way to the railroad station.

It was already midafternoon when we arrived. A strong north wind blew sand and dust into our faces as we joined our fellow students, most of whom were standing about, enfolded in tiny family groups. Then, as soon as the last junior classman appeared, all the draftees formed into a loose knot and walked onto the station platform. Puffing billows of white smoke into the air, a train was already waiting to carry them to an unknown destination where they would be trained in their role to help "liberate" the South.

*

Donald Chung, M.D.

One morning during the last week of July, the short, repetitive wails of the Chongjin city air-raid sirens interrupted our classroom activities for the very first time. All of us dropped whatever we were doing and, following orders, ran across the soccer field in as orderly a manner as we could manage to take cover in large sewer conduits that had been designated as our primary shelters. The huge concrete pipe sections were dry, which was fine with us, but they were buried beneath only a thin layer of soil, which did not inspire great confidence. There were only two manholes to enter this section of the sewers, so getting all of us safely below the ground took some time, and an understandably large amount of nervous energy was expended. Once inside the tunnel, we confronted an environment darker and cooler than that from which we had just come. I felt short of breath because of the poor ventilation and the excitement.

We heard the characteristic dull, throbbing roar of approaching large propellor-driven airplanes about thirty minutes later. This reminded me of the sound of the Russian aircraft I had heard flying over Harbin at the end of World War II. Then, however, the flights had not resulted in any fatalities or injuries. The situation was markedly different this time, for the whistling sound of the falling bombs and the massive shock of their detonations soon obscured the sound of the aircraft engines. The tunnel heaved, as though an earthquake had struck. Wind from the air displaced by the concussion pushed forcefully down the entire length of the confining concrete tube. One bomb dropped quite close to our shelter; I could clearly see the frightened faces of my fellow students in the sudden flash of its detonation.

The ordeal lasted only a few minutes. We could only hear and feel, but could not see, the planes or their payloads. At length, the dull throbbing from above

114

receded and died. Minutes later, the long wail of the sirens sounding the "all clear" penetrated the cool gloom of our sewer shelter, and we all climbed slowly, perhaps unsteadily, back to the daylit surface. We were shocked and grieved to learn that a girl student who had been seated in an angle of the tunnel had been killed by the massive pressure thrown off by the one near-miss. This was the first tragedy of the war we medical students had been party to, and we were all deeply chastened by its proximity to our lives.

Our soccer field had sustained a direct hit, and there was a huge hole—larger than an Olympic-sized swimming pool—less than a half-block's distance from our nearest entrance to the sewer shelter in which we had taken refuge. As these things go, that bomb barely missed wiping out the entire student body and faculty of Chongjin Medical College, a total of some two hundred people. News soon arrived that United States Air Force B-29 bombers had strewn hundreds of 500-pound bombs all across Chongjin, which was one of North Korea's major ports, a major steel-manufacturing center and the site of a Soviet-supported military supply complex. While the North Korean military authorities had been basking in the glory of their daily victories in the South, no serious thought had been given to the fact that the entire Korean peninsula could be reached by United States Air Force squadrons based in Japan.

Immediately after the raid, the entire student body was ordered to assemble at the college hospital, a short distance to the north of the college classroom building. There, we were each given a Red Cross armband and a first-aid kit containing bandages, injectable morphine, scissors, antiseptics and other items. When we were loaded aboard trucks drawn up at the hospital entrance, each of us was given a shovel. The excitement among our student group was palpable, as was several different kinds of fear: what had happened that required the aid of raw medical students; would we be placed in direct danger; what terrible sights would we see before this shocking day drew to a close; would our meager clinical training be adequate?

The trucks all headed in the direction of downtown Chongjin, which was obscured by a thick haze of smoke and dust. It was about a five-mile drive, during which the column of trucks slowly separated to cover as much of the downtown area as possible.

As my truck neared the edge of the downtown area, I could see that many of the tall buildings there had been gutted or demolished. The truck could not penetrate to the heart of the commercial area because rubble was blocking all the streets. Our leaders ordered us to dismount and form up into squads of four or five, which were sent in every direction. My group happened to pass the burned out ruin of the movie theater to which Chun Hae-jean had taken me during my "puppy love" days of 1947.

Hundreds of civilians—old, young, men, women, babies—lay dead or badly wounded in the twisted rubble. Many had bloody heads and faces while others had crushed or twisted limbs. Muscles were stripped from the arms and legs of some victims, or intestines lay beside their dead or dying bodies, while other corpses were unmarked, the victims' massive internal injuries resulting from the concussion of bomb detonations. Everywhere, arms, legs, heads and other parts of human bodies protruded from heaps of rubble and fallen concrete and balls of crazed steel reinforcing rods. The scene was too big and too horrible to comprehend in any but human terms and at a human scale; all we could do was find individual victims to treat as well as our limited supplies, experience and training would allow.

The first individual victim I confronted was a young woman who had been crushed between two great concrete slabs. I took in the fact that her left arm had been cleanly severed, then I noted that her wide-open eyes were turned upward and her mouth was open in a grotesque parody of surprise that must have been her last living impulse. I took a moment to hope that she had died swiftly, then turned to search for a living victim who retained a chance to survive with the aid of my meager ministrations.

Far from the ordered structure of the teaching hospital, we were forced to rely mainly upon instinct to conduct our treatment of wailing, screaming and sometimes stoic, victims. More often than not, treatment consisted wholly of a shot of morphine while rescue workers attempted to dig the dust-covered victims from the surface of the rubble. The area of destruction and the depth of the rubble in many places assured that most of the trapped victims would not even be found, much less rescued or saved by medical treatment.

Though I had listened attentively when the visiting Russian professor had lectured us on just the sort of treatment we were being called upon to deliver on this panic stricken day, I was dazed and overwhelmed, and I found it impossible to make decisions as quickly as I knew I should have. As I desperately dredged up all that I could recall of the Russian doctor's lecture, it dawned on me that he had not begun to cover the variety of traumatic injuries with which I was now confronted. I worked on in a drugged, almost catatonic state for hours, until the rescue effort was called off at sunset by the overwhelmed city authorities.

I came away from the trauma of that day of war with a deep, burning and lifelong hatred for war itself and for the faceless people who inflict it upon their fellow human beings. I was yet to be confronted by scenes and

117

acts far more personally threatening and physically devastating than those I saw in the bombed-out center of Chongjin, but it was there that the utmost of my feelings were attained and fixed.

From that day on, the air-raid sirens sounded with increasing frequency. There were even times when the bombing raids struck with no warning at all, when the bombers seemed to be headed elsewhere and then suddenly shifted course at the last moment.

*

The United States 8th Army, which had been built up over the first two months of the war from units stationed in Japan and brought in from the United states, took over the brunt of the fighting in South Korea while the defeated ROK Army tried to reform itself behind the American screen. Hammered incessantly by the advancing North Korean People's Army, the combined American and South Korean force eventually crossed behind the Naktong River and established a final defensive cordon on August 1 around the far-southern port city of Pusan.

It later came to light that the People's army suffered over 58,000 battle casualties in the opening months of the war, a staggering percentage of its original combat strength. The only mitigating factors were that it had all but destroyed the ROK Army and had achieved virtually all its objectives. Only the defeat of the final increment of the ROK Army and the ejection of the hard-pressed American 8th Army drawn up around Pusan stood between North Korean military forces and the forced reunification of the Korean nation.

The People's army committed eleven divisions—several of which were merely worn-down husks—to undertake a final effort to "push the 'American aggressors' into the sea and bring the final victory" which Premier Kim Il-sung wanted by August 15, the anniversary of Korean independence from Japanese rule.

Suddenly, even as victory lay within the grasp of the People's Army, the balance of power shifted with the arrival of fresh infusions of United Nations—mainly United States—troops at Pusan. Over 47,000 American soldiers had been committed in Korea by early August. Together with a reorganized ROK Army filled out with forced conscriptions, the United States commander controlled 92,000 against the 70,000 soldiers the North Korean People's Army was able to field around the broad Pusan Perimeter.

August 15 came and went, and Kim Il-sung's hopes for victory remained unfulfilled. The Naktong River valley was carpeted with the bodies of North Korean soldiers and their equipment.

*

During the middle and late summer, many wounded People's Army soldiers were evacuated to the Chongjin Medical College Hospital. We were no longer able to attend regular classes because of the frequency of the air-raids and the necessity of either awaiting or answering frequent calls for medical care throughout the city area. The sum total of the regional medical facilities was inadequate to bear the increasing patient load.

On the first day we admitted People's Army evacuees, I pushed around in his wheelchair a 23-year-old soldier who had suffered a large shrapnel wound in his right thigh. He was from a small farm near Chu-ul and had received his wound in a battle near Taejon. He knew almost nothing about the war—neither its aims nor any details of its progress—outside his own company's immediate activities. He proudly displayed a cigarette lighter, wristwatch and fountain pen he had "liberated" from a South Korean.

After our hospital began receiving military casualties, each new air-raid warning meant all medical students and staff nurses had an instant obligation; to shepherd the patients to safety. Ambulatory patients were led out of the building, followed by bedridden patients who were carried on litters and amputees who were pushed in wheelchairs across the adjacent fields toward the city's main shelters. These were located some two miles northeast of the hospital on a steep mountainside—the very area near the home of my aunt with whom I had once lived in happier, peaceful times.

From the mountainside shelters, we were able to look down on the ruins of Chongjin and beyond, far out into the Sea of Japan. The thrumming of aircraft motors would usually begin as we reached the base of the mountain, and the American warplanes would appear from out of the southeast, high over the Sea of Japan. Their path usually carried them over the southern outskirts of the miles-long city built on the narrow, curving coastal plain. Often, we could see the hundreds of pencil-thin bombs dropping in seesaw fashion from the bellies of the glinting, silver four-engined bombers. Then there would be the sight of the detonations and rising columns of smoke and dust, followed by the crescendo of explosions and, finally, the shaking of the very earth beneath us.

As the huge bombers departed, tiny, nimble swallow-like fighters flitted across the skyline to strafe buildings and streets or drop canisters of napalm, which burned in long, solid curtains of red-yellow fire suffused with billows of oily black smoke. The targets of the strafing and napalm were usually the city's rayon-manufacturing complex and the Mitsubishi steel mill that had been built by the Japanese before World War II.

There was no antiaircraft artillery committed to the defense of Chongjin's 100,000-plus souls or the city's important military and industrial centers. The only resistance was meted out by old Russian-made rifles aimed skyward as the fighters swooped low over the city's ruined downtown area.

As soon as the all-clear sounded, we would begin our return trek to the hospital to resume patient care. The trip was often made through a haze of acrid red-yellow smoke that drifted across the coastal plain in the twilight. It stung the eyes, bit into the nostrils, and tasted bitter and caustic.

The war had not reached a conclusion when, though classes had been suspended since mid-August, I was advanced to the junior class on September 1, 1950. The occasional bombings, which struck day or night, were by then being supplemented by naval bombardments undertaken by United States Navy warships standing offshore in the Sea of Japan.

*

The United Nations lines around Pusan continued to hold into the first half of September, 1950. By that time, the United Nations Supreme Commander, General Douglas MacArthur, had fashioned a bold stroke to defeat the North Korean People's Army.

MacArthur targeted the South Korean port of Inchon, on Korea's west-central coast, for a multi-division amphibious assault along the lines of the numerous amphibious assaults MacArthur himself had overseen against Japanese-held island bastions during the long Pacific War. He drew upon some elements fighting in the Pusan Perimeter, but relied mainly upon the bulk of two fresh divisions hurriedly reformed after the outbreak of the war in Japan and the United States.

121

Of all the armed nations of the world, only the United States had a sufficiency of experienced troops and equipment to mount so massive and ambitious an amphibious assault. MacArthur's plan envisioned an "end run" around the extended People's Army's right flank; the isolation of the People's Army south of a line between Inchon, Seoul and the east coast; and the eventual cracking of the main fighting strength of the seriously outnumbered People's Army between the bolstered Inchon invasion force and the revitalized 8th Army, which was to mount a drive out of the Pusan Perimeter at the earliest opportunity.

On September 15, 1950, a month to the day after Pusan was supposed to have fallen to the People's Army, the United States X Corps, composed of 1st Marine Division and 7th Infantry Division, swept from the amphibious transports that had carried it from Japan and began the process of overwhelming North Korean forces guarding the port and city of Inchon and the highway leading straight from the coast to Seoul. On the same day, 8th Army mounted a coordinated counteroffensive aimed at recrossing the Naktong River and driving all the way back to the 38th Parallel. General MacArthur's overall strategy was not aimed at merely driving the North Korean People's Army from South Korean soil, but in totally destroying the army as an effective fighting force.

Throughout the southern portion of the Korean peninsula, North Korean soldiers fled in confusion when confronted by the advancing elements of the sweeping pincers unleashed by Douglas MacArthur's fertile imagination and driving will.

CHAPTER TWELVE

Dr. Yang Jin-hong, the president of Chongjin Medical College, had been appointed by the Pyongyang government to work as one of the key people to reform and supervise Seoul National University during the temporary "liberation" of the South Korean capital. Following the Inchon landings in mid-September, however, Dr. Yang returned to Chongjin. As it turned out, he arrived in time to oversee the indefinite closure of the medical school and the assignment of all the junior class students to bolster the staffs of local hospitals throughout the region. I was assigned to work in Chu-ul and returned home by train.

By then, only Mother and my younger sister, Jung-hee, remained at home with Father's mother, a seventy-year-old who spent her waking hours badly hunched over because of crippling arthritis of the spine. We had not seen and had heard very little from Moon-hee since she left to become a prison guard. My second sister, Ok-bong, had married a lieutenant in the Security Police in 1947 and moved to Nanam, a small city between Chu-ul and Chongjin.

Father had long ago tired of selling used clothing in Chu-ul. He had joined the Korean Democratic Party in 1947 and soon became an unpaid volunteer officer. The party had been formed as a minority party by Choe Yong-kon, who was the North Korean Minister of National Defense, but the organization had no political representation in the national legislature. In a short time, Father became the unpaid chairman of the local party headquarters and, in 1948, soon after I advanced to Chongjin Medical College, he was called by the party central headquarters to serve in the party's central personnel office in Pyongyang.

123

Thus, after living off and on with his family for three years, Father once again found a valid excuse to leave. I was surprised to learn he even abandoned the woman he took during our first months in Chu-ul. However, loyalty seems never to have been one of Father's qualities. I have no doubt that my tall, slender, handsome, clothes-conscious father was never without female companionship during his years in the national capital.

There was no way I could satisfy my curiosity about Mother's reaction to his departure. I was unable to fathom her feelings, for she expressed no emotion regarding him in front of her children. She maintained her native dignity, showing neither dissatisfaction with nor unhappiness in the relationship.

The lines of communication between Father and the rest of us were growing weaker and weaker. He made an annual visit to Chu-ul (a duty visit to his mother, I suppose) and on one of them reported to Mother that he had been appointed manager of a factory in Pyongyang, owned by the People's Democratic Party.

*

I reported as instructed to Chu-ul City Hospital at eight o'clock on the morning after my return home. The facility was located in a small building with a single waiting room, a pharmacy, three examination rooms and one operating room. Dr. Kim, a general practitioner, was the director of the hospital and the only fully-qualified physician on the staff, which, until my arrival, comprised just him and three nurses and a number of consultants who maintained private practices in the area. I am certain that Dr. Kim, a tough-looking little man in his fifties, was a member of the Workers' Party. Whenever possible, I sat next to Dr. Kim while he examined patients. I wanted to learn as much as I could from him to bolster the extremely limited clinical experience I had thus far obtained at school.

There were several young men already seated in the waiting room, when I arrived for my first day of work. All of them had come to get letters that would give them excuses for avoiding conscription into the People's Army, which was calling up all the men of military age to replace the as-yet-unreported massive casualties sustained since the June 25th invasion of the South.

The first of the young men coughed constantly as he walked into the examination room, and his face was swollen and puffy. I took his history and found that he was twenty-four years old, an only son, the father of two and the sole support of his crippled father. He looked pale and malnourished. Dr. Kim provided a cursory examination and sent him for a chest X-ray. When the film came back, Dr. Kim explained to me that a great many conscriptees drank large quantities of soy sauce for a few days before the examination in the hope that "a congestive appearance of the lung fields showed up on film as tuberculosis." This man's attempts to malinger failed to pierce the scrutiny of the wily country doctor. I have no doubt that this man was soon on his way to the front lines.

The next patient was a chubby thirty-eight-year-old man who acted like an idiot and limped into the examination room with an expression of being in great pain. He told us that he experienced sharp pains in his right hip whenever he walked. Dr. Kim gave him an alcohol injection over his right hip and slapped him sharply in the buttocks. This caused an immediate stinging pain, which indicated that the man was faking.

By this time, I was convinced that Dr. Kim's entire practice consisted of the rooting out of military malingerers.

Donald Chung, M.D.

*

A week after joining Dr. Kim's staff, I received a notice from the medical school that the entire junior class was to be inducted into the People's Army. I was given a time and a place to report for duty.

Well, there it was. I was already older than many of the young men who had been conscripted into the People's Army, but, at eighteen, I certainly wasn't old enough to be a doctor, and my training was incomplete. Perhaps I would not even serve in a medical capacity, though that was difficult to imagine. Perhaps I had enough training to serve as an expendable front-line combat surgeon or a rear-area medical administrator. I certainly had no illusions about my meager qualifications and my virtual lack of clinical experience.

On the same morning as I received the notice, I was instructed by Dr. Kim to observe the first surgical procedure to take place at the Chu-ul City Hospital since my arrival there. I scrubbed, donned a surgical gown and sterile rubber gloves, and walked into the operating room on time, at precisely nine a.m. To my surprise, the surgeon turned out to be Professor Kim Pung-u, Chongjin Medical College's professor of surgical anatomy. This Dr. Kim was a successful surgeon, widely known in North Hamgyong Province. He was a gentle, soft-spoken intellectual, very well-liked by the students. While a consultant was administering the anesthesia, Professor Kim explained that the patient was a middle-aged woman with signs of cancer in the uterine area. He planned a total removal of the uterus. As soon as the patient showed signs of being deeply anesthetized, Professor Kim proceeded with an incision in her lower abdomen.

126

As the surgery progressed, the scrub nurse had to be sent from the room to fetch an additional retractor. I seized the opportunity to tell the professor about the induction notice I had received that morning. Cautiously he whispered in my ear, "South Korean and American armies have crossed the 38th Parallel and are even now rapidly pressing northward, you might well be killed just getting to the post assigned by the People's Army." Just then the nurse returned, silencing Professor Kim. Neverless, the brief spontaneous counsel of this mature intellectual I held in the highest esteem changed the course of my life.

Following the successful completion of the surgical procedure, I reported to the hospital director and told him that I had received an induction notice from the medical college and that I would not be returning to the hospital.

At that time, until hearing Professor Kim's report, I knew nothing about the progress of the war, for there had been little news—positive or negative—available to civilians since the early days of the armed conflict. I certainly had not heard any news of the Inchon landings nor the recapture of Seoul by United Nations forces.

As it happened, on September 30, 1950, General MacArthur called upon Kim Il-sung to surrender. Kim ignored the offer, and the ROK Army and United Nations forces drove northward across the 38th Parallel on October 1 crumbling resistance as it rolled forward.

*

I waited until after dinner to tell Mother of the induction notice I had received and of the war news told me by Professor Kim.

Although Mother had no formal education and lacked the power of articulate speech, she was a

127

fountainhead of wisdom. On hearing my announcement she asked no questions but simply rose and left the room. Soon she rejoined us with a small bag packed with a few of my essential belongings.

Wordlessly she led the whole household silently through the dark, moonless night toward her mother's house in Taehyang, about four miles further on the mountains, northwest of Chu-ul. Our progress was slow, requiring nearly two hours because of the crippled condition of my paternal grandmother who could not be hurried.

Throughout the long walk scenes from the past flashed across my memory. Only five years earlier we had trudged the same mountain road to Grandmother's farm on our exodus from Harbin. Joy had filled our hearts on that occasion, for we were settling down with our own extended family in our own free homeland.

There was no joy bubbling up from my heart on this night. I was going into hiding without any idea as to how long the ordeal might be, nor what the outcome might bring forth.

I was too young and too politically unsophisticated to realize the significance of my present actions. Alternating with scenes of the past rolling by on the screen of my mind, I replayed the strange events of the day: the unsettling call to arms; the frank and treasonous counsel of the professor who was more idol than doctor to me; the instantaneous reaction of Mother, like a lioness fiercely springing to defend her endangered young. I saw myself as a mere actor on a strange stage, unaware of the role I was to play. I seemed without self-will, following where events were leading me.

Mother, on the other hand, knew exactly what she was doing and where she was leading us. Her decision was her instinctual desire to keep her only son alive and out of harm's way. She was totally uncognizant of any political ramifications of what we were involved in. I was simply her beloved son, whose very conception led to hundreds of days of prayer on the nearby mountainside regardless of searing heat, drenching rain, or freezing snow. I was the sickly infant whom she had constantly attended during my first troubled months of life, the same son almost lost to a ruptured appendix in Harbin. There was no thought in her mind of loyalty to her native land. Her loyalty was to her son.

I had no personal opinions about the war nor even about the Communist system that had infiltrated virtually every aspect of life in North Korea. I recited Marxist-Leninist doctrine because everyone to whom I had been exposed in school recited Marxist-Leninist doctrine. I obeyed rules promulgated by the Communist leadership and orders issued by the hospital or civil authorities because I was obedient. I supported the war effort because my nation was at war. But I never *thought* about any of it. *Thinking* about events around me was not something that had ever occurred to me to do. I followed the leadership of others—my betters—in the conduct of my daily life, and now I was following my Mother—my better—into the mountains, toward an obscure fate. I was, as always, in someone else's hands.

*

Mother's only brother, Kim Dong-sik, was the head of the household. Uncle Dong-sik was very much like Mother: quick to hear and slow to speak. He was a model farmer and widely respected in Taehyang, the village in which both Mother and Father had been born and raised. In fact, Dong-sik was chairman of the village chapter of the Farmer's Union.

There was no room in the house to accommodate four extra guests—Mother, Grandmother, Jung-hee and

129

myself—so my sister and I spread a blanket on piles of rice straw we placed between the bags of rice and corn stored in the little straw-thatched barn behind the house. Next morning, however, Jung-hee and Grandmother returned to Chu-ul because the farm facilities simply could not accommodate more than two of us.

Uncle Dong-sik's house was about two hundred yards from the main country road between another small village to the northeast and Chu-ul, to the southwest. The farther village, in fact, is where the Hong family had taken me during my brief "medicinal" adoption as an infant.

I have no doubt that Mother discussed my situation in detail with Dong-sik. He certainly deserved to know precisely why Mother and I had inserted ourselves into his family's life, and to decide for himself if he wanted to bear the risk of harboring me. Of course, there was no doubt we were welcome.

Mother's mother was a very active woman, and she assumed the task of keeping her sharp eye out for any signs of interest on the part of the Security Police. Indeed, whenever there was the merest hint of trouble, Grandmother rushed to my hiding place, helped me climb into a large clay pot, and pulled the lid over my head. As soon as the uniforms disappeared from the area, Grandmother would return to knock on the lid, signaling that it was safe to come out. What a relief to breathe fresh air after being confined to my hideaway!

The time passed in endless stretches of crushing, unrelieved boredom. I had to stay in the barn to avoid being seen by casual observers as much as the prying eyes of the Security Police. I had long since become used to constant mental and physical activity during my waking hours, and now I was suddenly and utterly denied both.

Several times during my stay in the barn, small jet fighter-bombers, which the villagers called "swallow-planes," suddenly appeared over the tiny village of less than two hundred souls. As soon as the pilots chose their targets, the nimble warplanes banked very low and made their strafing runs. They shot at anyone wearing the yellow-green uniform of the North Korean People's Army, whether they were in the streets of the village, riding in a cart or motor vehicle, or even walking alone down a country lane. Often, they strafed farmers' carts and the village mill. I cannot imagine what the pilots thought the farmers were hauling in their carts or what was stored at the mill, and the farmers said that there were no soldiers stationed anywhere near their obscure and remote village, though it is true that the occasional soldier or small group of soldiers did traverse the roads through the area.

My tension grew daily. How it might turn out was still obscured though the more extreme possibilities were reasonably evident: I might be saved by the approaching armies from the south, or I might be captured by northerners.

I did not know it then, but the ROK Army had crossed the 38th Parallel on October 1 and, by mid-month, was halfway to the Yalu River, which marked the border between Korea and Manchuria. The ROK 3rd and Capital Divisions had raced 110 miles up the eastern coastal road and, though many South Korean soldiers marched on bleeding feet, the huge harbor at Wonsan fell on October 10. While the Capital Division continued northward, 3rd Division remained at Wonsan to screen landings by the United States X Corps, which had landed only a month earlier at Inchon. While the Americans scoured the area around Wonsan, the ROK Capital Division captured the major industrial city of Hamhung and the neighboring port of Hungnam, fifty miles north of

Wonsan and in the next province south of Chongjin. At the same time, to the west, the Americans surrounded Pyongyang on October 19.

By October 29, the leading regiment of the ROK Capital Division had reached Songjin. On November 5, the ROK soldiers captured Kilchu, which was directly linked by road to Chu-ul.

*

Beginning in mid-November, I could hear the sounds of artillery fire each day, and the night sky was invariably lit up by the flashes of battle far to the south. This went on for several days without any real hint that the war was progressing in my direction. The fact that the firing did not seem to be coming any closer made me even more apprehensive than I had been to that point. Was it possible that the People's Army had been able to stem the United Nations advance within earshot of my haven? Also by then, a cold front had moved down the northeast coast from Siberia, and temperatures were ranging from 10 to -30 Celsius. Paddy fields and the mountain roads within sight of Uncle Dong-sik's farm had a light covering of snow, and the older farmers were by then gathering every day at different houses for the endless round of wintertime card-playing and gossiping—the only entertainment available to residents of this tiny backwater sandwiched between the coastal mountain ranges to the northeast and southwest.

*

On the afternoon of November 21, 1950, I was seated in the barn when I heard a half-dozen shots break the silence of my sanctuary. Mother came rushing in and

132

whispered in my ear, "Look outside, over there. Lots of soldiers." Her face was a mask of fear.

A column of over two hundred North Korean soldiers was strung out across the snow-covered fields, marching from the mountains south of Taehyang toward the mountains to the north. The soldiers were clearly exhausted; many were limping and many others had bandages over their heads and on their arms and legs. I could see that many of the troops had no rifles, and almost all of them wore dirty, ragged uniforms. They all passed quickly through the village without speaking to any of the villagers.

Scarcely thirty minutes passed, when the silence of the village was again broken by the sounds of gunfire coming from the south. Mother again rushed to me, this time sporting a gentle, relieved smile. "Look out there," she pointed, "Different soldiers!"

CHAPTER THIRTEEN

I stood up to see a company-size formation of what I took to be ROK soldiers walking through the village in an extended column, the weapons of the troops pointed outward from the roadway in anticipation of trouble.

The scene before me marked a significant change. Only a few months earlier, the North Korean People's Army had been pushing these South Korean soldiers back into the tip of the peninsula. I frankly would not have believed the straits to which the People's Army had been reduced had I not seen a small splinter of the army in retreat. My mind's eye reviewed the scenes of the robust, tanned and well-equipped soldiers I had seen along the railway line from Chongjin to Chu-ul only five months earlier.

I could see that the new arrivals each had a skull insignia affixed to the right side of his helmet. I later learned that this was an element of the crack 18th Infantry Regiment, a part of the ROK Army's premier Capital Division. These were some of the toughest soldiers in the ROK Army, and they looked it when I first laid eyes on them.

It was not yet time to come out of my hiding place, for I had no idea how these no-nonsense combat infantrymen might treat a young man of military age in the newly-liberated but still-hostile northern half of their country. I knew I must leave my hiding sooner or later, but for now I was frankly terrified at the prospect of falling into the hands of men who sported so brutal a symbol as the 18th Regiment's death's head.

As I watched, the ROK soldiers split up into small groups and found shelter in homes throughout the village.

They all left in the morning to continue their pursuit of the shattered elements of the People's Army that had passed through the day before.

Finally, I knew which way the war .was really going; no more hearsay to accept or reject on faith, no more propaganda from far-off places. I had seen the difference between the two Korean armies with my own eyes.

The problem remained of how and when I might come out of hiding. I trusted neither army. If the northerners returned, they could easily assume that I was an evader or a deserter, and they might take immediate, ruthless action to make an example of me. If I was taken by southerners, they might consider me an enemy agent or, at best, a People's Army deserter. I could well imagine how I might be treated if either surmise were true.

Here, once again, Mother exhibited her profound wisdom. On the third day after the first ROK soldiers had passed through Taehyang, she said to me, "I will go down to Chu-ul and try to find some of your friends who have not gone to the war." And that is what she did. My former junior high school classmate, Choe Ik-hwan, assured her, by his open presence in the town as much as by his words, that it was safe for me to come out of hiding. Ik-hwan suggested that I return to the town hospital and reopen the clinic as a first-aid treatment center for the townspeople and villagers, who had had no medical care since all the doctors left town.

On November 25, the day Mother was in town collecting news from my friends, the main body of the ROK Capital Division captured Chongjin and the vital port and military support facilities that had survived the harrowing months of bombing. On that day, also, the Capital Division's forward headquarters moved into Chu-ul and set up a forward command post from which it would direct the final drive to the Manchurian border.

On that day, also, we had an unanticipated visitor. Father simply strolled into Grandmother's house—and, thus, back into our lives. He looked like one of the defeated soldiers who had trudged through days earlier. He was filthy and decked out in ragged clothing. He explained that he had left Pyongyang following its capture by the American 8th Army, then had walked for days and nights northeast toward Chu-ul, across the mountain wastes that cut through the heart of the northern peninsula.

The members of my family shared a few happy moments this day, though not all for the same reasons. Mother, of course, was always happy when her husband returned, and she was happy because her son was about to be set free. Father was probably just happy to have survived another of life's ordeals, and to have a place to stay. I was happy to be leaving the cramped, cold, and utterly boring confines of Uncle Dong-sik's barn.

That very afternoon, we moved from the country house back to our own house in Chu-ul. None of the many ROK soldiers we passed on the road or on the streets troubled me in the least. As soon as we got home, I removed the filthy clothes I had been wearing, then Mother cut my hair and prepared a hot bath for me. I sat in the tub for what seemed like hours, meticulously cleaning off the accumulated filth and stink of my six weeks of self-imposed captivity.

*

The next day I walked to the Chu-ul City Hospital, as my friends had suggested. There was no doctor, and I was the only civilian in town with medical training. Fortunately, Chu-ul had been untouched by bombing or even ground fighting, so there was no destruction and, more important, no civilian casualties. The street in front of the hospital was filled with rushing trucks bearing ROK soldiers and war materiel. My only concern was to keep from being run over. In the distance, I could hear the occasional crack of a rifle or pistol, and I assumed that snipers had been left behind by the retreating People's Army that had passed through days earlier.

When I arrived, I found that two of the three permanent nurses and several civilian volunteers had already opened the clinic. I toured the facilities as if I had always been the senior practitioner, and I got everyone to work cleaning the rooms and making them ready for any eventuality. I was tentative in my approach at first, but I found myself falling back on a hitherto unperceived self-reliance I imagine I had begun to develop during my summer of treating bombing victims in Chongjin.

Early that afternoon my work in readying the hospital for eventual patients was interrupted by the screech of brakes and loud deceleration of a heavy vehicle. A large truck pulled up and stopped directly in front of the hospital. Nervously I peered through the window to see what its ominous mission might portend. There, in the bed of the truck, were seven or eight young people. Among them I spotted my former junior high class-mate, Choe Ik-hwan. My fear abated, I rushed to the entrance to see what was happening. Upon seeing me, Ik-hwan called out, "Come along".

"What can I do?" I asked, wondering what it was he wanted of me.

"We just found a few dozen bodies up at the hot springs. I'd like for you to come along to help us identify them from photos we have of missing persons."

I had never had any experience with identifying dead people, but I was willing to do whatever I could to

138

help. I also knew that one of my aunts, the wife of Father's third brother, had been taken away by the Security Police a few days before the arrival of the ROK Army. I was afraid that one of the newly-discovered bodies might be hers.

The truck climbed slowly toward the hot springs area, which began about five miles to the northwest of the hospital on the mountainside road I had walked with such joy my first autumn back from Harbin. It was a fine, cold winter day with an endless clear, blue sky with the sun reflecting off isolated patches of ice covered ground. The road itself was slushy and muddy from the melted snow. As we reached the first hot springs, which were surrounded by Korean inns and Russian-style homes sporting bright blue and red roofs, I noticed how very quiet the surroundings were. Very few people were in evidence, and these were mainly women and young children. I thought of the young men who had undoubtedly gone to war from this beautiful and peaceful place—young men who had probably died upon distant battlefields or who might even be fighting on in the nearby mountains.

As the truck passed a suspension bridge over a particularly beautiful stretch of river gorge, I was overcome with nostalgia, for I had crossed the bridge with Chun Hae-jean during my puppy love days of 1948. Lost in my reverie, I could almost hear her laughter when I expressed my initial unwillingness to venture out upon the insubstantial and swinging span.

I pulled myself back from the happy past and saw that the truck had progressed up the narrow roadway past the center of the main village. We drove on another quarter-mile, then the driver pulled over and I followed the others when they jumped down from the back of the vehicle.

The scene before me was, in its way, more horrible than the brutal deaths I had witnessed in

Chongjin. Several dozen bodies, all female, lay naked and half-frozen in a roadside ditch. They were completely covered with a layer of melting snow. Every one appeared to have been in her thirties or forties, and every one of them had her hands bound with telephone wire to a wooden pole behind her back. The cause of death was particularly brutal, for these women had not been shot; their executioners had stabbed them repeatedly with sharp pointed sticks, which had been tossed into the ditch beside the bodies when the orgy of killing had ended. I noticed that many of the women had been repeatedly stabbed in their wombs and that a few still had sticks protruding from their vaginas.

We examined the bodies one at a time. Every one of the young men on the truck had come to find a wife or mother or aunt or sister, and most did. I was able to identify my aunt quite readily, for she had a distinctive burn scar on the right side of her neck. Late in the afternoon, we loaded the bodies aboard the truck and drove them back to Chu-ul, where we left those that we had identified at the homes of their relatives. The rest we turned over to the military authorities.

While on the drive back to town, I learned why these women had been slaughtered. Several weeks earlier, a number of young people between the ages of seventeen and twenty had resisted conscription into the People's Army and gone into hiding in the mountains. They soon formed an anti-Communist underground under the leadership of several adults who had built up a hatred of the Communist regime over the past five years and who had also fled from the town. The group acquired a radio and monitored the progress of the ROK Army and United Nations forces that were sweeping into North Korea. During the last week before the liberation of Chu-ul, as fighting raged around nearby Orang, the resisters became impatient with waiting and decided to strike a blow on their own. They mounted an attack against Chu-ul City Hall and the adjacent Security Police station, where they captured several rifles and some ammunition. During this same period, the underground youths crept into town at night to beg food from relatives and other townspeople they knew. The women we pulled out of the roadside ditch had all been picked up during the last sweep before the Security Police fled before the arrival of the ROK Army. Without trial or ample proof of the allegations, all the women had been executed on charges of aiding the hungry resisters.

On the day of my aunt's funeral, my family received another tragic jolt. A returning prisoner who had escaped from the northern coal mines told us that Father's fourth brother, Kil-yong, had perished in the mine to which he had been sentenced by the People's Court in 1946 for listening to south Korean radio broadcasts and attacking the arresting officer.

I had received a letter from Kil-yong in April, just two months before the outbreak of war. He had written to tell me that he had been selected as a model prisoner because he worked hard and behaved well. He was hoping to be pardoned soon, before his five-year term was up. In any case, he promised to take me on a fishing trip as soon as he returned home.

The escaped prisoner explained that the entrance to the coal mine had been sealed with explosives by the prison officials when they joined the retreating People's Army. All the prisoners who happened to be working in the mine, including Uncle Kil-yong, were killed in the blast.

I cried for many hours as I asked myself over and over why such things happened. My elder sister had been raped by Russian soldiers, my uncle had been sent to prison mainly for listening to the radio, my aunt had been brutally murdered by her own people for feeding hungry

141

boys, and my uncle had been entombed in a coal mine by his fellow Koreans. I knew, also, that two women in Chu-ul had been brutally and repeatedly raped by an ROK Army sergeant and several of his men, and that at least 12,000 civilians in Hamhung had been slaughtered at the order of North Korean authorities. In fact, the stories of brutalities, large and small, were mounting with each passing day. As a surgeon, so many instances of brutality eventually had a numbing effect.

Was the brutality something we had unconsciously learned from our former Japanese overlords? Had we fallen under the spell of evil madmen? Was it something we knew from instinct, to issue forth from some dark corner of everyman's soul when circumstances threw off the restraints of civilization?

I did not know then and do not know now why or what good was supposed to flow from it, but I did know that the entire Korean nation, north and south, had succumbed to the unrestrained insanity of a fratricidal civil war.

CHAPTER FOURTEEN

I spent on the average about four to six hours a day at the city hospital, serving the civilians in the Chu-ul area. Most of the services rendered consisted of treating minor injuries and dispensing simple medication for less serious illnesses such as diarrhea, stomach-aches, coughs and assorted aches and pains. Thankfully, everything was within my limited—though growing—expertise.

On the morning of December 2 I was asked to visit a small mountain village about ten miles northwest of town to examine and treat sick villagers who could not be efficiently brought in to the hospital. There was no pressing appointment needing my attention so I grabbed my emergency medical kit and loaded it with the medicines usually prescribed for the various internal disorders I expected to encounter. I set off in the company of one of the volunteer medical workers who had joined me at the hospital in the past few weeks. The illnesses I treated at the village were indeed routine, and I was able to start back down the road to Chu-ul in the early afternoon.

I arrived in downtown Chu-ul at about four in the afternoon, just as the light was beginning to fade. It grew dark early in Chu-ul because the sun slipped behind the high mountains that hemmed in the town on all sides but the east, where Chu-ul overlooked the Sea of Japan. A light snow had been falling all day and, as long as there was sun, the reflection of sunlight on the white surface had actually had an insulating effect upon the otherwise bitterly cold air. Now, with the sun gone, there was a rapid onset of inhuman cold. Snowflakes that had earlier

143

melted when they came in contact with my face, now clung heavily to it and covered my coat and woollen scarf.

Nearing home, I was astonished to come upon hundreds of ROK soldiers marching southward in long snake-like columns stretching out as far as I could see on both sides of the main road. Each of the soldiers was burdened with a heavy field pack and weapons. Rolling slowly along the center of the roadway were long columns of military vehicles carrying other soldiers or immense loads of equipment and supplies. But what impressed me even more were vast columns composed of many thousands of civilians who were trudging along on foot through the fields on either side of the roadway.

I stopped and watched in complete bewilderment. It was clear that a retreat was in progress, but I could not believe that this powerful and well-equipped army had anything more to fear in North Korea. Certainly, the ragtag North Korean People's Army I had seen in miserable retreat was incapable of forcing so large and mighty an army to give up what it had so recently won. More mystifying, there was no audible sign of distant heavy fighting. In fact, I heard no sounds of gunfire or artillery, light or heavy, near or far.

Military policemen were everywhere, directing this mass movement with frantic arm signals and even more frantic blasts of whistles. Completely puzzled, I stood by the side of the road and watched the moving crowd go by. As I stood, the snow continued to build up on my clothing and exposed skin. I thought that if those passing by happened to notice me, I must have appeared to them as an incongruous snowman.

After about fifteen minutes I approached a military policeman who was standing at a nearby intersection. I asked him where the ROK Army was going and why it was moving south, but he kept on with his job as if he did not hear me. Perhaps he simply chose not to answer.

After my repeated questioning, he shouted at me without interrupting his hand signals, "Young man, this is only a three-day tactical retreat." My military experience was so slight that I readily accepted his explanation. Perhaps it was the reason given by his superiors, and they by theirs.

*

Mother and my youngest sister, Jung-hee, were preparing dinner when I reached the house. They appeared happy and peaceful because the majority of the family was back together once again, following the United Nations victory over the People's Army and the Communist regime. Indeed, Mother had virtually blossomed out, showing signs of absolute euphoria for many days. I had thought several times over the past week that I had never seen this work-worn woman of forty-eight as happy and relieved as she then appeared to be. She actually hummed lilting tunes as she bustled happily through her daily chores. For the first time since I had become a sentient being, I was able to see a bit of the girl in her.

The thought of shattering Mother's illusion of security was painful to me, but I sensed I had no choice. Even if the mass movement *was* only a three-day tactical retreat, I was well aware that the vacuum could be filled by a renascent People's Army and, in its wake, the dreaded Security Police. After standing silently in the doorway for a moment, I blurted out the news of what I had just witnessed.

"The South Korean Army is retreating south and a crowd of civilians is following along with it!"

My news came as a tremendous shock, for neither Mother nor Jung-hee had any idea of the mass movement that was going on only a few streets away. Father was out visiting a friend, but he would soon find out because he would have to cross the road taken over by the southbound columns in order to get home.

Mother was unable to speak for several minutes. And just as suddenly as her youthful, joyous spirit had reappeared, it vanished as my words reached her consciousness. Aware of this devastating change that was overtaking her, I had to go on with my spoken thoughts, regardless of how much I would have preferred to spare her the sorrow I knew my next words would cause her.

"I have to follow them. Otherwise, I might be killed by the Security Police when they get back to Chu-ul," I fairly blurted out the words, aware of their bluntness.

The shock to Mother that I feared was as harrowing to me as it was to her, but I knew that this was the moment for making my own decision about whether I should risk being killed at Mother's side, or save my life by following the retreating southern forces.

Finally, recovering slightly from her agonized silence, Mother insisted that I once again hide in Grandmother's countryside barn. Jung-hee, then only eleven years old, had been listening to the conversation in silence, but she suddenly enfolded me in her arms and hugged me tightly to her body, "Please don't leave us," she stammered in her childish voice, fighting back her tears. "Hide in a foxhole in the mountainside and I will bring your meals every day. Please! Please, Brother! You're the only brother I have. Don't leave me!"

Her words seared into my very inmost being. At her frantic insistence, I absently shoveled several spoonfuls of rice into my mouth. The moist globs stuck in my throat, and, choking violently, I gave up trying to eat and rushed from the table.

Ignorant of what lay before me, I instinctively knew that I must in some way prepare myself for a journey whose destination and length of time were both unknown to me.

I left the room and changed my clothing. First, I put on a thick layer of clean underwear and covered it with my blue school uniform and my long woolen topcoat. While I was dressing, Mother came to the realization that the preservation of my life dictated my following the ROK Army out of Chu-ul. With her usual serenity which was as familiar to me as her very presence, she packed a small knapsack with a three-day supply of rice, some dry, seasoned cuttlefish, and three pairs of clean socks. She also hung around my neck my identification booklet from Chongjin Medical College, and topped it off with her only white silk scarf, one of her few personal treasures.

I was anxious to get out of town as soon as possible, for I felt that the North Korean People's Army might be arriving as quickly as had the ROK Army in its wake only a few short weeks before. I hefted my knapsack and emergency medical kit to my shoulder and prepared to embrace Mother at the open outside door.

At this moment, the calm and stoic exterior she had worn every day of my life finally gave way. Convulsively she clutched at my sleeve with her crippled, arthritic fingers. Her voice was a cry that would sound in my ears for years to come, sometimes receding into the recesses of my brain, but always lingering like a haunting melody, pulling me back into an unrecoverable past.

"My Son! My only Son! Don't leave me. You have been my whole life." As though those words were the sum total of her life, her voice became a tiny whimper, ending in a resignation to fate which had in these few brief moments ended, for all practical purposes, her life.

I knew the depth of the simple words just spoken, their inviolate truth, but an even greater truth loomed before me—I could delay no longer.

Outside, the snow continued to descend like a billowing lacy curtain. The air was bitterly cold, but I knew that more than the icy wind was tearing at my mother's face. The thoughts of losing her only son, the son who meant the whole world to her, cut into her being with the ferocity of the cutting edge of an iceberg.

Desperately we clung to one another in the open doorway of the house, my fear mounting with each passing moment. I sensed this might be my last opportunity to evade the dreaded Security Police. I knew I had to leave. For the first time in my life I berated my beloved mother. My voice was harsh though my instincts longed to gather this tiny specter in my arms and shield her from all the world's ills.

"Didn't I tell you it's only for three days? I'll be back in three days, and then we can live together in peace forever." Then, gently but firmly, I pushed her away from me, back into the house.

I felt a quiver course through her thin, emaciated body, like a harp string continuing to quiver after the sound has seemed to stop. Her face, lined and aged beyond her years, became a stolid, wrinkled mask, her eyes hiding any human feeling. As I disengaged myself from her grasping embrace, the last thing I was to remember was the roughness of her poor, gnarled fingers, still trying desperately to cling to me just a few seconds more.

Unable to face her longer, I swung around and gave Jung-hee a final hurried embrace, then rushed into the void. Only then did I realize that tears, like a gushing waterfall, had been streaming from my eyes, for in the raw and bitter cold they had frozen on my face.

Surging blindly forward, refusing to turn my head for one last glimpse of Mother and the home I was leaving behind, I soon joined the waves of refugees and soldiers moving on to some unknown—unknowable—destination to the south.

The wind was blowing hard and wet snowflakes swirled in the gleam of headlights of army vehicles. Soon, the engulfing darkness and pelting snow banished from my line of vision any last vestige of my home, even had I been emotionally able to seek one last glimpse.

It was four-forty-five on the afternoon of December 2, 1950.

*

The cause for the retreat was not, as I thought for some time afterward, the resurgence of the North Korean People's Army. Rather, the threat was far greater, for the recently-declared People's Republic of China was afraid that the United Nations army closing on its Manchurian provincial border by way of North Korea might eventually carry its anti-Communist crusade on into China.

As early as October 25, elements of the Red Chinese People's Liberation Army—so-called "volunteers"—had gone into action against United Nations troops in both northwestern and northeastern Korea. Following initial successes in large probes against modern Western military units, the People's Liberation Army had committed literally hundreds of thousands of its soldiers to a secret infiltration of the vast mountainous wastes in north-central Korea. On November 25, division after Chinese division of the Chinese infiltrators struck at United States 8th Army units in northwestern Korea. On November 27, many Chinese divisions hammered United States X Corps and ROK Army units throughout northeastern Korea. The

United Nations units in the west disintegrated under unremitting pressure. The disorganized remnants fled southward to Pyongyang and beyond. In the east, and only a fewscore miles southwest of Chu-ul, the Chinese divisions came up against just about the only United Nations units determined to hold them back. At several places on the eighty-mile road between the port of Hungnam and the mountain town of Yudam-ni, on the shore of the man-made Changjin (or Chosin) Reservoir, elements of the United States 1st Marine Division and 7th Infantry Division held their ground against Chinese assaults that should have been overwhelming—assaults similar to those that had indeed been overwhelming everywhere else they encountered United States or ROK forces.

On November 30, following consultations in Tokyo with General Douglas MacArthur, the commanding general of the United States X Corps, still holding its own around the Changjin Reservoir, ordered a total but organized withdrawal of United States forces in his sector. At this time, the ROK Army I Corps—which was operating near the coast to the north of X Corps—had its headquarters in Songjin while its subordinate components, the Capital and 3rd Divisions, had headquarters located respectively at Chongjin and Kilchu. (Capital Division's forward command post was at Chu-ul.) Elements of the U.S. X Corps and the ROK I Corps had penetrated all the way to the Tumen River border with Manchuria.

As soon as the American corps commander ordered a withdrawal from the Changjin Reservoir area to the port of Hungnam, the ROK I Corps commander was obliged to follow suit. Orders were issued to the Capital and 3rd Division commanders on the night of November 30 and, though the ROK units were in no way as severely pressed as the U.S. X Corps, the bulk of Capital Division

150

reached the outskirts of Chu-ul by the night of December 1.

The vast array of soldiers and equipment I joined on the afternoon of December 2 were the rear units of Capital Division following orders to retreat southward.

CHAPTER FIFTEEN

The night I fled Chu-ul it was ominously dark. Snow crunched underfoot and covered the surrounding terrain, made visible by headlights of the motorized division. The longest trek I had ever made was the three-hour homeward journey on foot from the racetrack in Harbin, the day Father bet and lost our bus fare. It didn't take a statistical genius to calculate that that earlier record stood no chance of survival at the ordeal stretching out before me.

Limping along on sore or frozen feet were people of all ages, both male and female. Their number grew as hour after hour of the fearful night passed by. Many older men and women hobbled along using canes and occasionally even on crutches. Not unexpectedly, they fell farther and farther behind, unable to match the pace of the forward moving throng. Occasionally younger family members would slow to assist their elders, but many younger refugees tried desperately at all costs to keep up with the line of soldiers and trucks of the retreating army.

The farther south the march penetrated, the greater grew the throng. Many ox-drawn carts, heavily overburdened with household goods and human cargo, slipped off the treacherous icy roads into ditches filled with ice and slush. If the oxen could not regain their footing on the road, the soldiers, no doubt following orders, shot them as they hopelessly struggled.

As was to be expected, more and more of those fleeing southward fell farther and farther behind. I, being young and in good health and driven by my relentless fear, managed to keep pace with the main body of death's-head troops I had followed out of Chu-ul.

We arrived at Myungchon as the sun was coming up on December 3. At that moment, the soldiers stopped at the local school and trudged into the yard to light fires and cook their breakfasts. I walked on to a farmhouse on the far outskirts of the town and begged for food and a place to take a brief rest. The farmer was most gracious considering the circumstances. He welcomed me into his home and placed before me a warm breakfast consisting of a baked potato, a small dollop of rice and some hot soybean soup with cabbage.

As I was eating, I noticed that one of the farmer's young sons had an infected wound on his right thigh. "Why hasn't this wound been treated?" I asked. "The war has driven away our local medical practitioner," the farmer replied. As soon as I had wolfed down the last of the hot breakfast, I cleansed the wound and gave the farmer several packets of sulfa from my emergency medical kit. I was happy to be able to do something to repay this man for his extraordinary kindness. I settled down for a short, sound nap then rushed off amidst mutual good wishes to rejoin the military column.

The next day, December 4, came and went as I followed alongside the ROK Army motorized column. The third day, December 5, was the day I had promised Mother I would return home. Why I had made such a rash and impossible promise I do not know. The words had merely issued from my mouth, conceived not with any conscious thought of mine, but with a heedless rush as though by prerecorded rote. Aware of my unfulfilled promise, I kept my direction headed south though my spirit fled my body and must have hovered over the little house in Chu-ul where dwelled my mother.

By now I felt as though I, too, were motorized, being driven by the pressing rush of events outside my control. I was lost in time, oblivious to everything except the fact of moving forward. I ate the last of the rice and cuttlefish Mother had packed into my knapsack. I put on the last of the three pairs of socks she had supplied. I was weary, confused, and frightened.

We arrived at the large town of Kilchu on the afternoon of December 6. As I wandered through the streets in search of food or a warm or simply sheltered place to rest, I saw a dozen young men sitting in a group in the town schoolyard. All of the men wore armbands that read "Local Volunteer Youth Group." I assumed, correctly, that the group had been formed to somehow assist the ROK Army. I sneaked into the yard and plopped myself down behind the resting group. When the young men rose sometime later, I went with them.

We all wound up at the nearby home of the group leader. The man did not seem to have a firm idea of how things were going, but he announced, "The ROK Army is retreating back to South Korea." We were then fed a substantial dinner of steaming hot rice, hot soup and kimchee, Korean pickled cabbage. During the meal, I ventured to introduce myself to as many of the others as I could. This very mixed bag included men of all ages, up to the age of fifty. I found that, as usual, I was one of the youngest. There were brothers and fathers and sons, professors and students. Most of the men were well-educated college students or graduates. I gathered that many, perhaps most, of the men harbored strong anti-Communist sentiments. However, most claimed to have fallen in with the slowly-growing group more out of a sense that there was safety in numbers than out of political conviction. I was not sure what we were supposed to be doing for the ROK Army, nor what the rewards were supposed to be. As happened so often in my life, I was content to pull the distinctive armband up the sleeve of my topcoat and follow along. I certainly did not question why I was so readily taken in.

155

*

At noon on the following day, December 7, our group marched back to the school at which I had first found it. The word was passed around that we would be receiving instructions from ROK Army soldiers. It was a clear day and much warmer than it had been since before I left Chu-ul. Marching was made difficult through streets slushy with melting snow.

Kilchu was filled with ROK soldiers, army vehicles, and countless thousands of refugees seeking shelter from the wind on the sidewalks or under the eaves of houses.

As I marched along, grateful for the warmer air which lessened the earlier biting sting, I was stunned to see Father sitting in front of a house, soaking his feet in a basin of water. With him was my third uncle, the one whose wife had been so brutally murdered at the Chu-ul hot springs and whose body I had identified. Uncle was leaning on a cane, his feet bound in bandages.

Breaking free from the Volunteer Youth Group I rushed toward them. "Father," I shouted, "I knew you would be coming with me."

At the moment all the years of emotional deprivation I had suffered because of this cold and distant figure fell away as I instinctively reached out my arms to hug him. He returned my embrace with vigor, something he had never before done. All the animosities built up over the years seemed suddenly and swiftly washed away. It felt like the beginning of something new and wonderful.

Father looked totally wasted. Besides the blisters on his soaking feet, his lips were a mass of fever blisters. Gone, too, was his erstwhile meticulous clothing, replaced by ragged clothing such as my own. Despite their utter exhaustion, Father and Uncle seemed to

156

brighten at the sight of me, Dong-kyu, standing before them.

Instantly, Father opened his pack and pulled out two pieces of rice cake which he gave to me. Hesitating briefly, I took one small bite. Then, as though the present rushed in over me like a tidal wave, I hastily mumbled, "Good-bye. Soon we shall meet again in the South," and rushed off to rejoin the Volunteer Youth Group.

Whether it was a resurgence of lifelong loyalty to Mother and the imbedded memories of Father's denial of any fatherly affection, I disregarded the momentary filial reaction I felt upon seeing Father in his piteous condition. Now it was I who directed my steps as I saw my real future beckoning, knowing that the past, like a long-held umbilical cord, was finally and irrevocably cut from my body.

*

The Volunteer Youth Group was not assigned any duties by the ROK Army that day—or ever, really—but we did receive definite orders to get to Songjin as soon as possible.

Much later, I learned that large units of the North Korean People's Army, backed by even larger units of the Chinese People's Liberation Army, had been moving steadily south from the Chongjin area and had arrived on the north side of Myungchon on December 7. On the same day, a regiment of the ROK 3rd Division had been in contact with North Korean soldiers before retreating through Kilchu and on to Songjin to be evacuated by ship with the main body of the division.

A light snow began to fall late in the night of December 8. The column of the Volunteer Youth Group had reached the top of another seemingly endless series of mountain passes. Gone was the warm air of the previous day. The road we stumbled along was slippery with slush. A bitter north wind drove the falling snow against our backs. One thought alone got us all over that pass. We knew that at the bottom of the long slope that rolled away to the south was the port of Songjin.

At the top of the pass, a checkpoint had been set up by the ROK military police. Every refugee was given a thorough inspection before being allowed to decend into the city.

As if the progress of this human phalanx had not already been mercilessly impeded by its own hunger, fatigue, sickness, and the cruelty of the weather, it was now forced in its thousands upon thousands, to huddle standing up in the bitter onslaught of the elements, snared in a bureaucratic Catch-22.

Eventually my group reached the checkpoint. Our Volunteer Youth Group armbands were prominently displayed as the MPs flashed their torches over our bodies and into our faces. At length, the light, searing in the stygian dark, found my face. I heard a disembodied voice admonish me to move on.

With that, our group, now numbering over 200, reformed and marched quickly down the mountain toward the city. The landscape before us lay in near-total darkness. Only a few gleams of dim, widely dispersed light shone from an occasional house here and there.

Long after midnight, we were guided to an empty factory warehouse and told to get some sleep. This was one of the easiest orders I have ever had to obey. I simply blacked out as soon as my head touched my knapsack, so profound was the accumulated physical and emotional strain I had experienced throughout the previous week.

*

"Get up and meet outside immediately."

Thus was I awakened on the morning of December 9, 1950. It was still dark. A cold wind blew as we shuffled sleepily into line outside the warehouse. I could see masses of ROK Army vehicles, soldiers and refugees in the dark gloom, and all seemed to be moving toward the port. After a brief wait, we filed into the endless column, following the cone of light from the group leader's flashlight.

To my surprise and relief, the docks were only a few blocks from the warehouse. After waiting for most of the army vehicles, equipment and troops to be loaded on the huge, grey-painted ship tied up at the pier, my group was guided up the gangway by a military policeman—as though we were somehow especially privileged beings.

A guide met us at the top of the ramp and led us to the very bottom of an open hold that held army vehicles and equipment. I thought of the tens of thousands of refugees from all over northeastern Korea stranded outside the port area. Each one was desperately hoping to secure a spot aboard one of the few overcrowded vessels. All around me in the hold I noticed that men, mostly young, comprised the majority of refugees. What agonies they must have endured in deciding to follow the ROK Army singly aboard ship, rather than waiting to see if they might all be rescued with their families intact.

I was lost in such dark thoughts when, at about one o'clock in the afternoon, the gangway was raised and our ship—the United States Navy transport *St. Wind*—got underway. I was later told by men who were standing outside on the main deck that hundreds of refugees had plunged into the icy waters and drowned as the entire mass of waiting humanity surged forward in a final convulsion of hope and fear. The sea was stained by blotches of blood, and the faces of many of the men on deck were rimed with their frozen tears.

As soon as we cleared the harbor, I set out in search of Father and Uncle. Though I searched through as much of the ship as I could, I was unable to find either of them.

*

This was the first time I had ever been aboard a large ship sailing on the open sea. It was quite different from the Saturday night steamboat cruises on the Sungari River my family had enjoyed in Harbin before the end of World War II. Then, we had been feted with good food, comfortable seating and good music, and the sailing had been so smooth that the wine in Father's glass had never moved. Now, here I was, on a vast grey whale of a ship proceeding slowly out to sea. The ride was neither as smooth nor as comfortable, but I felt happier to be making it than I ever had on those long-ago cruises on the Sungari. I stood on deck and watched until the dock I had crossed in the dark of the morning finally passed from sight. In time, I could no longer see land.

The ship came to a bumpy stop late in the night, but I could not see enough to figure out where. Someone in my group later reported that we were docked at Hungnam, and I learned years later that the 105,000 Americans comprising the United States X Corps were embarked from this great port over a ten-day period along with 91,000 North Korean civilian refugees, 17,500 vehicles and 350,000 tons of supplies and equipment. In all, some one hundred nine oceangoing vessels undertook a total of one hundred ninety-three round trips between South Korean ports and Hungnam and other North Korean eastern ports.

When we left Hungnam on the night of December 10, the wind was blowing fiercely and the sea was rough. I felt as though my stomach had turned upside down, and I vomited copiously until only a yellow bile came up. I knew that I had become dehydrated, so I tried to crawl out onto the main deck to get some fresh air and find some water to roll around in my foul-tasting mouth. I got to a hatchway and felt more movement than I had below. I could see that waves were breaking across the rails. There were no lights showing on the main deck or from the high bridge, nor in any direction away from the ship.

I had eaten nothing since the ship left Songjin on December 9; there was no food aboard for refugees. Besides, I was too sick to hold any food down. My dehydrated and weakened state made me confused, perhaps a bit delirious. In the pitch blackness, I managed to climb aboard an ROK Army truck that had been lashed to the deck and covered with a canvas tarpaulin. I reached into the rear compartment and grabbed a handful of something from a large container. Clutching my find to my chest, I weaved to the nearest bathroom without looking at what I had stolen, for I was afraid of being waylaid by the ROK military policemen who patrolled the ship. When I reached light, I opened my hand and discovered that I had stolen dried, salted anchovies destined for the ROK mess hall. I was so hungry that I fought all the anchovies down my gullet without thinking about the consequences. I licked my hand clean and started back to rejoin the Volunteer Youth Group. I was overcome with a powerful thirst within a minute, but my frantic search through that part of the ship turned up no drinking water. I finally fell into an exhausted heap on the deck between the trucks stored in the hold.

*

Donald Chung, M.D.

I was awakened on the morning of December 12 by the sound of many people walking out on the main deck. I tried to get up, but I found that I was weak and dizzy, which I vaguely recognized as the results of severe dehydration and malnutrition. At length, I managed to pull myself out to the deck and breathed in fresh air, which made me feel a little better.

A round, red sun was rising in the east, far out to sea. To the west was my first sight of land since boarding the ship. I noticed that the storm winds had abated and the sea was calm. As the ship neared shore, I saw that the land was brown, not white with snow. As we came closer to shore, I was amazed to see women walking along the mountain paths overlooking the sea with heavy loads atop their heads, not wearing overcoats, though it was the middle of winter. Then I noticed for the first time that the air was balmy, and not a single cloud flecked the sky.

The *St. Wind* docked at the tiny southern port of Kuryongpo-ri at about eight o'clock in the morning of December 12, 1950. It had been ten days since I had left Chu-ul, and I was seven days overdue making good my last promise to Mother.

It took a long time to unload the military vehicles, equipment and soldiers. I stood in a corner of the deck to watch, but I could not control the thoughts racing through my mind as I looked out over the village and upon the mountain behind it.

I kept telling myself, "Kuryongpo-ri is a part of the motherland. Its people are my people. They speak my language." I knew that, before World War II, every country boy's dream had been to go to Seoul to study at the Imperial University. Now, I thought, Seoul is the capital of half the Korean nation, the half to which I have been denied access since my years back from Manchuria. Here I am, looking across a tiny Korean port in a part of

162

the land that calls itself the Republic of Korea. I come from a part of the land that calls itself the Democratic People's Republic of Korea. Both are home. But they have become different because of the policies of two alien powers, the United States and the Soviet Union, and because of the clashing political convictions of the rabid Communists and rabid anti-Communists who have won the support of one or the other of those alien powers.

I could not keep my thoughts untangled, for I had had the precepts of Marxist-Leninist doctrine hammered into my mind for five long years. I was alienated from my southern cousins for five years because, my leaders told me, they had been seduced by the impure doctrines of capitalist-imperialist avarice. I had been led to believe that on June 25, just six months ago, these mad-dog cousins I am about to face had been induced to mount, suddenly and without any excuse, a military adventure against my—and their—peaceloving kinsmen.

I stood ready to take my first step onto South Korean soil, not because I really wanted to, and certainly not out of any conviction that one half of the Korean nation's people were any more right than the other half. I was here because I had opted to be saved from peremptory execution by placing myself in the care of the army of my southern cousins, and that army had—almost as an afterthought—allowed me to tag along in its wake as it returned to its part of the motherland.

It occurred to me that I should start trying to find my third and fourth cousins, who had come south from Chu-ul in 1947. Then I got sidetracked thinking about all the cars and luxurious possessions these southerners surely owned.

As I waded through my confused emotions and outlandish daydreams, the hour approached noon, and the Volunteer Youth Group was ordered from the ship.

PART III
The South
(December, 1950 - August, 1962)

CHAPTER SIXTEEN

I was snapped back from my reveries and dreams by the bawling of a loud voice. As I looked down from the deck to the quay, I could see that a uniformed stranger was beckoning me to leave the ship. I was still a bit lost in my thoughts, but I looked around in surprise and saw that everyone—soldiers and refugees alike—had already evacuated the ship and that I alone remained on deck. I tried to rush, but my weakness and excitement slowed my progress, left my legs quite feeble, and I barely managed to make it safely across the narrow, undulating gangway.

The sky was still a gorgeous blue, though a few cotton-puff clouds were now in evidence. It was a bright, sunshiny day, a comfortable and pleasant new beginning for a weary, starved refugee. When at last I reached the quay, I saw just over two hundred young North Korean men sitting or squatting along the beach. All appeared to be as physically and emotionally drained as I was, but I am certain that each and every one of their minds was rolling with the thoughts in which I had been immersed only minutes earlier: we had arrived safely following a harrowing journey to a land we supposed held out the twin promises of freedom and opportunity.

For now, however, everyone's priority was to get some food and water.

The village fronted by the beach seemed peaceful and somehow filled with hope. I had no way of knowing then that, in July, a sizable portion of the ROK 3rd Division had been hemmed in along this peaceful strand by a superior North Korean force. Only the intercession of a United States Navy cruiser had allowed the trapped

167

South Korean units to board a flotilla of small coastal vessels and United States Navy transports, which carried them farther south, to Pusan. Through the month of August, this nondescript place had been the northeastern anchor of the Pusan Perimeter, and had been hotly contested well into September.

I moved quietly around the crowd of refugees and sat down among the rear ranks. I asked the time and was told that it was close to noon. The sun seemed unusually warm.

A squad of ROK soldiers arrived with baskets of food and cans of drinking water. The distribution began in the front rows, and the food and water were slowly passed from rank to rank. It took a great deal of time before any of the food or water reached me. In the meantime, I was tortured by thirst and hunger and the memories of my desperation aboard the ship, when I had eaten the dried, salted anchovies. My eyes were riveted on the steady but slow progress of the food handlers. Finally, my turn came. I received a fist-sized rice ball that had been dipped in salt water. No food I had ever eaten seemed fitter than that hunger-allaying lunch. I took tiny, tiny bites and chewed and savored each for as long as I could. Somehow, the skimpy meal seemed to build up my blood sugars, and I could feel the restored energy coursing through my bloodstream. I could think and even see much more clearly.

As soon as we had all finished eating, a tough-looking ROK Army sergeant came out of one of the nearby buildings and delivered a brief speech about how we ought to find ways to show gratitude for the new opportunities we had been afforded by the Republic of Korea. As these things go—and I was by then something of an expert—this was a pretty mild and unskilled exhortation. As the sergeant finished speaking, forms were handed through the crowd, and we were all urged to complete and sign them. No one said what would happen if we did not, and none of us took the trouble to find out.

What I got was a personal-history form that served as enlistment papers for the ROK Army.

How ironic, I thought. I have just gone through many days of perilous, life-threatening hardship precisely because I wanted to avoid military service—at least long enough to complete my medical education. So here I am, squatting on a South Korean beach and filling out a form and enlisting in an army that is at war with my mother, my sisters, my brothers-in-law, my closest friends. I was certain I had seen the last of my student days. Then an odd new thought struck me, a concept that might just carry me through the ordeal that lay ahead: If all the refugees on this beach, and no one knows how many others, became exemplary soldiers and fought as hard as we could, we might contribute to ending the war and the killing much sooner. It made no difference to me whatsoever which side won, as long as the war was ended. I happened to have landed in the South, so I would do my utmost—not for the Republic of Korea, but for the Korean nation, for all Koreans. Only in this way, I reasoned with a newfound and utterly clear sense of purpose, will we northerners be able to return safely to our part of our fractured motherland and rejoin the loved ones we have left behind.

I completed the form and handed it in. I feared the future, but I also looked forward to finishing the ordeal that still lay before me.

In time, the ROK sergeant told us that we were all members of the 23rd Infantry Regiment Reconnaissance Company.

*

Donald Chung, M.D.

My "company" of refugee soldiers was ordered to its feet in the late afternoon and marched off through the town. Someone shouted, "Remain in line! Do not break ranks without permission; don't even stop by the roadside to urinate without making a formal request of a superior and without the superior's permission." I noticed that we were closely watched by ROK soldiers armed with rifles.

No one told us differently, so I supposed that we were marching directly into battle, and that frightened me half out of my wits—not so much because I feared a fight (I certainly did!), but because none of us had been given weapons.

The march—fueled with the energy of one rice ball per man—continued, with only brief rests, well into the night. The mountain road was narrow, but the moon was full and I could see well enough in its silvery light. It was quiet but for our footfalls and heavy breathing. After a long time, the sergeant began singing a popular southern song of the day. It was new to us northerners, but I was swept with a feeling of nostalgia when the melody led to a line that said: "Ah, ah, in the moonlight of Silla, the bell of Pulguk Temple is heard . . ." The unified Silla Kingdom that had ruled most of the Korean peninsula from 668 to 936 had produced some of the most beautiful Buddhist temples and works of art in Korean history. Among these was the Pulguk Temple.

The sergeant boomed out the song over and over and before long we refugees were singing along with him. We marched into a large city shortly after midnight. Someone whispered in my ear that this was Kyongju— the capital of the old Silla Kingdom!

We were now some twenty miles southwest of Kuryongpo-ri, where we had landed that morning, and just over fifty miles northeast of Pusan. The "company" was broken down into small groups and each group was

170

sent with an armed soldier to be put up in private homes. During the process of counting us off into the small groups, the sergeant learned that nearly two dozen of his refugee soldiers had mustered the courage to run away during the march. He was not happy, but we thought there was nothing he could do to us, for we had stayed.

A breakfast of steamed rice and hot soybean soup arrived in midmorning. After eating, we were given free time to spend in the open market, where there was plenty of good food on sale. The food caught my eye and the aroma filled my nose as soon as I neared the market. I was particularly attracted to sticks of glutinous rice candy, but I realized that I had not come equipped with any money. It dawned on me after a time that I would not be needing my thick, blue Russian-style topcoat in the balmy atmosphere they offered in the Republic of Korea. I asked the candy seller, "Will you trade some of your candy for my coat?" The old man took the overcoat in hand and shrewdly tested its thick nap and peered at all the seams, from collar to cuff. At last, he made his offer: "I'll give you a half-dozen sticks of candy for it." That was a poor bargain, I knew, but I was desperate for the candy, so agreed. I had pushed down two sticks of the candy within a minute, and shared two more with two of the refugees I had met in Kilchu. I was in heaven.

We were marched to the train station by way of the royal tombs of the Silla kings. Without any idea of where we would be taken, we climbed aboard freight cars and watched as the doors were slid closed. Those of us near the walls of the freight car could see little through some tiny cracks. All we knew was that the sun was shining outside and the train was moving.

*

171

The 23rd Infantry Regiment was one of the three infantry regiments of the 3rd Infantry Division, a component of the ROK II Corps. The regiment had been part of the ROK Army's premier Capital Division in North Korea, but had been transferred immediately after the evacuation, perhaps for not quite measuring up to the high standard of the division's other regiments. I learned that the 23rd Regiment had been evacuated from Songjin, and that a large component had come out aboard the USS *St. Wind,* the ship that had carried me to the South.

The main body of 3rd Infantry Division had marched or been moved by train from various staging areas along the Kyongju-Yongchon-Andong-Yongju-Chechon-Wonju-Hongchon axis by December 20, 1950. On December 23, the entire 23rd Infantry Regiment reassembled at Hongchon. For the time being, we were held in divisional reserve while the balance of the division moved northward to the vicinity of Inje to establish a main line of resistance and help prevent the Chinese People's Liberation Army and the renascent North Korean People's Army from overrunning South Korea.

It remained reasonably warm during the days, but the temperature at night often reached -20 Celsius, which is an incredible drop. The army in which I had enlisted had made no move so far to equip me, so I naturally regretted having given up my overcoat in exchange for candy. It was on one of these freezing cold nights, around midnight, that the 23rd Regiment Reconnaissance Company marched on foot into Hongchon from Wonju. As usual, the company was broken down into small groups, which were billeted in houses. My group drew a vacant farmhouse with a thatched roof.

It was bitterly cold when we got indoors, and there was no light. It was infinitely better than being outside, for the cold drafts throughout the house could not

172

begin to compare with the chill night wind to which we had been exposed on the march.

We lay back on our knapsacks, all huddled together to help keep one another warm. I quickly fell asleep, but one of the older men woke me. "Listen," he said, "the Christians are out carolling." I adjusted my hearing and picked up the distant strains: "Silent night, holy night, all is calm, all is bright."

When the carollers had passed beyond hearing, the older man explained what the singing was all about, for most of us knew nothing about Christianity. "It is now the morning of December 25," he explained, "Baby Jesus of Nazareth was born 1,950 years ago today." He paused, then quoted, "For God so loved the world that He gave His only begotten Son so that anyone who believes in Him shall not perish; but, will have eternal life." He said that he was quoting from "the Christian book, The Bible." It was all new to me, though I could vividly recall how Christian students had been discriminated against at school, and how they had been prevented from attending Christmas programs at the churches in the North. I had no inkling then of Christianity, and the older man's lecture was merely interesting. As I drifted off to sleep again, however, I gave a moment's fleeting thought to this new way to compare the North with the South.

*

Christmas morning dawned sunny and bright, though it remained very cold outside. The company was mustered and led across a small country bridge to the regimental headquarters area. Following a quick hot breakfast outside the headquarters mess hall, we were marched to a large quonset hut. By this time, only 156 of the original two hundred members of the company

173

remained; all the rest had deserted during the long journey to Hongchon.

We were formed into several long lines and marched into the prefabricated building, where we were confronted by very long tables in an otherwise bare room. Our sergeant ordered the lines of men to approach the tables and remove all articles of civilian clothing— everything—and place them on the table. In time, my own clothing was replaced by stacks of army clothing: a cap, a steel helmet, a summer fatigue uniform, a pack, boots and several changes of socks. I felt a pang of regret as I stripped off my blue school uniform and exchanged it for the olive green of the ROK Army uniform, for now I knew beyond a doubt that I was well on my way to fighting my own countrymen, which translated to Mother, Moon-hee, Ok-bong and Jung-hee.

As I put my old clothing on the table I was aware of one item I had to keep—Mother's treasured white silk scarf. Just at that moment a corporal strode up to me and grabbed the muffler from my hands. I grabbed it back with my left hand and emphatically signalled "No!" with my right. "I can't give this up," I implored. "It was the last thing given me by my mother as I was leaving home."

The corporal seemed made of stone, showed no trace of emotion, and paid no heed to my imploring words. In the end, I was bereft of my one and only valuable possession, the one item my mother treasured which she sacrificed for me. I was, though, able to keep the tiny ID book with my school records which Mother had hung around my neck. Small recompense then, but it was to prove to come in handy at a later time.

After dressing, we were all provided with ancient rifles captured from the North Korean People's Army. Most of the weapons were of Japanese or Chinese manufacture, though there were several Russian-made "burpguns". Next, we were assembled to hear a lecture on the care and use of our weapons. This was easy for me to pick up, for I had already learned about precisely these weapons in my college military training classes. Some of the weapons had remained loaded after capture and, in the midst of the safety lecture, several rounds were accidentally discharged. Several soldiers sitting along the wall of the room pitched over, and two of them proved to be dead.

Following the furor created by the accidental discharges and horrifying sudden deaths, I mentioned to one of the sergeants that I had been an advanced medical student in the North. He ignored me. It turned out that I was one of several medical students in the refugee group, and there were many others whose educational backgrounds could have provided the ROK Army and the Republic of Korea with some valuable assistance for conducting the war. However, it was the policy of the ROK Army that groups such as ours be maintained without any individual detachments because, it was felt, making any exceptions would weaken the group as a whole. Thus, valuable human resources stood the chance of being frittered away in the dangerous exploits that would certainly be the fare of an ill-prepared infantry reconnaissance company.

After lunch, the company broke down into platoons and squads, which were placed in the care of experienced ROK Army corporals and sergeants. Except for these leaders, the entire company was composed of North Koreans, mainly men from my own North Hamgyong Province. We were organized into a company headquarters and two platoons of three squads each. I was assigned to the 2nd Squad of the 1st Platoon.

Following a light dinner at the training camp, we were marched back—as real soldiers, we thought—to the houses in which we had spent the previous night.

Next morning, December 26, the entire company, except for the noncommissioned officers, was mustered outside the company headquarters tent. All of us were shivering from the cold, because we were only wearing the light summer uniforms we had received on Christmas Day. After a brief wait, an officer strode out of the tent. This was Lieutenant Kim Hyun-min, a twenty-three-year-old native of Kunsan and a former enlisted man.

"I am your company commander," Lieutenant Kim began. "When I say that the snow is black, you must accept that the snow is black, even if your eyes deceive you into believing that the snow is white." He directed a steady gaze from one member to another of the group, his eyes boring into each soldier's brain. "Do you understand?" The entire group bellowed, "Yes!" He went on: "There is a tradition in our army that, when any member of a unit violates the rules, the entire unit gets punished. I have it from reliable sources that last night someone in your unit traded his newly-issued underwear to a villager for some rice cakes. Now is the time for your group punishment."

As soon as the lieutenant finished speaking, the company first sergeant came out of the headquarters tent carrying a dozen stout wooden sticks. Beginning with the first man in the 1st Squad of the 1st Platoon, the lieutenant ordered each soldier, one by one, to lie on the ground and bare his legs. He then delivered several punishing blows to each pair of legs. Lieutenant Kim was a very strong man, and he struck with all his might. I could see that blood was oozing from many of the injured legs, and Kim broke many of the wooden sticks across bleeding shins. One of the soldiers bolted after being hit the first time, and the officer chased him, but only for a short distance. This was only four places away from me, and I was sure that the company commander's frustration

176

and rage would be amply expressed in the course of future beatings. To my amazement and delight, the lieutenant indicated that he had had enough and the sentence was commuted.

Many of the soldiers who had been beaten limped away on badly damaged legs when, at last, the company was ordered to break formation. I wondered about an army that condoned the damaging of infantrymen's legs in time of war—or anytime. The points Lieutenant Kim had wanted to make were amply made. We knew beyond doubt that we were responsible for how our fellow soldiers conducted themselves, and we knew that punishment would be swift and brutal. Lieutenant Kim was bound to have a disciplined company at his disposal, but if punishments such as the one I witnessed this day were the norm, the ultimate cost in permanently damaged limbs and disabled soldiers might prove exorbitant in the end. I had never seen such wild and brutal punishment in my life.

CHAPTER SEVENTEEN

Our ROK Army 3rd Division was facing the North Korean 2nd Division across the battle lines centered on Inje. As with most North Korean units that had been returned to the war following the disastrous battles of September and October, the People's Army 2nd Division had been substantially reorganized. Our information indicated that our immediate adversaries were mostly raw conscripts who were short of arms and generally suffering from logistical deficiencies brought on by very long lines of supply and inadequate transportation.

The first of our refugee soldiers to be committed to the war went off on a squad-sized search mission a few days after Christmas. These new soldiers returned to our company area late in the afternoon of the same day without having made contact with the enemy—our northern cousins—but they were exhilarated from having risked their lives and survived.

On December 31, 1950, the North Korean People's Army (supported by Chinese units, which we did not then know had entered the war in November) mounted an offensive along most of the battle line, which roughly approximated the 38th Parallel. By late afternoon, the ROK 9th Division, on our 3rd Division's immediate right, was overrun in the vicinity of Hyun-ri. To our left, we heard, the ROK 7th Division had also fallen apart north of Chunchon, thus opening a gap between the ROK II Corps and the United States X Corps.

On New Year's eve, following the arrival of all the bad news, Lieutenant Kim sent out one of his squad leaders, Sergeant Yim, and two corporals to reconnoiter a small village on a mountain road south of Hongchon. Sergeant Yim was by then something of a legend in the company. A native North Korean, he had served in the Imperial Japanese Army in World War II and had attained the rank of sergeant. He had come to live in the South after the war and had naturally gravitated into the fledgling ROK Army of the immediate post-war period. He was a big, tough-looking man who could get from here to there and back again faster than anyone else in the Reconnaissance Company. Yim was well-known for his courage and stamina, and he was acknowledged even by my contingent of unschooled refugees as a man everyone wanted for a leader. It was said that no one who stayed close to him and followed his orders could be killed in combat.

The three scouts donned the clothing and white headbands typically worn by Korean farmers, and Yim tucked a pistol and a short knife into his waistband, while the corporals carried bundles concealing American-made M1 rifles. They left the company headquarters tent very late on New Year's Eve and made their way quickly to the mountain village.

The three ROK non-commissioned officers approached a farmhouse that had smoke rising from the chimney and was lighted from within by kerosene lamps. When Yim got close enough, he could hear several voices within the house speaking in a North Korean dialect. The sergeant was certain that the house was sheltering North Korean soldiers, so he ordered the corporals to cover him from behind a nearby tree with their rifles. Then he adopted the typical farmer's plodding gait and walked right up to the house with his hands clasped behind his back. Much to the surprise of the watching corporals, three North Korean soldiers with their hands held high emerged from the house a few minutes after Yim went in. The sergeant was right behind them, his pistol cocked and held at shoulder level to cover his prisoners. Yim's prisoners proved to be a People's Army officer and two privates.

After the prisoners were sent to Regimental Headquarters for interrogation, the story of Sergeant Yim's latest exploit quickly made the rounds through the company. In later weeks, the story would be used as a point of instruction, a model we all might emulate when our turns came to bring in prisoners.

*

On the morning of January 1, 1951, the company was fed a special New Year's breakfast. For the first time since our arrival at Hongchon, we received beef soup to go along with our rice. The soup was oily, but no one actually managed to find any meat in his bowl. Someone laconically suggested that "The cow must have just walked through it."

In the middle of the afternoon we received special orders to move north, though the whys and wherefores were withheld from us. I clapped on my oversized GI helmet—which had been designed for larger American heads—and slung on a backpack containing a few days' supply of food and my small horde of clothing. I shouldered my long Japanese bolt-action rifle and buckled on my ammunition belt with my bayonet over my right hip. I weighed 118 pounds and stood just five-feet, four-inches, so I was quite burdened down.

We marched north up the mountain on both sides of the snow-covered main road. Many other units and scores of vehicles were using the center of the roadway to move south, past us, away from the front. As we huffed past a crossroads, I looked up in time to see Choe Ik-hwan, the former student-body president of Chu-ul Junior High School, the same former classmate who had asked me to help identify the women's bodies found at

181

the hot springs following my return to Chu-ul from Chongjin. Like me, Ik-hwan was decked out in an ROK Army uniform, but he also had on a long, woollen GI overcoat. Since he was marching southward, we only had time to wave and beam at one another in surprise and pleasure.

The country road was very quiet by the time we reached the northern outskirts of Hongchon. Over one hundred fifty members of the 23rd Regiment Reconnaissance Company were strung out in two long columns on either side of the roadway, following Lieutenant Kim and our platoon sergeants and squad leaders. High mountains rose on our left, and rice paddies to our right ran back into more mountains.

Shortly after sunset, someone called out an alarm. We saw that he was pointing at a lone man wearing a backpack who was across the rice paddies, toward the mountains to the north. Lieutenant Kim ordered some of the men to give chase, but the man stayed well ahead of them, so they stopped to fire at him. The runner eventually ran from sight and our men gave up and returned to the main body of the company.

Ten minutes later, we entered a small village and fanned out to inspect all the buildings. Several of our men entered two triangular straw huts right at the entrance to the village and found charred wood and hot ashes inside. Other soldiers found a large iron kettle filled with steaming rice in another house. Before his soldiers dug in, Lieutenant Kim used the quantity of rice to guess how many enemy soldiers had been billeted in the village and told us that the running man had probably been their last lookout.

Sentries were posted all around the village and the password for the night, *"namu-jike"*—"wood A-frame"—was issued to everyone. The bulk of the company was broken down into four- and six-man teams and allowed to forage for sleeping space in the abandoned huts and houses.

By this time, I had come to Lieutenant Kim's notice as the youngest soldier in the company, and he had made me his unofficial orderly. I was thus assigned with four other soldiers to sleep in the company headquarters. There was still an old woman living in the house, though her entire family had fled along with all the other villagers. She served us a dinner of steamed rice with kimchee. The village became very quiet after the company had finished eating and settling in for the night. Lieutenant Kim and our headquarters team quickly fell asleep, but we were constantly awakened by the old woman's coughing fits. Through the fog of my interrupted sleep, I absently deduced that she might have a chronic bronchial condition.

I was pulled abruptly and irretrievably from my sleep around midnight by an excited order from Lieutenant Kim. As I oriented myself to my surroundings, I heard a flurry of gunfire from far in the distance. Kim and one or two of the others who had seen combat thought aloud that the gunfire was friendly, for they could pick out the distinctive low-pitched thud typical of M1 rifles. I had no way of knowing then if they were right or wrong. Our anxiety steadily mounted as the sounds became louder and louder. When it seemed as if the gunfire was right on top of us, all the noise abruptly ceased; there was dead silence everywhere.

We waited in tense fear. The man beside me whispered, "What's going on here? I don't like it. It's scary."

He no sooner finished speaking than automatic-rifle fire exploded all around the village. It sounded to me like popping corn. I was suddenly aware that there were many men running past the house yelling *"Namu-jike!"* and "Come on!" and "We're moving out!"

None of us, not even Lieutenant Kim, knew quite what to do. It was extremely dark out, and confusion reigned all around us. In the end, I carefully peeked out through a small chink in the door. I could see that all of the ROK soldiers in the street were holding their hands high, and that other men dressed in People's Army uniforms had leveled rifles at them.

I turned back to report, and I saw that only two other men remained in the room. The others, including the company commander, had fled out the rear door, away from the center of the village. All three of us were new recruits, and we were frozen in place by the terror of this unexpected midnight contact with the enemy. I managed to throw off my numbing panic and turned to follow those who had already left.

The old woman remained sitting in the back room, calmly smoking her long-stemmed clay pipe. I imagine that living so close to the 38th Parallel had caused her to see Northern and Southern soldiers take and retake her village many times. She showed neither surprise nor fear over the fact of the latest changeover. I told her that we three were going to be hiding out in the small barn where her family had formerly stabled its oxen. I begged her, "Please don't reveal our hiding place to the North Korean soldiers if they inquire about us."

We ran into the thatch-sided barn, which opened into the fenced farmyard, and lay down. It was very dark and we were well-concealed from view, but we were able to see anyone approaching through the farmyard because the back room of the house was lighted by the old woman's kerosene lamp. Our hiding place smelled foul, and we soon discovered that we had bedded ourselves down in decomposing ox dung. There was nothing we could do, and no time to do it, for a pair of North Korean soldiers swinging the muzzles of their automatic rifles soon appeared in the yard. When one saw the old woman seated in the back room of the house, he asked in a loud voice, "Are any ROK soldiers here?"

My heart was gripped in fear, but I could see that she remained impassive, giving no indication of even having heard the question. The armed man at her door repeated himself, to which she firmly replied, "I told you before that I haven't seen any!"

I had remained motionless throughout the exchange, though I had pointed my rifle at the North Koreans as soon as they entered the farmyard. The last thing in the world I wanted to do was to open fire on those two men, but I was mentally prepared to shoot them as a last resort if they approached the barn. Thankfully, the old woman's firm response seemed to convince the two, for they lowered their weapons and strode briskly from the yard.

There was still a considerable commotion emanating from the road side of the house, beyond our range of vision. It was clear that we could not stay where we were much longer, and certainly not until daylight. Leaving through the yard was out of the question, so I frantically searched along the barn's walls in the hope of finding a way out. My search was rewarded when my fingers made out the edge of a wooden cover over a small hole which I guessed had allowed the family dog to enter and leave the farm compound. We three could barely squeeze our bodies through the tiny opening, and we had to leave our packs and helmets behind, though we pushed our rifles through ahead of us.

Once clear of the barn, we entered a flat area covered with rice paddies. There was absolutely no cover, and the nearest ROK Army units were in the mountains miles to the south. We ran desperately across the pitch-dark paddies.

I was breathless and nearly exhausted from panic and the unaccustomed physical exertion when, only

185

fifteen minutes after clearing the barn, I saw that our track was converging with that of several columns of what had to be North Korean soldiers marching southward across the snow-covered paddies. We threw ourselves down into a shallow irrigation ditch between two paddies and less than one hundred yards from the nearest enemy infantry. As the long line of men passed, I could see that a number of my companions of the past few weeks were marching in their midst, bound and constantly covered by numerous weapons. Now and then, the North Koreans prodded or hissed curses at one or another of the captives in an effort to hurry them along.

As soon as the near column had marched from sight toward the mountains to the south, my two companions and I left the ditch and dog-trotted along the base of the nearest hill. We lost all sense of direction in the early-morning fog, but we finally managed to stumble blindly into the lines of an ROK Army unit.

We had come through the ordeal dressed only in the light summer uniforms that had been issued to us a week earlier. I was freezing from the cold and the loss of body heat brought on by the tough physical exertion of my running escape. As we sat shivering in a tent in an ROK Army battalion headquarters compound, someone threw blankets across our shoulders and told us that the battalion commander wanted to interview us.

We found ourselves standing stiffly before a nattily-attired lieutenant colonel, whose hard, impassive expression led us to believe he might have us executed for having run away from our company. At his brusque urging, we reported all that we knew about the events of the night: the sudden, swift attack; the ensuing confusion; our escape; our near run-in with the People's Army columns. The officer seemed to warm to the last bit of news, and he beckoned us over to a large map hung on the wall behind his field desk. Though we were unable to

pinpoint the exact direction in which the enemy column
had been marching, we apparently provided enough
information to allow the officer to make some educated
deductions. At once he had picked up the field telephone
on his desk and was busily plotting a fire mission with
the commander of an artillery battery.

My comrades and I were escorted back to the
Reconnaissance Company bivouac, where we found other
members of the company, including Lieutenant Kim,
waiting. By mid-morning, a large portion of the company
had dribbled in from virtually all points of the compass.
Some tales I heard were as harrowing as my own. A
group of late arrivals claimed to have escaped captivity
during a heavy artillery bombardment late in the morning.

When we counted noses, it was learned that
about a dozen members of the company had been killed or
captured. All were members of the group that left Songjin.
We pieced enough stories together to figure out that our
password, *namu-jike,* had been leaked when North
Korean scouts captured one of the sentries guarding the
edge of the village. Thus, the North Koreans had been
able to bluff their way into the center of our company
area.

We were now blooded veterans, though our
baptism had been something less than auspicious.

*

By January 8, 1951, our ROK 3rd Division had
gradually withdrawn from Hongchon to a line through
Wonju, Chechon and Yongwol. During the redeployment
phase, we refugee soldiers were finally supplied with
warmer clothing: a special reversible cotton-lined
uniform, including a soft cap that was khaki-colored on
the outside and white on the inside. We were also issued
American-made M1 rifles, a semi-automatic weapon of

good repute that fired an easily-loaded eight-round clip. Though we also received boots and gloves, neither they nor the reversible uniforms were really warm enough to withstand the bitter weather.

Between January and April, 1951, the 23rd Infantry Regiment constantly moved back and forth, north and south, across the 38th Parallel. Battle lines in the east-central area were fluid, and enemy troops were as apt to be encountered behind our lines as in front of them. During this period, the Reconnaissance Company was usually deployed as far north as other elements of the regiment so that we could search out enemy positions and attempt to evaluate the strength of enemy units.

As time went on, it became clearer and clearer why the ROK Army kept so many well-educated and potentially more-useful North Koreans at work as reconnaissance soldiers. Though all Koreans spoke the same language, there were some differences between the dialects of the North and South, and those differences could bring forth important results when certain of us were sent out to cross the lines to collect information. Also, nearly all of us had received military training in the North, so we knew procedures and the like. At times, certain of us donned People's Army uniforms and posed as People's Army soldiers or officers when crossing the lines. Unfortunately, the number of men who were able to carry off such subterfuges dwindled, for more and more of them failed to return from their often-solitary trips. Whether they were found out and killed or simply deserted I do not know, though I would rather think the former than the latter.

For days on end during our endless search operations we were unable to change our socks or remove our boots. We marched with rain pelting down on us through mud, snow, and slush and across swollen rivers and streams. It was no wonder many of us suffered from various degrees of frostbite. I was no exception. I watched my hands turn blue and swell from frostbite. Then, as the roughened skin cracked open I saw a clear fluid ooze from the openings. At that point it was almost impossible to use my hands. I seldom slung my rifle over my shoulder, preferring to keep my hands on it at the ready when in the field. My hands were particularly vulnerable because as a student and medical assistant I was not used to hard manual labor and as a lad at home before that I was never asked to do any strenuous work. But one thing was in my favor—my feet were saved from the tormenting condition afflicting my hands, possibly because so much time was spent in exercising them by our interminable marches.

The fluidity of the lines and the consequent movement brought on problems in keeping us adequately provisioned. There were many days when we had to get along without any food issued through army channels. On those days, if we were lucky, we subsisted on the scant supplies of dried corn, frozen potatoes and rice we pillaged from the many abandoned farmsteads we encountered deep in the mountains during our reconnaissance sweeps. In addition to what we could scrounge, we occasionally received a six-ounce bag or two of dried biscuits, which we set aside as emergency rations for use when all else failed. We usually carried our supplies on our backs, lashed to farmers' A-frames, as we moved across the trackless mountains that were our preserve.

The smokers among us suffered a great deal during those frequent periods when the cigarette supply was interrupted and their reserves had been used up. In ordinary circumstances, everyone was issued two packs of cigarettes per day. When the supply system balked, most of the smokers limited themselves to one cigarette after each meal. If supplies did not get through for a very long time, then the smokers shared a single after-meal cigarette among three or four or even five men. When all the cigarettes had been consumed, half the company or more could be found pacing around, nervous and irritable. Things got so bad once that one of the smokers dug through the snow to find yellowed autumn leaves that had not yet decomposed. When he had all he could find, he dried them over an open fire and rolled them in some paper he dug out of his pack. Finally, he lit up and inhaled the harsh smoke into his lungs, following which he gagged, coughed and spluttered as torrents of tears erupted from his eyes. Surprisingly, the fit cleared up and he seemed to gain much enjoyment from his efforts. A non-smoker, I felt nothing but pity for these poor nicotine addicts.

We played endless rounds of blackjack whenever there was a lull in our work. Since, for reasons we were to learn months later, we were never paid, we usually bet cigarettes. By the end of a marathon game, most of the cigarettes lost half or more of their tobacco. When I first joined the company, I had obligingly given my cigarettes to the smokers among my friends. When I became addicted to blackjack, I kept them for my betting. It was during one of these card games that I tried my first cigarette. Within a few minutes after I had inhaled two or three puffs, I became dizzy and nauseous. In the beginning, I did not like smoking at all. I'm not sure why, but I kept practicing until, within a few months, I was consuming all the cigarettes I could get my hands on, an average of two packs per day.

*

One day in January, when part of our company was moving northward through a line of hills, another soldier and I were assigned to scout about a thousand yards ahead of the main body. As I had been instructed, I walked with my M1 pointed to the front and my eyes sweeping the ground ahead and on all sides. After a time, the road ahead ran north along a small hill which connected a ridge between high mountains to the north and south. To the left of the road was a steep slope with a noisy stream tumbling southward. As we approached the hill, I could discern a dark-green object at the summit. I ducked down behind the only available cover, a tiny rock, and stared hard at the alien presence while, at the same time, I passed a hand signal cautioning the main body to stop in its tracks.

I strained my eyes for long seconds, and even rubbed them in the hope my vision would sharpen enough to positively identify the object on the hill. I considered the possibility that it was merely a tree stump or a rock, and that a trick of the light made it appear to be green. My companion and I watched for ten long minutes, during which time we both thought the object moved slightly. Since we knew that staring eyes frequently perceived movement when there was none, we continued our patient vigil. Had I been willing to shatter my concentration, I am sure I would have thought that, though this was one of my first combat patrols, I was epitomizing the role of the veteran scout.

At long last, the object really did move. And several similar objects appeared next to it. Then many more appeared. They were . . . heads!

All of a sudden, a great many green-clad soldiers were firing at my companion and me. Many of the bullets hit the rock I was hiding behind, a rock that was barely large enough to protect just my head. I heard one round hit the back of my steel helmet, but I was so numb with fright that I could not tell if it or any of the others had penetrated my flesh.

In desperation, I rolled to my left and allowed my body to slip down the bank of the stream paralleling the road. Once I was certain it was safe to stand, I ran southward through the shallow water until I came to a sharp turn, at which point I clambered back up to the roadway, where I found the main body. Only then did I notice that I had left my helmet and rifle behind the small rock. Even more disconcerting, I also discovered that the bullet I had heard hitting my helmet had grazed my left shoulder blade, leaving a shallow wound that seeped small quantities of blood. But it could have been much worse and I was thankful for my continued good fortune.

The main body drove forward through diminishing fire and, by the time we topped the small hill, the enemy soldiers had all fled from sight.

So now I was an authentic blooded veteran and, except for leaving my helmet and rifle behind, I felt I had handled myself well in my first direct confrontation with the enemy. I frankly thought I had saved the main body of my company from marching into an ambush.

*

One day we occupied a hill atop which all the trees had been burned off by napalm canisters dropped by United States Air Force jet fighter-bombers similar to the ones that had attacked Chongjin during the Autumn. The hill was strewn with hundreds of charred North Korean corpses. In the midst of the bodies, we found large rectangular red and yellow plastic mats, which United Nations forces used to identify and mark their positions for the pilots of fast-moving friendly warplanes. It was clear that the enemy had attempted to use these captured panels to fool the airmen. Unfortunately for them, they did not know the required pattern in which the markers had to be set out, a pattern that was changed every day.

Another time, a small group of us that had been sent out to scout an enemy position picked up a Chinese-language broadcast on the walkie-talkie radio we had taken to communicate with our headquarters. Until then, I had not even heard that the Chinese had intervened in the war on the side of North Korea. In fact, even then I thought I was hearing a broadcast from China that had somehow bled onto our tactical channel. When we returned safely later in the day and reported the incident, we were all astounded to learn the truth of the matter.

The routine of constant patrolling carried us into the spring of 1951, by which time the natural attrition of combat had left the company with a solid core of competent survivors.

During an advance around Inje that spring, my platoon was trudging across a small field at the head of a high valley when someone spotted a pair of North Korean soldiers about a thousand yards away. The platoon leader bellowed, "Get your hands up and surrender!" One of the enemy soldiers dropped his rifle and shot his hands into the air, as ordered, but the other man jumped into a ditch and opened fire with his burpgun. The entire platoon blazed away at the shooter until his weapon fell silent. A squad that moved cautiously forward to secure the prisoner found the shooter in the ditch, dead with a single round through his brain. He had colonel's insignia on his shoulders.

The prisoner was a baby-faced private, only fourteen years old. He told us he had been accompanying the colonel, who was carrying maps and documents in his thin leather backpack, since they had been separated from their unit during an American airstrike some days before. The two had been wandering around these mountain wastes in search of a friendly unit. The youngster was bright and appeared to be well-trained. He demonstrated that he could read maps and comprehend the basic small-unit tactics employed by the People's Army.

The captured documents and maps were passed up the chain to regimental headquarters, but the boy was taken to the small mountain hut in which our company headquarters was located. We identified ourselves as northerners and offered the prisoner a clean ROK Army uniform and good food. Our doing so would have been considered highly irregular by superior headquarters, but we often sought to bolster our steadily-declining numbers by making such offers to likely candidates, and many accepted. This boy, however, refused the clothes and food, and even refused to say any more to us for several days; he preferred to sit outside for hours on end and watch American fighter-bombers dropping high explosives and napalm upon North Korean positions in the mountains to the north. Gradually, he warmed up to me in particular, at least enough to accept food I offered. Though he had been our enemy, we also took to him. In time, he revealed that he was from a town near Chu-ul and that he had been conscripted right out of his junior high school classroom a few months earlier. In time, though he would not talk about his own political convictions, he seemed to understand why so many of his fellow North Koreans had come South with a dream of living in a democratic and free society.

Such a dream was not to be his, for one night a few months after his capture, and after he had been accepted as a sort of non-participating company mascot, the youngster was squatting beside me in a trench. Abruptly, without warning, his former People's Army comrades launched a sudden assault. As soon as the attack was repulsed, I turned to say something to the boy. Whatever the words might have been, he never heard them, for he lay dead beside me, a bullet through the head.

Once again I wanted to lash out at the futility and inhumanity of war which took its toll of innocent youth and cast a deathly pall over combatants and noncombatants alike, the only victors being those who, like our youthful mascot, died instantaneously.

CHAPTER EIGHTEEN

While we refugee soldiers of the 23rd Regiment Reconnaissance Company were learning to be soldiers and suffering our first losses, the command structure of the ROK and United Nations forces was undergoing numerous changes.

Lieutenant General Walton Walker, the U.S. 8th Army commander, was killed in a jeep accident on an icy road north of Seoul on December 23, 1950. He was replaced by Lieutenant General Matthew Ridgway, then the United States Army Deputy Chief of Staff. On April 15, 1951, Lieutenant General James Van Fleet replaced Ridgway, who replaced General Douglas MacArthur when MacArthur was relieved by President Harry Truman on April 11 following an open disagreement between the president and the general over the conduct of the war. It is hard to say how these changes impacted on us, but it is true that the command styles of all the generals differed, definitely affecting the conduct of the war at my level.

The Communist First Spring Offensive got underway on the night of April 22, when the Chinese mounted massed infantry assaults against the UN lines. These assaults were typically accompanied by the sound of whistles, bugles, gongs and shepherd's horns. The People's Liberation Army divisions cracked General Van Fleet's line at the weakest point, which was held by the ROK 6th Division. The disintegration of the ROK division left a huge gap between the U.S. 24th Division in the west and the U.S. 1st Marine Division in the east. Enemy troops poured through and cut the road leading northwest from Seoul. By the end of April, 8th Army had been forced to withdraw to a new defensive line known as "No-Name Line." This defensive barrier ran in a fairly

197

straight line from the west coast about one-third the way across the peninsula, then slanted northeastward. Only the eastern tip of the line projected above the 38th Parallel.

On May 9, 1951, the ROK III Corps, consisting of the 3rd and 9th Divisions, moved up to No-Name Line and established a main line of resistance there. My own 3rd Division was the corps right wing, with headquarters in Hyun-ri. The 22nd Infantry Regiment held the divisional right flank, and the 18th was on the left. The 23rd Infantry Regiment was the divisional reserve. The 9th Division established its headquarters in Yongpo, about three miles east and slightly south of Hyun-ri. Its 30th and 28th Infantry Regiments were deployed on the right and left, respectively, and the 29th Infantry Regiment was in reserve. The entire line in the III Corps sector was several miles south of our old positions, which had been centered in Inje.

The Hyun-ri front was hemmed in by steep ridges to the west; often, the slopes were in excess of sixty degrees and the peaks varied from 2,000 to 5,000 feet. The valley of Hyun-ri was very deep, and the Soyang River ran through it in a southwesterly direction. The river was a major barrier, from 165 to 330 feet wide and six to sixteen feet deep. Crossing the Soyang on foot was almost impossible. One of the Soyang's tributaries, the Naeinchun River, ran through Yongpo, Hyun-ri and Inje. This river was 65 to 300 feet wide, but it was relatively shallow and could be forded on foot. The main supply route from III Corps Headquarters was along a mountain road so narrow that two cars could not pass one another. Wireless communications across the mountainous terrain was difficult to maintain. At the altitude of the valley, even in early May, patches of snow persisted and it was extremely cold at night.

Twelve Chinese People's Liberation Army divisions struck along a twenty-mile front between Naepyong-ri and Nodong at five o'clock on the afternoon of May 16, 1951. The main blow fell upon the ROK 5th and 7th Divisions in the vicinity of Hangye-ri. Both ROK divisions disintegrated, and the Chinese exploited their breakthrough by swinging east into the rear of the ROK III Corps.

The defenders enjoyed an advantage in geography, and should have been aided in the defense by a full moon. However, a Chinese human wave assault succeeded in breaking through at the eastern corner of the 22nd Infantry Regiment's sector at around four o'clock on the morning of May 17. At the same time, another Chinese attack severed the single road connection to the south.

My company was transported by truck to 3rd Division Headquarters, in Hyun-ri, arriving without incident at about noon, May 17. We simply sat at the outskirts of the village, awaiting orders.

In mid-afternoon, the commanding general of ROK III Corps flew into Hyun-ri's tiny airstrip to observe the situation at the front and receive face-to-face reports from commanding generals of his 3rd and 9th Divisions. Following the discussion, one battalion of the 9th Division's 29th Infantry Regiment was dispatched to retake Omachi Mountain and reopen the road to the south. Even with strong artillery support, the battalion was unable to dislodge the Chinese. So much ammunition had been expended by then that United States Air Force transports had to re-supply III Corps by parachute drop. The bulk of the fresh supplies landed on and around the Hyun-ri airstrip, but many loads fell into enemy hands.

As it grew dark, all six infantry regiments of the 3rd and 9th Divisions, plus support units, completed a general withdrawal to Hyrun-ri. Hundreds of army vehicles and artillery pieces were packed bumper-to-bumper on the narrow country road running south through the town, and many thousands of soldiers sat in the stalled trucks or stretched out on the ground. All the soldiers I saw looked exhausted from the fighting and the rigors of the withdrawal. Like me, many had not been given any food since the day before.

The night ground slowly onward and the chill steadily increased. The thousands of soldiers in and around the town were given no orders by their senior commanders. From time to time the sound of rockets and mortars split the air as they left the enemy stronghold at the Omachi Mountain pass to the south.

I spent the interminably long night sitting with two other men in the back of a truck loaded with company supplies. These two men were my helpers. Like me, they were North Koreans, had even come from villages near the far northeastern coast. But unlike me, they were prisoners of war. They had been under my orders since the early Spring, when I was put in charge of all the food supplies for the company mess. One was a sergeant and the other a private, and both had been captured by Reconnaissance Company near Inje. I never knew if the two requested or merely agreed to stay with the company, but they had long been an integral part of it. There were numerous occasions when I spent long periods of time alone with these two, far from any help, herding them along lonely mountain trails as we carried food to outlying platoon outposts. To fear them never entered my mind, even when we had to pass through enemy lines to get from our headquarters to the isolated outposts.

Later that night another attempt was made to re-open the road to the south so elements of the two divisions bottled up between Hyun-ri and Yongpo could move again. The new attack was launched by 9th

Division's 30th Infantry Regiment and 3rd Division's 18th Infantry Regiment. My unit not being involved, we three simply continued to sit in the truck and listen to the sounds of the escalating battle. Instead of receding, the noise of battle increased steadily, becoming not only louder but obviously coming closer! Just before midnight, enemy shells were falling right into Hyun-ri for the first time since the Chinese offensive had been launched.

Rapid-fire orders were passed along the line of waiting soldiers: all vehicles were to be burned. The jeeps were pushed into roadside ditches and trucks were set ablaze on the roadway with gasoline. Thousands of soldiers around the village began fleeing into the surrounding hills in a complete and disorderly rout. Panic, like the gasoline-fed fires engulfing the vehicles, swept over the main strength of the III Corps.

Preparing to follow orders to destroy the truck we three sat in, I jumped from it, expecting my two helpers to assist in setting it ablaze. To my astonishment they had vanished into the surrounding pandemonium, gone for good as it turned out. Had anyone asked me, I would have had to admit I could not blame them.

*

In short order I became one with the disorganized retreat. Climbing a nearby mountain, I paused to look back. Hyun-ri was a blazing inferno of houses, trucks, and supply dumps. The night air was filled with the noise of vast stores of ammunition firing off in the intense heat.

In the eerie flickering light, I made my way upward through a stand of trees and outcroppings of huge blocks of rock. All around me were other men scrambling upward, the same as I. But as I ascended, the darkness grew more intense and everything beyond a few paces

201

before me blanked out. I seemed to be alone on the inhospitable mountainside.

All night I plodded on, fording streams, straining eyes and ears, trying desperately to determine my direction. Occasionally the sound of a voice would reach me and the underbrush crackled as someone pushed through. I had no way of knowing it might be an enemy or comrade, so I pushed on alone, strenghtened only by fear.

In the first pale streaks of light of the dawn of May 18, 1951, the scene around me gradually began to take shape. I discerned the outlines of trees, and high in their branches birds, as was their natural instinct, began singing sweetly to greet the new day. My mind, clinging to reality despite my exhaustion, thought of the incongruity of man and nature. Somehow, in some way, I silently prayed that mankind would at last accede to nature's law of survival of the species and leave behind the futile human destructiveness of war!

As if to taunt my fervent prayer, a bird of another sort, also on the wing with the rising sun, swooped low in the direction of Hyun-ri, trailing curtains of the distinctive oily flame of napalm, out to make sure nothing but death and desolation remained to the enemy. So much for my prayer!

As I continued to clamber up the steep mountainside in the growing light, I began to distinguish other ROK soldiers doing the same. Their appearance was startling, until I realized they had all removed their insignia of rank from their uniforms and had discarded everything but the clothes they were wearing.

I allied myself with the group and climbed along with them. By midmorning, our company, increasing by other ROK soldiers converging on the area, had reached a small stream near Pangdaesan. Our throats parched from lack of any liquid and our mouths dry with fear, we scrambled down the bank to quench our thirst. Lifting my head after drinking, I stared straight into the face of a fellow townsman from Chu-ul. I recognized him as a student at the Teachers' College in Chongjin while I was attending medical school there. Eager to express my surprise and pleasure at this unexpected meeting with someone from home, I opened my mouth to speak. But no words issued forth, for suddenly in that very moment, the air around us was rent by the sharp crackle of bullets. An enemy patrol had beat us to the mountaintop!

Before I could automatically react, hundreds of bullets fell in our midst, kicking up the dirt at our feet and snapping off branches all around us. Seized by an overpowering panic, I ran wildly in the direction away from the source of the firings. I noticed my fellow townsman was running beside me, but in another instant I saw him tumble face-forward to the ground. Taking a longer glance, I saw that he had been shot in the ankle. My instant reflex was to stop and give him whatever help I could—try to get him back up on his feet or carry him away. But before I could act upon it, so swift was the onslaught from the enemy, that I was literally frozen in my tracks. That my life, too, was on the line didn't register on my consciousness, so horrifying was the scene I witnessed. For as I turned to render whatever assistance I could, I saw the top of his head explode in a gush of blood, bone, and brains. Never in all my experiences as a medical assistant during the air raids on Chongjin, had I witnessed such a brutal attack on a human being. I was galvanized into action by the hideously revolting sight, and retching as I went, I blindly fought my way out of the firing action.

When I reached a small hill about a quarter-mile from the stream, I saw that an ROK soldier of undetermined rank was trying to stop the fleeing men and form them up to fight back. "Stop," he yelled. "We can hold here!" I thought his efforts were noble but absurd, for I was one of a pitifully small proportion of the fleeing soldiers who had retained possession of his personal weapons. I plunged past him, heading south with the herd.

During the next five days of desperate retreat, my group, which constantly swelled and receded, covered over forty miles of rough terrain and escaped or evaded numerous enemy efforts to bring us to captivity or death. We managed to subsist on wild mountain greens and some dried corn and potatoes we found in abandoned farmsteads. On May 23, we reached Hajinbu-ri, where a new defensive line was being established. By the time I arrived, only about one-third of 3rd Division troops had reported back.

*

Before that time, and while I was evading Communist perils in the mountains, General Van Fleet had decided to allow the enemy to continue their advance south from Inje while the U.S. 3rd Infantry Division and the reinforced U.S. 185th Airborne Regiment were rushed across the peninsula from the U.S. X Corps sector. During this redeployment, the ROK III Corps was dissolved, and my division was transferred to the ROK I Corps.

The U.S. 3rd Infantry Division was sent into combat along the southern limit of the new Communist salient. Over five times the normal ammunition allowance for such an operation was fired by the artillery units supporting the American counterattack. The power of the Chinese advance was dissipated by the weight of the bombardment and the unexpected American counterthrust. By the end of the day, May 19, it was obvious that the Chinese would be unable to achieve their goals. On May 20, the American reinforcements had stabilized their holding line while the ROK 8th Division was moved up to plug part of the hole left by the routed and now-dissolved ROK III Corps.

The Communist Second Spring Offensive ended after only four days, having achieved a relatively narrow penetration on what amounted to a secondary front. This was the third, and final, attempt by a Communist army to conquer South Korea. It ended in a carnage unparalleled by events before or since in Korea. Many supporting Chinese died in curtains of napalm and high explosives carried to the front by unchallenged United Nations warplanes, and from bullets and large-caliber rounds fired by massed United Nations and ROK Army weapons. In just two weeks of fighting, over 17,000 Chinese prisoners were taken by United Nations forces in our sector alone. It is true that a large part of the ROK Army suffered grievous harm at the start of the Chinese offensive, but it was clear in the end that there was no longer any hope of unifying Korea on Communist terms. In fact, the Chinese opened negotiations with the United Nations command within a month of their failure on the II Corps front.

A new United Nations general offensive was initiated immediately in the wake of the Communist Second Spring Offensive. By the end of May, the U.S. X Corps was back to the Soyang River, and Kaesong was in the hands of the ROK I Corps. By the beginning of June, all of the land below the 38th Parallel, except for a small salient west in Inje, was in the hands of the ROK Army and its free-world allies.

HYUN-RI RETREAT

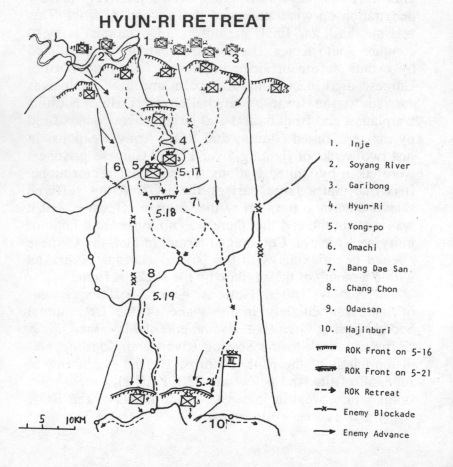

1. Inje
2. Soyang River
3. Garibong
4. Hyun-Ri
5. Yong-po
6. Omachi
7. Bang Dae San
8. Chang Chon
9. Odaesan
10. Hajinburi
〜〜〜 ROK Front on 5-16
〜〜〜 ROK Front on 5-21
– – → ROK Retreat
✕✕✕ Enemy Blockade
——→ Enemy Advance

CHAPTER NINETEEN

On June 1, 1951, my regiment was being redeployed and refitted in the rear. We refugee soldiers of the "Local Volunteer Group" formed in Kilchu in early December of 1950 had survived our baptism of fire. We were told during this period in the rear that we had completed our period of probation in the ROK Army. This was the first mention that we had been fighting since New Year's Day as something less than full-fledged soldiers of the Republic of Korea. It also made clear why none of us had drawn any pay during the past five months of intense combat.

Looking back on my bizarre life as a "probationary" combat infantryman, I recalled my feelings on the deck of the USS *St. Wind*, I gazed in a semi-delirium on the beach at Kuryongpo-ri. At that moment I was convinced I would be able to meet my family once again and live with them in peace and freedom. There had to be a way to unite the North and South into one democratic nation. I had given the Republic of Korea the benefit of the doubt as I stumbled off the ship, willing to take up arms in the hope of that reunification. Even when I learned that that nation had placed my life in jeopardy without affording me the basic right of recognizing my existence on its army rolls, I maintained that hope. My fellow refugees and I had served faithfully as ghost soldiers, without ever receiving even the pittance regular soldiers were paid. There was no show of gratitude by the Republic of Korea for our efforts, for our accomplishments and obedience. I felt childish in not realizing all that time that regular soldiers were paid. But all that was insignificant to my feelings when I tallied our numbers and realized that fully one-fourth of the original 156 volunteers were either dead, wounded, or missing in action by the time the rest of us were officially inducted into the ROK Army. There had been many brave soldiers among those dead, wounded, or missing; they and all the rest had risked the perilous journey to the South out of an honest conviction that at the end of the unknowable road, they would have the opportunity to enjoy freedom and a better life. It was a bitter realization that these brave compatriots would never, in all likelihood, be accorded any recognition for their ultimate sacrifices.

But as time unfolds its rolls of honor, these dedicated ghost soldiers will find their names enshrined thereon, if not graven in the stone, then immortalized in the hearts and minds of all who fought alongside them, and those who later learned of their exploits.

When my regiment was sent to the east-coast sector after refitting, I went as Private First Class Chung Dong-kyu, 0722012. Shortly thereafter, on June 25, 1951, the anniversary of the outbreak of the war, all the surviving refugee soldiers were unexpectedly rewarded for our efforts by promotion to the rank of corporal. Next, on August 15, the anniversary of Korean independence from Japanese colonial rule, we were all promoted again, this time to the rank of sergeant. By then, we were also receiving our monthly pay. By late 1951, I was an assistant squad leader.

*

Early in 1952, after months of "routine" action near Inje, our 3rd Division replaced the ROK 6th Division on "Gary Line," on the east-central front to the right of the U.S. IX Corps. For many days, we had no significant contact with the enemy, who appeared hesitant to meet United Nation forces. This may have been due, in part, to the absolute superiority of UN air and artillery power at this stage of the war.

The 23rd Infantry Reconnaissance Company was split into very small groups each night and sent out to set up ambushes near enemy positions. Our main purpose in going out was the capture of enemy soldiers, who were desperately required by higher headquarters to help determine enemy intentions, deployments, troop strength, order of battle, and morale. Each of us carried only two hand grenades, which we fastened to our chest straps by their handles, and an M2 carbine carrying only one clip of fifteen .30-caliber bullets. Sometimes, we were armed with shotguns and birdshot in the hope of sufficiently wounding a would-be prisoner to bring him down without killing him. No matter how we were armed, we were invariably admonished to hold our fire unless we were in immediate personal danger.

We usually crawled out to our posts in the bitter cold after midnight, our faces painted over with black camouflage cream so as not to reflect the moonlight. When we reached our posts, we usually concealed ourselves in ditches and gullies or behind trees and shrubs. We waited there for enemy patrols to pass and fall into our hands. We were not allowed to talk and could barely move for fear of making noise. Smoking, of course, was absolutely forbidden. If nothing prevented it, we would usually return to our own lines between four o'clock in the morning and sunrise.

Despite all the precautions and suffering, we failed to secure a single prisoner over the course of many weeks. It was quite clear that our northern cousins and their Chinese allies had no intention of approaching us. In fact, I would not have been surprised to learn that they knew every one of our hiding places and simply skirted them on their own nocturnal forays.

Since there was nothing to do while waiting for prisoners to fall into our trap, I spent many lonely hours thinking of home, and most of my thoughts centered on Mother. The more I thought of home, the more my mind brought into focus my last picture of my piteous, grieving Mother. With the growing likelihood I would never again see home or Mother, my depression deepened into a near-manic condition. My imminent death beneath the moonlit skies of the war-torn no-man's-land in which I lay shivering every night became an obsession. I reflected at great length on my last, unkept promise to Mother—my promise to return in three days. Though the three days were long gone, to fulfill that promise was the lodestone that drew me back from the brink of total despair.

*

The commanding general of the U.S. IX Corps, to which our ROK 3rd Division was attached, ordered Operation "Clam-up" to commence at six o'clock on the evening of February 10 and end at six o'clock on the morning of February 16, 1952. The intent of the exercise was to mislead the enemy into thinking that United Nations units had withdrawn from our sector of the IX Corps front. It was hoped that the enemy would venture forth to investigate or occupy the "abandoned" positions and, thus, fall into our hands.

Our company moved stealthily to the 3rd Division's northernmost outpost, Hill 662, to join the 23rd Infantry Regiment's 9th Company, which had been there for some weeks. The move was completed by four o'clock on the morning of February 10. As soon as we had set up, the 9th Company relayed information via voice radio—which we assumed was being monitored—that it was beginning its ordered withdrawal. Then, with great ostentation, the infantry company began moving to the rear. The whole scheme was designed to fool the enemy into thinking that Hill 662's defensive complex was being left vacant.

The defenses were as good as any I had ever seen. There were many well-constructed reinforced pillboxes circling the forward crown and top of the hill, and ample bombproof bunkers on the rear slope. Each pillbox had a five-foot-long-by-one-foot-high firing and observation port facing the enemy hills, and there were hundreds of hand grenades and thousands of .30-caliber rounds stored in each structure. The pillbox occupied by my squad was crowded but not uncomfortable.

Hill 662 was connected to Hill 748, to the south, by a narrow saddle. From the firing port, I could easily see the nearest enemy outpost, on Hill 674, about two-thirds of a mile to the north.

Despite the noisy withdrawal by our 9th Company, the enemy restricted his movements to two or three squad-sized sweeps around the summit of Hill 674; he made no move whatsoever in our direction. We naturally hoped that our move to Hill 662 had not been observed, and we redoubled our efforts to remain under cover and out of sight. Lieutenant Kang Dae-yoo, our temporary company commander (Lieutenant Kim was on leave), ordered absolute silence and cold meals for everyone; no lights and certainly no cook fires were to be shown. Only one soldier per pillbox was placed on guard and everyone else was cautioned to remain as motionless as possible.

Days passed without the enemy paying us the slightest attention. The only movement to and from Hill 662 was by civilian porters, who carried in food—usually only steamed rice balls, all we had to eat. I have no idea why canned food was withheld. Going outside during the day to relieve our bladders and bowels was also forbidden. When our steel outer helmets, which we were

211

using for toilets, were filled, we had no choice but to use a corner of our crowded pillbox. This naturally led to greatly increased discomfort, and the odor was appalling even to veterans who had long ago become inured to the more-disgusting aspects of life in the field.

Lack of activity put everyone on edge. One night, I was all of a minute late reporting for guard duty at one of the night observation posts. The company first sergeant did not say anything to me, but simply swung a great roundhouse punch that knocked me off my feet.

Enemy activity began to increase late on the night of February 14, the fifth day of Operation Clam-up. At about one-thirty in the morning, an enemy infantry platoon was seen approaching the eastern side of Hill 662. The corporal who made the initial sighting passed hand signals to his platoon leader, an inexperienced second lieutenant who could not possibly have seen the enemy soldiers from his platoon command post. As soon as the lieutenant understood the corporal's signals, he set off a line of command-detonated land mines. Everyone who could bring a weapon to bear opened fire as well, but the enemy platoon fled at once. Our reaction squad found three dead Chinese soldiers on the lower slope of our hill, but no prisoners were taken.

Having met with resistance, a sure sign that Hill 662 had not been abandoned, the Chinese commenced with their usual tactics aimed at unsettling unwanted adversaries—the incessant sounding of bugles, flutes, shepherds' horns, drums, rattles, gongs and whistles. All this had no perceptible influence upon the veteran reconnaissance specialists occupying Hill 662; we were all too excited over the coming prospect of taking some prisoners after sitting in the damp cold for five interminably boring days. To us, the rising crescendo of cacophonous noises signalled an end to the waiting. We prepared ourselves for the final battle as the silvery moonlight was reflected off the snow-covered lunar landscape.

Lieutenant Kang passed his orders over the network of walkie-talkies that bound the company together: "We will put up our strongest resistance. In order to avoid exposing our positions or revealing our full ability to defend ourselves, do not open fire until the last possible moment. If possible, allow the enemy advance guard to penetrate our main line so that we can take prisoners."

The Chinese fired a white smoke shell over the top of Hill 662 at about five minutes to two on the morning of February 15. Within a minute, our hilltop defenses were being peppered by light small-arms' fire. Minutes later, machine guns emplaced atop Hill 674 were raking our line of combat pillboxes. Mortar rounds impacting to the rear of the hill severed wire links with headquarters and made us solely dependent upon our voice radios.

At twenty after two, the Chinese fired several blue-smoke rounds, and the incoming rifle and machine-gun fire abruptly ceased as the enemy mortars shortened range and began hitting Hill 662. At the same time, we began receiving hits from enemy medium caliber enemy artillery. Over three hundred mortar and artillery shells struck our hill during the next twenty-five minutes. I heard an unending stream of reports over the squad walkie-talkie indicating that pillboxes and many of the men in them were being neutralized by the incoming fire. I was certain that a number of my fellow refugee solders were being killed. Next, I heard the news that Chinese infantry platoons were advancing from Hill 674 under cover of the artillery and mortar bombardment. I looked out through my pillbox's firing aperture, but I could see none of the attacking infantrymen through the curtain of bursting shells.

The Chinese advanced directly up the forward slope of Hill 662 and rapidly engaged the men deployed in the forwardmost pillboxes. By three twenty-five, the fighting was general throughout the compound, with reports of savage hand-to-hand combat emanating from my walkie-talkie. I peered out of my pillbox's firing aperture and could hardly distinguish friend from foe among the ghostly figures that darted through my field of vision. Members of my squad on either side of me were firing at anything that moved, though our pillbox had not yet been directly threatened.

With our communications to the rear irretrievably shattered and many of our fighting positions overrun, Lieutenant Kang finally passed the word: "Withdraw to Hill 748 by way of the saddle. Every man for himself!" I left my pillbox in the dark, just after moonset, and followed a clump of dark human figures across the saddle. When I reached Hill 748 just before sunrise, I found that the remnants of the company were reforming under Lieutenant Kang. As soon as the flow of survivors stopped, Kang led us rearward, all the way to our regimental command post.

Many of our comrades had failed to join us, but those of us who tended to look at things in a positive light realized that the vast majority of the company was comprised of self-reliant veterans well used to moving cross-country under extremely adverse conditions. We knew we had lost many comrades in the fierce combat against overwhelming numbers of Chinese, but we expected many of the missing to trickle in. Many did return, but not nearly as many as we had hoped.

The attempt to capture enemy scouts by tricking them into reconnoitering our hill had failed at great expense, mainly due to a new lieutenant's attack of first-combat jitters and the enemy's quick offensive reaction. Adding to our own misery was the fact that 8th Army had lost an important hilltop fighting position as a result of our failed subterfuge.

After we had eaten and rested a bit, Lieutenant Kang ordered the survivors of the battle to line up in a large tent. He told us, "Our company is to recapture Hill 662 with the support of an artillery battalion." He wanted to select only a few men to form a special squad that would be sent to retake the hill just lost by our entire company. To a man, our chins dropped to our chests and our eyes found promising objects on the floor to keep them occupied. I knew that our exhaustion had eradicated any hint of bravery from those eyes. I also knew that I would be excluded from the special assault squad because I had acquired a tiny shrapnel wound in the palm of my left hand, which was wrapped in a clean, white bandage.

When no one volunteered for the death squad—for that is what we all thought of it as being—Lieutenant Kang stalked down the line of survivors and called aloud the names of the men he selected for the duty. After a bowl of rice wine and a cigarette per man, the squad shambled from the tent and boarded jeeps waiting by the entrance to take them up the hill to the regimental observation post to receive final orders. Mentally I checked off more names from the dwindling list of survivors of the group which over a year before this disastrous day I had joined in Kilchu.

Operation Clam-up was called off at two in the afternoon of February 15 rather than at six in the morning of February 16, as originally planned. As a result, Lieutenant Kang's death squad was reprieved. The regiment ordered the 3rd Battalion to mount a full-scale assault to retake Hill 662, and our condemned comrades were returned to us. The ROK artillery battalion supporting the 23rd Infantry Regiment directed the fires of all its guns against Hill 662 as soon as the 3rd Battalion attack had been arranged, and the infantry battalion advanced on schedule. Following a grim uphill fight and the use of grenades, bayonets and fists, the Chinese were driven from Hill 662 at twilight. I heard that the snow atop the hill was a carpet of bright red in places.

*

After Hill 662 was retaken and the front settled down to more-routine forms of mutual terror, our company was ordered to the main line to take up positions alongside the regiment's rifle companies. By this time, I calculated that half of the 156 refugee soldiers who had arrived from North Korea were gone—killed, wounded or missing.

The front was quiescent during this period, with no major attacks instigated by either side. We remained at full alert, however, never knowing when something might occur. Our security was fairly good; the front was shielded by a hundred-yard-wide band of land mines and tripflares which were supposed to go off if anyone came in contact with them or the wires to which they were attached.

One of the flares went off one dark night, and hundreds of ROK soldiers opened fire with rifles and machine-guns. I, too, fired wildly into the dark as I watched the yellow-red tails of thousands of tracer rounds stitching phantasmagoric patterns through the black sky. The firing remained continuous and rapid for a very long time; the only time anyone stopped firing was to allow the barrel of his weapon to cool down. Order was finally restored after about thirty minutes, and everyone who could went back to sleep. I had become so inured to the specter of combat by then that I didn't know I had fallen asleep until I was awakened just before dawn. A patrol sent to investigate the front at dawn found that an enemy patrol had thrown a blanket across our forwardmost wire barrier and had, thus, set off the flare that had precipitated our mad gunfire. Three bullet-riddled bodies, barely recognizable as enemy soldiers, were found on the near side of the wire. It looked as though they had been cutting a gap to prepare the way for a raid on our lines by a larger force.

*

At this time, the food supply system had broken down to the point where we were ravenously hungry most of the time. Corruption was rampant throughout the ROK Army; supplies of every type were routinely siphoned off at every command level leading down to the companies and platoons manning the front, and only a tiny fraction of our allocations actually reached us. Most mornings, each of us received as our daily ration less than a cupful of rice, which we had to cook in our canteen cups, and some pickled vegetables.

The effect upon our morale was staggering. One morning in the early spring, three members of my original group of refugee soldiers went down to the forwardmost listening post and talked their way out into no man's land by telling the sentries that they hoped to bring back edible greens or the final gleanings of some war-shattered farm buildings. The three had not returned by the next morning, and a Korean Central Intelligence Agency operative who was permanently attached to the regiment made his way to the front to interrogate every one of the surviving refugee soldiers. He wanted to know if the three had been spies or had planned their escape with our connivance. In fact, I had heard the three grousing about the corruption and talking about deserting, but they were far from the only ones taking part in such discussions. I had not given their defection any thought until I heard they had really left.

My brave refugee comrades, long used to ranging far afield each night, were growing bored and restless as a result of the company's relative inactivity during this period. Sitting around in trenches day and night was fairly safe, but it was too constricting for us. We had little to do but think or talk about our painfully empty stomachs. One late spring day, six or seven of my comrades came by my trench to trade tales of their experiences over the past eighteen months of combat. Talk inevitably turned to our growling stomachs. One of my visitors had been the regimental commander's personal driver, and he had seen much of the corruption going on at higher levels. Another, an older man, had served for a time as a truck driver with the regimental supply company. At length, the older man proposed a plan he must have been thinking about for a long time. He suggested that we steal one of the supply trucks and drive south to Chiri-san, the tallest mountain in South Korea. He had heard that the vast rugged terrain was infested with Communist guerrillas who would welcome us into their ranks. I heard him out, but I did not commit myself either way.

On a very hot summer afternoon some weeks later, I saw that most of the soldiers who had discussed desertion with me were gathering one by one in my trench to conduct another meeting. I was not up to the discussion, for all my muscles ached and I had an excruciating headache. About thirty minutes into the animated session, I felt the onset of bone-wracking chills. Despite the heat, I felt it was too cold for me to sit still, so I crawled out of the confining trench and squatted above the group, hoping the afternoon sun on my face would warm me up. Soon, I was shivering so badly I was grinding my teeth. This went on for nearly an hour before I simply keeled over. My body felt like jelly, and sweat was pouring from my skin. I slowly pulled myself to my feet and staggered from the meeting, which was still going on in my corner of the trench.

My platoon leader sent me down to the regimental dispensary, where they eventually told me I had been suffering from the paroxyms of malaria. I was treated intravenously with an arsenic compound called Sarbarsan and ordered to remain in the dispensary overnight for observation by the medical staff. Early that evening, my left arm, which was bruised from the injection, began to swell and hurt badly. Apparently, some of the Sarbarsan had leaked from the vein into the surrounding muscle tissue. The medics gave me several aspirin and treated the swelling with hot, wet compresses. Despite the soothing treatment, I was unable to fall asleep that night because of the pain. I cried out for Mother's love and care as I recalled with haunting clarity the long night following my emergency appendectomy in Harbin—just seven summers earlier. How I longed to find her dozing beside me, holding my hand in hers, as I awakened in the morning.

Apparently that single treatment with the arsenic compound killed the malaria parasite, for I never again suffered those paroxyms and chills.

I also heard nothing more of the planned defection.

CHAPTER TWENTY

Several days after my malarial attack abated, Lieutenant Kim, my company commander, asked me to do a personal favor. Kim had been saving a part of his pay. He wanted me to deliver the cash to his fiancee, who lived in Pusan, the port city at the southern tip of the peninsula that had played so vital a role at the start of the Korean War. Since I was going, the company first sergeant asked me to stop by his sister's house in Taegu, where ROK Army Headquarters was located, to pick up the Russian-made revolver he had captured in combat and left behind on his last leave. The journey would amount to a six-day leave, my very first trip to the rear of the combat zones since my arrival in South Korea two years earlier. Now I could gain a sense of what I had been fighting for all that time. Naturally, I was extremely excited, particularly since Lieutenant Kim provided me with what seemed like a princely sum of spending money.

As I packed a few days' supply of rice and some extra socks in my backpack for emergency use, I was again taken back to my last day at home in Chu-ul, when Mother had packed rice and socks for me.

Wearing my helmet, green summer fatigue uniform and my webbed belt with bayonet, I left the front on the regimental supply truck. As always, I carried my M2 carbine slung on my right shoulder. The truck took me only as far as regimental headquarters, where I was obliged to stand on the edge of the roadway to hitch another ride. It was a long wait, and I began thinking of my first semester of commuting between Chu-ul and Chongjin Medical-Technical High School. I was preparing to boost myself into the rear compartment of a passing truck when a U.S. Army 3/4-ton truck stopped in the dust

221

beside me. There was the driver and another man in the front, and two American soldiers in the rear. The driver signalled me to jump on.

At about noon, the truck pulled off the road at the camp of a United States Army battalion. The driver motioned an invitation that I join him for a meal. Though I had learned Chinese, German, Latin, Russian, Japanese and Korean in my travels, I neither spoke nor understood a word of English, so I tagged along close to my host as we got into the self-service cafeteria-style serving line. Following the driver's lead, I cut myself a thick slab of meatloaf, spooned out steamed mixed vegetables and fresh salad, and took a big bowl of vegetable soup with bread-and-butter. I was surprised to see that there was still room on my tray, so I grabbed a huge piece of chocolate cake and topped the whole thing off with a cup of hot coffee with lots of cream and sugar. I had not seen so much or such good food since my last dinner with my family before we left Harbin in 1945. Without uttering a single word, I shoveled all this delicious repast into my mouth, using my spoon and fork and, where necessary, my fingers. I ate every last crumb and drank every last drop, and even felt a little distress as I pushed my tray away.

As we left the mess hall after a satisfying smoke, the chubby mess attendant pressed several chocolate bars into my hand. I could not understand what he said to me, but I suppose it must have been something like, "Hey, Shorty, you look so hungry, and you ate so much, you deserve to have these to eat along the way."

This was my first real contact with Americans, and I came away impressed and awed with the marvelous meal and the even-more marvelous generosity of my hosts. It is something I have never forgotten.

The truck passed through Seoul in mid-afternoon. This was my first look at the South Korean capital, one of

the world's largest cities. It was still pretty much a ruin
as a result of the vicious street-by-street fighting
required to recapture it from the North Korean People's
Army in September, 1950. Soon we were on a narrow
country road that wound across low hills hemmed in
between high mountains. For the fourth time that day. I
was drawn back to memories of home, for this could have
been the road between Chu-ul and Chongjin.

Sunset caught us at a high altitude in the
mountains. It was so cold that I began to shiver, for all I
had on were my thin summer fatigues. The Americans all
had parkas, but there was none for me, so I huddled up
between the two men in the rear compartment as we
passed through Taejon, scene of a major North Korean
victory against American troops very early in the war.

We came to my first stop, Taegu, near midnight.
The friendly driver pulled off the main road and drove all
the way to the railroad station to drop me off. He offered
his hand, which I shook, and he pulled away as I bowed
over and over again in the correct Korean style.

There were many small inns near the railroad
station, which is why I suppose the American dropped
me there. I chose one of the cheaper ones, which proved
to be fortunate. The innkeeper, a woman, answered my
inquiries in my own dialect. "Where are you from," she
asked.

"Chu-ul, in North Hamgyong Province."

"Ah, you will find many local merchants at the
city's open market who are also from your region."

I was very excited to hear this, for there was a
chance I might learn the whereabouts of someone I had
known in the north. My head was all filled with visions of
home and familiar faces as the kindly innkeeper led me to
my small room for the best, most comfortable night's
sleep I had enjoyed in over two years.

*

Very early, before breakfast, I was on my way to the city market. I arrived just as it was opening for business. There were rows and rows of stalls down the center of the road. Many of them were manned by refugees selling anything and everything. I stopped at the first one and asked the merchant, "Do you know anyone from Chu-ul?" I deliberately used my local dialect in the hopes that a passerby or nearby merchant might overhear and recognize it.

"I know a lady from your hometown," he answered, and he dropped everything to lead me to her.

It turned out that the woman knew many refugees from the Chu-ul area. In fact, she knew my fourth cousin, Chung Chun-duk, who was twelve years older than I and whom I had had hopes of finding at the time I arrived in the South at the end of 1950. Cousin Chun-duk had arrived in Harbin looking for work when I was in the first grade. He had lived with my family until he got settled. In fact, Father had helped him find a job. He came south with his wife at the end of World War II. Now, the woman in the Taegu market gave me Chun-duk's address, which was right there, in Taegu! She also told me, "In every major city in South Korea there is an open market, and every open market has a high percentage of refugees from the north. You will probably locate many relatives and friends."

It was still very early, and I still had not eaten, but my excitement overwhelmed me. After asking directions, I walked so fast that I soon felt the sweat pouring off me. I eventually found my cousin's nameplate in front of a small apartment building, and I strode right up to the door and knocked. After only a moment's nervous wait, a woman answered the door. She was Chun-duk's wife, who welcomed me into her home as soon as I blurted out who I was. Chun-duk jumped up from the breakfast table and rushed to the doorway to greet me. I was overjoyed at this meeting, and so was he. He explained that he was a captain in the ROK Army and worked at Army Headquarters overseeing the map production department. In fact, after I was fed a good breakfast, Chun-duk insisted that I go to work with him. I spent a pleasant enough day while Chun-duk explained his art.

We spent the evening camped out in Chun-duk's sitting room, catching up on all the years since our last meeting. I told my cousin how, on the front lines, I spent every day wondering if I would live long enough to keep the promise I had made to Mother as I left her home for the last time. Then I lost my composure and begged my cousin, "Please get me out of the hell into which I have been thrust. I know I have more than fulfilled any obligation I owed to South Korea for saving me from the People's Army and Security Police. Is this not my very first respite since arriving in the South? Rescue me; help me find a worthy job away from the fighting." I spoke my plea through a shower of tears. Chun-duk listened intently, without once interrupting me. He knew very well that I was the only son, the only one who could carry on my family line. He was Korean; he knew what that entailed. Finally, when I had spent myself, he calmly promised, "I will see what can be done to help you."

I learned from Chun-duk that my third cousin, Chung Mong-ho, was an ROK Army lieutenant colonel and the senior intelligence officer on the staff of the ROK 8th Division, at the front.

*

I took the train to Pusan the next morning. After seeing to my errand of taking money to Lieutenant Kim's fiancée, I resorted to the advice I had received from the woman refugee merchant in Taegu and went directly to the central open market in the hope of finding refugee merchants who might know the whereabouts of friends from Chu-ul. There were as many refugees in Pusan as there were in Taegu, and I quickly found a former Chongjin Medical College classmate selling used books in the open market. He told me that several of our former classmates were then attending the Seoul National University College of Medicine, which had been moved into a Buddhist Temple near the center of Pusan for the duration of the war.

After leaving my former classmate, I made straight for the temple campus, where I ran right into my former roommate and friend, Yi Jung-gi.

The last time I had seen Jung-gi was on the platform of the Chongjin central railroad station, when I saw him off to the North Korean People's Army and a wildly uncertain fate. I was sure he had died since then, which made the unexpected reunion all the more emotional. In the rush of words that followed our initial embrace, I learned that he was a part-time student and a part-time civilian doctors' assistant at the local military hospital. The job was not an obligation, but strictly for the money, for he had to make his own way through school in South Korea. Three other old friends from Chongjin Medical College were also enrolled in the Seoul National University College of Medicine. All of them, and Jung-gi, had served as front-line medical officers in the People's Army, and all of them, including Jung-gi, had deserted at the first opportunity. Unlike me, however, none had been conscripted into the ROK Army.

One of Jung-gi's best pieces of information was that Dr. Kim Pung-u, the noted surgeon who had advised me to flee before I was conscripted into the North Korean People's Army, had made it safely to the South. He was running a small clinic in Pusan, so I went straight there after Jung-gi had to leave for classes. The professor remembered me, and seemed very glad to see me, but he was so busy with patients that he could spend only a few minutes to hear my tale. As I was leaving, Dr. Kim pressed some money into my hand and urged me to eat a good lunch, which I did. I never saw Dr. Kim again, but I have always felt that I owe him my life.

*

I was ecstatic the whole way back to the front, and for many days afterward. I was no longer alone among strangers in this strange land; some of my treasured past was within my grasp. I also had a prospect for safely leaving the front and all its dangers, for Cousin Chun-duk might contact me any day with news of a transfer to a safe job.

It occurred to me that I should be thankful for my bone-crushing bout of malaria, for it had prevented me from taking part in the stupid venture with the would-be deserters (the desertion never came off) and undoubtedly put me in line for the only leave I had in my years as a combat reconnaissance soldier.

Each day after my return to my company seemed longer than the one before. Naturally, I grew increasingly anxious and I found myself repeating over and over in my head, "I have to survive the war until the day Cousin Chun-duk can arrange my transfer away from this hell." At the same time that I was praying so fervently, my head was filled with dreams of spending the war among the sons and relatives of generals, government officials and legislators—safely in the rear. I knew that I was cannon fodder, that my years of medical training were deemed to be of no value to a nation at war. I became increasingly certain that, despite the upward mobility of early, pre-war refugees like my two officer cousins, the South Korean nation had little use for refugees who had arrived since the start of the war.

I received a letter from my cousin, Captain Chung Chun-duk, in December, 1952, months after I had seen him in Taegu. The letter read, in part, "Who would there be to fight in the front to defend our nation against the Communist aggression if everyone were to try to work in the rear just because he was the son or relative of this or that man who holds high rank in the government or the army?" My one hope vanished with those words, and my future darkened before my eyes. I was naive enough, despite my hard years in the ROK Army, to accept my cousin's judgment and to consider myself overly selfish. I considered Chun-duk to be one of the most patriotic men I had ever met, and I am certain he wrote from an honest conviction. It did not enter my mind, then, that running the ROK Army's map production department in Taegu could hardly be considered standing at the forefront of the nation's defenses.

It took me until the early Spring of 1953 to get in touch with my third cousin, Lieutenant Colonel Chung Mong-ho, who was still serving as the ROK 8th Division's senior intelligence staff officer. It happened that the 8th Division was operating quite close to the line held by my own 3rd Division, so Cousin Mong-ho called me by phone as soon as he received my letter. I had met him only a few times in Chu-ul after we returned from Harbin, for in early 1947 he had escaped to the South because he had acquired an early and violent dislike of the Communist system that was then just gaining real power over our lives.

A few days after the call, I took leave and visited Cousin Mong-ho at his divisional headquarters. After exchanging information, I came right out and asked if he could arrange a transfer to his staff, and he promised that

228

he would do what he could. Again, my hopes soared. I knew that a divisional headquarters was not as safe as a map-production facility in Taegu, but it certainly had to be safer than the life I lived as a member of the 23rd Infantry Regiment Reconnaissance Company.

From that day on, I stopped by my company headquarters every day to ask the first sergeant if my transfer orders had arrived. It got to be something of a joke until, about a month after my visit with Cousin Mong-ho, the first sergeant told me that my name had shown up on new orders, that I was being transferred to 8th Division headquarters. The first thing I thought of was that now I would be able to stop watching my friends die, one by one.

As I began to realize that freedom was in my grasp, I realized also that Lieutenant Kim might not want to release me from his command. I was, after all, one of the few really experienced non-commissioned solders remaining in the unit. That very night, I packed all my gear and walked back to the regimental command post, where I boarded a truck that happened to be going my way. I reported to Cousin Mong-ho as soon as I arrived at the 8th Division command post, but I did not mention that I had expedited my orders without telling my former commanding officer. Mong-ho assigned me to his staff and told me to report for work in the morning.

When Lieutenant Kim discovered that I had left without first reporting to him, he became extremely angry and complained through official channels. That very morning, I was ordered to report back to him immediately, which frightened me only because I thought I might have to remain with his company. I had always been on excellent terms with Kim, and had served in his company command group off and on for all my time under his command. I was extremely surprised, then, when he ordered, "Sergeant Chung, stand at attention!" and slapped my face with all his considerable strength. Kim ordered me to return to my platoon: "Never, absolutely never, seek to leave my company again!" I was shattered and could think of nothing but my twisted plight until, late that evening, I received word that Kim wanted to see me at the company command post. I arrived, as ordered, and Kim told me, "I am approving your orders. Return to 8th Division headquarters in the morning, as set out in your transfer orders." I pulled myself up to my full height, braced at perfect attention and saluted Kim as smartly as I had ever saluted anyone. I felt the hot sting of tears in my eyes and on my cheeks as he returned my salute. I continued to cry as I returned to my tent to collect my belongings and to say a proper good-bye to the comrades with whom I had shared so much danger since my arrival in Kilchu in December, 1950. Of the 156 who had reformed Kim's company, only about forty were left.

I served on Cousin Mong-ho's staff for only a few weeks, then was transferred to the 8th Division's medical battalion. Mong-ho told me that he could not understand why my superb qualifications had been overlooked for so long. Though 8th Division participated in some hard combat in the Spring, my only exposure to real danger came when everyone available was pressed into service to carry ammunition to the top of a hotly-contested hill. To a soldier of my experience, this hardly qualified as combat, though we did suffer casualties in an artillery barrage.

CHAPTER TWENTY-ONE

On March 28, 1953, the Communists announced their willingness to accept a United Nations offer to exchange sick and wounded prisoners of war. The agreement, which was signed on April 11, cleared the way for reopening truce negotiations, which had broken down in October over the issue of involuntary prisoner exchanges. (The Communists wanted all prisoners of war returned to their hands, whether or not individual prisoners wanted to remain in South Korea.) Full-scale talks resumed at Panmunjon on April 26, when the Communists acceded to the United Nations' demand that no prisoner be repatriated against his will.

The armistice signed on July 27, 1953, established a two-and-a-half-mile-wide buffer zone following existing battle lines right across the Korean Peninsula. One result of the agreement was that South Korea wound up with about 1,500 square miles of new territory. The armistice agreement also established a commission of neutral nations to supervise the truce and provided for a political conference to be convened to reach a peaceful settlement of the "Korean question." To date, no such settlement has been reached.

*

I received my first letter from Yi Jung-gi in December, 1953, months after the fighting had ended. He wrote that he was attending medical school during the day and working at night, pretty much as he had been doing in the summer of 1952, when we had met in Pusan. However, he explained that he had been drafted into the ROK Army shortly after we had met and he had served out the war in the Pusan military hospital in which he had previously been employed as a civilian doctors' aide. The letter went on to say that he had been released from the army and had returned to school as soon as the war had ended. So, after serving in armies on both sides of the 38th Parallel, Jung-gi managed to get back into school.

Something in the letter prompted me to make some inquiries, and I learned that anyone who had been drafted out of school into the ROK Army—whether as a high school or college student—had been released from duty to continue his education. On the other hand, I and former North Korean students who had not attended school in the South—and who had almost invariably served with combat units—were not being granted similar benefits. This was so great a disappointment to me that I decided to make the army a career. What else could I do? The Republic of Korea had not considered me fit material for anything but menial military work, so it was not about to help me complete my education. However, I re-enlisted mainly because the war had ended without my nation being reunified. There was no way I could return home, no way at all to fulfill my last promise to mother. I re-enlisted because I was despondent.

*

In the Spring of 1954, I was assigned with soldiers from many ROK Army medical units to temporary duty with the U.S. 7th Infantry Division in Dong-duchun. After reaching the division, I was sent to the 17th Infantry Regiment Medical Company, which was located just below the Demilitarized Zone. This was my first contact with Americans since my 1952 trip to Taegu.

As soon as I reported to the medical company, I was issued a new set of U.S. Army uniforms and ordered

232

to report to the company commander, Captain Robinson, who turned me over to Captain Scott, the company medical officer and the first black man with whom I had ever spoken. In his turn, Dr. Scott led me to my quarters, a neat-appearing staff non-commissioned officers' tent (I was by then a Sergeant First Class), and motioned that the top of one of the bunk beds was mine. Scott left, but the occupant of the bottom bunk, another black man, gave me a big smile and said some words of welcome. He was a big, burly man named Sergeant Phillip.

On my very first evening in these strange surroundings, Phillip led me to the Non-commissioned Officers' Mess and saw that I was fed a dinner that seemed about as large as the American meal I had eaten nearly two years earlier on the road to Taegu. As if that wasn't enough, Phillip led me to the snack bar near the center of the company and bought me a glass of beer Asahi, from Japan—and a chocolate bar. I could not understand a word Phillip said to me that evening, but it was clear that I had been accepted and that I was among friends.

I reported the following day to observe at the company's busy outpatient clinic. I was just as interested in how the medical officers went about their examinations as I was in the conclusions they drew and the treatments they prescribed. I was able by then to read from English medical texts, but I had a long way to go before I would comprehend most of what was said at the clinic. I was especially surprised at the huge number of venereal disease cases, mainly gonorrhea, spread among the various illness and non-combat injuries that had to be treated. Soldiers who showed any significant abnormal findings were evacuated to a field hospital for further management while we treated only simple cases. This was very different from the ROK Army method of treating most cases as close to the parent unit as possible, even those requiring in-patient care such as the case of my malarial attack in 1952. The clinic also provided health care for Korean civilians who worked in the compound. We frequently diagnosed tuberculosis of the lungs among this group. In time, I rotated from the clinic to the X-ray section, where I learned to take and examine X-rays, and I also assisted in the cast room.

I was eating well, my English was improving steadily, and I was gaining valuable practical medical knowledge.

*

In a way, the most important aspect of my time with the 17th Infantry Regiment Medical Company was getting to know Americans. Their ways were alien to my ways, but I found them a likable if somewhat excessive people.

One Saturday after lunch, a Canadian-born sergeant asked me to join him at the Non-commissioned Officers' Club, where he bought a full case of Kirin beer, twenty-four bottles. "Let's drink together," he said. I agreed, though I was not much of a drinker and could only down one bottle in the first thirty minutes. As I started my second bottle, I felt that my heart was beating far too fast. Then I had to rush to finish it so I could run to the latrine to void it. From that point on, I managed to keep on drinking the beer slowly but steadily into the evening. We had a quick hamburger for dinner just as many other non-commissioned officers got off duty and joined us in the club to see the evening's stage show. After uncountable trips to the bathroom, we just managed to finish the last of the twenty-four bottles when the club closed at midnight. After ten hours of steady alcohol consumption, I could barely reach my tent and climb into my bunk. My face was still flushed in the morning, and I exuded a beery odor with every time I exhaled. My head ached and my stomach was sour.

The beer binge was the most fun I had had in a long, long time, for my ability to get out and around was severely limited by the fact that, while the Americans took care of room and board, I was paid in Korean won, which could not be used to purchase extras in the American compound. For that, I needed dollars.

On the evening of the day the American soldiers were paid, I noticed that there was some sort of gambling going on in every tent. Most of the Americans played blackjack while they smoked and drank in excessive quantities. Many "kibitzers" hung around watching and taking part in the general merriment. As such evenings wore on, someone was invariably needed to run down to the snack bar to get food, beer and cigarettes for the gamblers and the onlookers. I was often asked to run the errands, and I usually received a tip for my work. Once in awhile I got a really big tip if I happened to be helping a big winner. Since I was paid in dollars and American coins, I eventually wound up with my own spending money, which made my life bearable.

At times, usually on payday evenings, fights would break out in some of the tents. As a rule the only weapons used were fists, but there were times when the medical company had to treat knife wounds or even the results of blows from shovels and other exotic weapons. I noticed that many fights broke out between aggressive Caucasian soldiers and members of other races.

The matter of race had never been much of a factor in Korea, but it seemed to be a big deal among Americans. I had noted, of course, that there were men of all races in the medical company compound and, I imagined, throughout the U.S. Army. What surprised me was how under-educated many of the Americans were, regardless of race. That there were men who could not

235

read or write was surprising but I learned of several who did not even know their own ages. When I asked how that could be, I was told that their mothers had not told them their birthdates. I thought someone was kidding, but apparently it was the truth.

As I picked up more English, I unwittingly picked up many of the crude slang expressions the soldiers habitually threw around in their close-knit all-male world. In this, they were no different from Korean soldiers, but I had no way of knowing what could be repeated in polite company and what could not.

Each weekend, several soldiers from each tent were given an opportunity to fly to Japan for rest and recreation. I was constantly approached by these men who wanted to learn Japanese phrases they could use to pick up Japanese girls. Many of the men received letters from geishas and Japanese girls after they returned and I was asked to translate. Sometimes, I was even asked to write responses in Japanese. All these requests were very easy for me to fulfill because I had learned all my schoolwork up through seventh grade in Japanese. I became very popular after awhile. For good measure, I taught some soldiers Japanese songs, which I understand really impressed the girls they met in Japan. Of course, all this effort on my part earned me needed spending money.

I was truly unhappy when my duty with the 17th Infantry Regiment Medical Company came to an end. I liked these free and easy Americans and their casual ways, and I enjoyed the freedom I shared when I was in their company.

I returned to my own 8th Division medical battalion, but was soon transferred to the 3rd Medical Battalion, based near Seoul, where I worked as a clerk until it became clear that the absence of a hot war had caused the ROK Army to reassess its needs for what it considered to be highly-paid staff non-commissioned officers. The whole idea of making the army a career had long ago gone sour and I had stayed in only because I could think of no alternatives. When morale among career staff non-commissioned officers reached a depth I could no longer ignore, I decided to leave the army and see what civilian life had to offer.

CHAPTER TWENTY-TWO

At morning parade on July 27, 1956, Sergeant First Class Chung Dong-kyu joined the ranks in front of 3rd Medical Battalion along with others called from the roster. I there received my honorable discharge from the Republic of Korea Army along with a bonus of one month's salary. I executed a final sharp salute to the battalion commander and joined my buddies for a final round of handshakes.

An air of finality—not festivity—permeated the activities. There were no bands playing, no adulatory speeches. No words of praise or thanks. Just a piece of paper dismissing me with perfunctory honor—not for the services I had performed, but a mere stipulation I had committed no transgressions against the military code.

I thought of the years of my youth given over to the military. The ideals, the high hopes I had held that I was fighting to make my nation whole again, even as my profession was to make a human being's body whole. Was I over-zealous in believing that the sacrifices I had made, the many hells I had traveled through, the illnesses, the wounds, the psychological traumas I had sustained were worthy of more recognition than this passing out of a paltry piece of paper dismissing me from military duty? It wasn't medals I wanted or singular recognition of what I, one refugee ghost soldier, had tried to give the Republic of Korea. What I felt that my comrades and I needed to hear were words of sincere congratulations for a job well done, words of thanks for our years of service in line of duty to a cause in which we believed.

Well, in a way we had put on our own celebratory show during the years of combat when tracer bullets patterned the night's darkness and bombs and shells like peacetime fireworks brightened the sky. It is a good thing that the thought process is a quick one, for all these transitory ruminations passed quickly through my mind as I walked from the parade ground out the gate of the battalion compound for the last time and made my way to the nearby bus station.

My sole possession was a small duffle bag slung over my right shoulder. In it were some old clothes, an extra pair of boots, and a few days' supply of rice. Together with the pay bonus, that represented all I received for my five years, eight months' military service to the Republic of Korea. I had served two years, seven months in combat, knowing no future benefits were promised. And when I reenlisted at the end of the Korean War, I was still aware that no veterans' benefits and no pensions down the line were in order. In a sense, I had less going for me than I had had when I left home in Chu-ul, for on that dark wintry day I still had a burning hope that I would return to my family.

Leaving the army meant I was on my own. I realized I would probably never see my family again. As I rode the bus into Seoul, my thoughts journeyed back to that snowy day in December of 1950 in Chu-ul. The haunting, wraithful figure of Mother rode along with me, and I could not stop the tears welling up in my eyes as I was transported through time and space to relive Mother's last embrace.

Vainly I tried to distract myself by counting the telephone poles as they rushed past my window. The effort failed and I allowed the memories to flood over me as they had each time I had faced momentous decisions over the past six years. My thoughts turned from time to time to the horrors I had experienced in life: the rape of my sister, the bombings of Chongjin, the rout at Hyun-ri, and all the "minor" violence of the war I had survived more through luck than skill.

I sensed great changes within me—a distinct loss of one part of my innocence—but I also realized that there were parts of me kept immature by my years of extra duty in the ROK Army. Before me this day loomed a "normal" future. I had cast myself into the real world and I frankly had my doubts as to my ability to survive. I was not certain I had acquired the needed survival skills despite all the hard years I had lived. My apprehension grew as the bus flew over the road to Seoul for it struck me only then that I had in no way planned a means for earning a living. When I alighted from the bus that evening, no one awaited my arrival, and I had nowhere to go.

My first impulse was to look up my friend, Yi Jung-gi, now a senior classman at the Seoul National University College of Medicine. On reaching him, I learned he was living in the house of a retired ROK Army colonel who was from Jung-gi's hometown. The colonel was a gracious man who offered to put me up for awhile until I got my feet on the ground. I sensed he did this not only because I was Jung-gi's friend, but also because I had so recently come from the army. In the case of the latter, this was about the only tangible benefit arising out of my service.

After resting myself for a few days, I began looking for something to do. I first looked up a fellow former refugee soldier who owned a small stand in the open market from which he repaired and sold oddments such as fountain pens and cigarette lighters. I knew that he was at the stand all day long, no matter the weather, and still he could barely afford two meals a day and the rental on a small sleeping room. I found that he was happy despite his circumstances and he suggested that I take up a similar trade. I might have considered the suggestion, but I did not have nearly enough to launch even so modest a venture.

All I did have, besides a little cash, were the clothes on my back, my uniform and boots. I spent a little of the cash having the uniform dyed what I thought would be a more-fashionable black. However, even I realized that there was no way I could go searching for a respectable job looking neat and healthy if I had to dress in that odd-looking uniform. Besides, I quickly learned that there were few jobs—respectable or not—to be had at that time, particularly for veterans who had somehow fallen from grace now that the war was but a distant memory for most civilians. I was not overly surprised that I could not even land a job as a busboy in a third-rate Chinese restaurant. Day after day, I returned to the colonel's house in a state of deeper disappointment, which was steadily turning to despair. My small horde of cash was rapidly dwindling.

*

After a month-long diet of steady rejection, I decided to look up another old army buddy, Sergeant Chang, a refugee soldier now stationed in Seoul as a member of the ROK Army CIA. Chang, who had also served as a sergeant in the North Korean People's Army, was one of the smartest soldiers I ever met, a factor that was recognized by our superiors who had moved him to our regimental counter-intelligence contingent after many months of superb performance behind and between the battle lines. He was glad to see me, and suggested that I might get some needed relaxation by joining him for a swim in the public pool at Uidong, just north of Seoul. While we were driving through Seoul's busy streets, we naturally reminisced about the many tough combat missions we had shared during the war. At length, Chang urged me to keep trying; he was most encouraging about my future, though I frankly could not see what encouraged him.

The swimming pool was about a quarter-mile from the parking lot. It was a hot, humid day, and we were sweating copiously as we made our way up the narrow mountain path. A refreshing swim seemed a better and better idea with each step, and I was nearly lost in the thought when a bell in my subconscious brought me to instant alertness. My attention was smartly drawn to a tall, somewhat obese gentleman with gray hair and wearing dark glasses who was coming down the path toward me. The man was carrying a baby boy and walking beside a beautiful young woman. I knew that I knew him, but it took me a moment to figure out the connection. Then, as we were about to pass one another, I became certain that he was my former physiology professor at Chongjin Medical College. Without any more thought, I hailed him by asking, "Aren't you Professor Park?"

The man stopped in his tracks, nearly overwhelmed by the unexpected contact. He took off his sunglasses and peered down at me with a look of mixed surprise and shrewdness. Then he broke into a full, beaming smile and placed his arm gently across my shoulders. "You're Chung, aren't you?"

I had taken Dr. Park Suk-ryun's physiology course during my sophomore year, in 1949—seven years before—and he still knew me! I suppose it was doubly fortunate that his course was one of those I liked the best and excelled in the most. I had received a top grade from Dr. Park, and had even assisted him in several extracurricular experiments. I was only mildly surprised, but deeply gratified, that he had identified me after only a momentary glance.

Dr. Park asked how I was doing, and listened attentively as I described my desperate situation. When I had finished talking, he looked at the beautiful lady at his side, then back at me. "Why don't you move into my clinic with us right away? We might have a job for you." The lady nodded in agreement.

Only then did Dr. Park introduce his new wife, the mother of the infant in his arms. I gathered that his former wife had been unable or, perhaps, unwilling to escape to the South when Dr. Park had fled. This was very common among the more than 100,000 North Korean men living in the south, so it did not suprise me at all. (Many years later, I learned, Dr. Park's oldest son was traveling in Europe when he was contacted by agents of the North Korean government and given a message to Dr. Park from his first wife. She had waited for all those years for her husband to return. This, sadly, was quite common among North Korean refugees of Dr. Park's generation, though many of the left-behind wives also remarried.)

The doctor gave me his address and telephone number, urged me to enjoy my swim, and extracted a promise that I would meet him at the clinic that evening.

What an exciting moment that was! I could hardly contain my tears and laughter, and I all but hugged Sergeant Chang for inadvertently engineering the fortuitous encounter. I had lost all interest in the anticipated swim, and Chang, who was as genuinely excited and happy as I, pulled me down the path to the parking lot so he could drive me straight to the colonel's house to collect my belongings. There, as Chang waited with the jeep, I quickly packed my meager belongings and offered my profuse gratitude to the kindly colonel, who in return expressed his extreme and heartfelt pleasure at my newfound hope.

*

After a really fine (free) meal at one of my friend's favorite restaurants where I was his guest, I arrived at Dr. Park's clinic in Sergeant Chang's jeep early that evening, as promised. The clinic was located just across from the main gate of Sunggungwan University, in the northeast section of Seoul known as Myungyundong. It was housed in a two-story split-level wood-paneled building of approximately 3,000 square feet and accommodated the Park family as well. When we pulled up before the clinic the whole Park family came into the small yard inside the wooden gate to greet me. After I shook hands with sergeant Chang and promised to stay in touch, Dr. Park led me into the house. I was told to leave my duffel bag in a large open room on the second floor, which was used as the admitting ward for from four to six patients at a time. Dr. Park took me on a tour of the building. Also on the second floor were his consultation room and the pharmacy which had a small ticket-booth-type window opening out onto the adjacent patient waiting room; on the first floor were an X-ray room, a small laboratory, and a bathroom which also opened into the family living quarters, located in the lower split level.

The clinic staff consisted of a nice-looking young nurse, a physician-assistant who was a senior classman with Yi Jung-gi at the Seoul National University College of Medicine, and Dr. Park's sister-in-law, who dispensed medicine and took care of billing.

My first assignment the very next morning was to help both the nurse and the doctor-assistant in their treatment of patients. That morning, I was the first one up. I swept the front yard and the street in front of the clinic. In the evening I helped the nurse clean up the clinic and scrub the floors of all the rooms, including the bathroom. Gradually, I was given greater responsibility; I began undertaking the microscopic examinations of stool samples, running urine tests and blood counts, and taking and developing the simpler X-rays, such as chests and bones. It was not long before Dr. Park had me dispensing medicines as well. The hours were long and the work was hard; I took no breaks, for the clinic was open from dawn until dusk seven days a week every day of the year except for a half-day on New Year's Day.

Dr. Park studied at every free moment, between patients and during his lunch periods. He was working through a massive text on internal medicine. *The Textbook of Internal Medicine* by the American, Dr. Russell Cecil. I was urged to read this text while Dr. Park drew me into explanations and discussions of some of his more interesting cases. Slowly, Dr. Park worked me back into the medical disciplines. Busy as we all were, it was clear that he had high hopes for me. Instructing me enabled him to fulfill his urge to teach. something from which he had acquired a great deal of obvious pleasure during his time at Chongjin Medical College.

Working my way through Cecil's English-language text on internal medicine created a whole new set of problems for me. My first language had been Japanese, though we always spoke Korean at home. Then I had learned a dialect of Chinese in Harbin, and next I had had to learn written Korean when we returned to Chu-ul in 1945. My years at Chongjin Medical-Technical School and Chongjin Medical College had increased my linguistic diet to include Latin, then German, then Russian. However, I had had no chance to truly master the latter three by the time the Korean War engulfed me. I had learned what I assumed was English during my brief tour with the U.S. 17th Infantry Regiment Medical Company, but it was absurd to think that that brief exposure would serve my purpose when I tackled the convoluted formal text of the thorough but truly massive book Dr. Cecil had inflicted upon the world of medical science.

The days were long, the work was hard, and the pay was woefully inadequate. But I awoke up every morning overwhelmed by a deep excitement over my prospects for learning and helping my fellow man. Before each new day dawned, I was ready for the unique challenges that can only be provided through the study and practice of medicine. This was exactly the opposite of my experience in the army, where each day, in both peace and war, was dreaded protraction of an unremitting spiritual pain.

I hated only two aspects of my work at the clinic. The first was having to travel around Seoul to collect unpaid bills during the last few weeks of the year. According to Korean custom, all a person's accounts should be settled in full so the new year could be started free from debt. It was obvious that most of the people I saw hated to see me—being yet another in what I suppose was a long line of bill collectors—coming to their doors flourishing a statement of account. some debtors were highly abusive in words and demeanor, and sadly I took it personally.

The other thing I really hated was late-night house calls. I would finally drop off into a deep sleep after a long, hard day's work only to be awakened by sharp rapping on the front door of the clinic. The routine hardly ever varied. Half-awake and dazed, I would slowly realize that I was being pulled from my sleep with calls for help by someone who would be repeating Dr. Park's name over and over. I invariably rolled onto my back, blinking my sleep-starved eyes, hoping that someone else would answer the door before I had to. Then I would hear Dr. Park's voice: "Chung! Why aren't you out there helping the patient?"

Donald Chung, M.D.

There were no vacations, no recreation, no exercise program, no chance to meet people or spend time with a woman (even if I had known a woman who wanted to spend time with me). We were there, on call, all day, every day. I had a roof over my head and ample good food in my stomach, and I reveled in the work. But still I craved more. For, though I was certainly back in medicine, I was really going nowhere.

CHAPTER TWENTY-THREE

In the Spring of 1957, during my seventh month at the clinic, Dr. Park told me that the women's medical school at which he lectured once a week was opening up an entrance examination for transfer students and men. He urged me to apply.

Despite the fact that I was earning a small wage and my keep, I still could not afford to purchase any new clothing. I wore the same things every day: my black-dyed army uniform and a pair of cheap white rubber shoes. I was frankly aghast at the notion of seeking admission to a medical college if all I had to wear to my interview were these rags. However, my urgent desire to enter the medical community as a full-fledged member overcame my shame, and I applied for an interview with the Dean of Admissions of Soodoo Medical College.

The screening interview was conducted during the first week of March, 1957. The dean, Dr. Koo Guk-hae, was an imposing individual of about forty-five, with greying hair and a very large build for a Korean. He had an attitude to match his imposing physical attributes; he stared at me from over the top of his eyeglasses—appraisingly but without any sign of what he was thinking—as he tried to rip my story to shreds. The only credential I had was the small identification book from Chongjin Medical college, which I still carried around my neck as the only totem of my former life in the north. It had a photograph taken when I was fifteen (I was by then twenty-five) plus a record of the courses I had taken, and my grades. I suppose I could have called upon Dr. Park to attest to the veracity of my claims, but it never came to that (unless, of course, my friend and mentor had already taken such action on his own, but that proved to be unnecessary). Between the written record I presented and my answers to his coldly probing questions, Dr. Koo allowed that I was what I said I was.

Far from securing a position in the student body, Dr. Koo granted permission for me to take an examination to gain one of the three openings in the sophomore class. I was both ecstatic and disappointed; ecstatic to have the opportunity, disappointed at the prospect of repeating my second year of medical school. I could well understand the dean's apprehension, for it had been nearly seven years since I had attended any classes. I had also come to realize and, to a degree, accept the pattern of my fortunes. It seemed to me that I was destined to take two long steps to gain one short forward step's progress in life. I had started my career in medical education as a fresh youngster, and now I might have an opportunity to continue with it as a jaded old man. I only hoped, if I passed the hurdle of the examination, that old age and senility would not overtake me before I actually attained my doctorate.

Thus buoyed, I began studying for the test that could very well get at least an aspect of my life on course.

I was rusty. The haphazard medical retraining I had received under Dr. Park's helpful guidance was child's play compared to what lay between my interview and the test. I had fallen out of the habit of study, and mere simple thinking was an old acquaintance I had barely encountered in my years in the South.

Finally came the big day. I was seated along with other applicants waiting to take the written examination. Anxiety swept over me as I opened the examination booklet and pored over the questions. Reading each one, I felt the weight on my shoulders lighten. I was confident I could accurately answer all the problems set before me. But then came the nagging fear that most likely all the other candidates could do the same, lessening my chances of being accepted.

These others were an imposing lot, apparently older and more mature than I and, most distressing of all, they were all well dressed. This was a reminder of the odds I faced during the 1946 examination to enter Chongjin Medical-Technical School. I was an unremarkable cynosure in my black-dyed uniform and tacky rubber shoes.

A week later, at nine o'clock in the morning, I stood with palpitating heart among my fellow-hopefuls before a sheet of paper posted on the entrance of the admissions office of Soodoo Medical College. Imprinted on that innocent sheet of paper would be the results of the examinations given the week before. The list was headed by over one hundred names, half of them belonging to males who would become the new freshman class. At the bottom of the list I finally found my name. My disappointment was staggering until I read a notation in fine print beside my name: I was accepted as a probationary student pending results of first-semester examinations. If I scored average or better, I would then be accepted as a regular student.

My disappointment turned to elation. I had made it. The conditions were more than fair and I accepted them with a light heart, secure in my ability to succeed.

But the battle was just beginning. Now I faced an even bigger challenge. The tuition for this private medical college was very high, 120,000 won per year, about $6000. I was poleaxed by the news. I had no savings to speak of; not enough for tuition much less enough to live on. It was nearing mid-March, and classes were due to begin April 1.

After worrying myself sick over the next few days, I finally came up with a truly desperate plan of action. I had nothing to lose and everything to gain, so I would look up old classmates from the North and old army buddies who owned small businesses or had jobs, and I would ask them for money. It took me about ten days to piece together a list of their addresses. That mere collection of data almost did me in because my friends were scattered across the length and breadth of South Korea. I had no choice; I begged Dr. Park to give me a few weeks' unpaid leave from my duties at the clinic. He was most understanding.

I scoured four provinces and six major cities in my quest. Some of my old school friends were just getting established in their own medical practices while the others and most of my army buddies, were selling books, repairing fountain pens or selling used shoes. I presented each of them with an outline of my plight and bluntly asked for funds to help pay my tuition. None was rich and most were not even well off, but they all gave generously. More important, every one of them provided me with a stiff measure of moral support and enthusiastic encouragement. By the time I returned to Seoul, I actually had taken in a bit more money than I needed to pay the college.

On the morning of April 1, 1957, I left Dr. Park's clinic and walked the two blocks to the medical school to attend my first day of classes in over seven years. As I made my way down the hall to the sophomore class homeroom, I was able to see inside through the glass windows that faced the hall. There were fifteen rows of long tables that ascended in steps from a podium with a blackboard to the back wall. Three aisles ran from front to rear, one on either side and one in the center. Nearly all the seats were already occupied—by nearly one hundred women! When I got to the door, I was stopped in my tracks by the pungent odor of their combined preferences in perfume. I hesitated for an instant, thinking in a flash about how those provocative odors, and all that they implied, would take my mind from the important purpose at hand. I had spent nearly six years in an all-male environment, and had had only an inadequate, celibate seven-month transition at Dr. Park's clinic. I was not ready for any of the many things that *might* happen in this predominantly female enclave.

My native shyness prevented me from committing myself to entering just yet. I stood in the doorway, unable to advance and unwilling to retreat. The heat of blushing cheeks in no way helped me resolve my dilemma and the piercing realization that I was yet decked out in my black uniform and white rubber shoes nearly undid my resolve. I could not help thinking how I would smell to them.

My personal stalemate was broken when one of the young ladies strode from her seat to the podium. She was, I soon learned, the sophomore class president, and she informed us that there would be no class during the first period. Then she asked, sweetly, "Will all the new *male* students please come down to the front of the room to introduce yourselves?" I found this very difficult, much more so than any of the combat forays in which I had participated. After all, I knew I would not die here, though that seemed a splendid solution to my overwhelming attack of diminished vanity. When my turn came to speak, it was all I could do to stammer out my name. My hands were sweating and I could feel a deepening of the scarlet flush on my cheeks spreading to the roots of my hair.

*

The curriculum for the sophomore year included pathology, microbiology, pharmacology, parasitology, surgical anatomy, preventive medicine, hygiene, diagnostics, general surgery and clinical laboratory.

Fortunately, I had studied and excelled in many of these subjects at Chongjin Medical School.

At nine o'clock that morning, after a brief recess, the pathology professor—Dr. Koo, the imposing Dean of Admissions I had earlier encountered—entered the homeroom, placed his notebook on top of the lectern and, without any introduction whatsoever, began reciting his lecture and writing notes on the blackboard. Most of the medical terms he used were in English, which my classmates had no difficulty transcribing into their notebooks. I was unprepared for so much English, though certainly not surprised that it replaced the Russian medical terminology my North Korean teachers had had to use in their lectures. My befuddlement increased as my mind raced in a vain attempt to translate the terms that were pouring out of Dr. Koo's mouth at far too-rapid a rate for my comprehension. I fell farther and farther behind and finally lost the thread of his meaning. I literally shook my head to clear it of the cacophonous rubbish that filled it, in an effort to start fresh. Naturally, the professor saw my emphatic head-shake and stopped lecturing. "Do you have any questions or comments to pose, Mr. Chung?" The sudden, unexpected and wholly unwanted attention intimidated me, and I barely had enough control left to blurt out, "No! No, sir!" in a voice several screeching octaves higher than normal.

Most of the students around me managed to take four or more pages of notes during the fifty-minute lecture while I had managed to pick up about a dozen pathology terms by the time the professor slammed his notebook closed and strode briskly from the room. No sooner had he gone, however, than the sweet-looking stranger who was sitting behind me asked if I would care to borrow her notebook to flesh out my own inadequate notes. All I could do was nod my head and stammer my thanks. I needed to do a lot more than just fill in a few blanks, and it was soon clear that she knew I needed more than just a few notes. After a brief pause, she graciously offered to let me keep her notes overnight. I was deeply embarrassed, but I knew I needed any help I could get and was grateful for it. What I really needed, I knew, was an instant grasp of English.

Only three hours of lectures were presented the first day, but I was utterly drained by the time I left for the clinic, where a great deal of work still awaited my attention. That evening, my hands shook as I tried to transcribe notes, and my legs felt like rubber bands. Despite the emotional and physical strain, or because of it, I was able to sleep soundly for the few hours I still had before I had to return to school for an even more grueling second day of classes.

I knew that my disadvantages were adding up early. In addition to my inadequate English, I did not have nearly enough money to purchase the required medical texts. That meant that I had to resort to transcribing from school-owned or borrowed texts on top of taking copious lecture notes. The only thing to do was sacrifice sleep which would not help my attention span in class.

I soon fell into a routine of undertaking four to five hours of study and transcription each night after the clinic closed. By the time I had reviewed the subjects covered in a day's lectures and brought my notebooks up to date it was usually between one and three o'clock in the morning. In time, however, I noticed that the number of pages of notes I was able to take down during lectures was growing daily. The loss of sleep was something I handled internally, just as I had during years of terror-filled days and nights in the war zone.

Several weeks into the semester, the class was scheduled to observe a post-mortem examination in the operating theater. The pathology professor, Dr. Koo, decked out in his white mask, laboratory coat and rubber gloves, stood next to the naked cadaver on the table in the center of the room and lectured in his non-stop style. I was in one of the rear ranks of students, looking down over and between many of my female classmates. At the conclusion of his introductory lecture, Dr. Koo pointed his finger directly at me and announced that "Mr. Chung will come forward to record the post-mortem examination for the class." I had no choice; there was no way out; I came to the fore of the class and prepared to take notes at lightning speed. The professor made his incisions and explored the cadaver with his darting scalpel as he droned out his findings to the class at large and me in particular. Once the autopsy was complete, he stated in a loud voice that I write up my notes and deliver them to his office, then he strode out of the operating room.

Once again, and thankfully, I accepted help from the young woman who had provided me with her notebook on the first day of classes. We worked together for over an hour to get the autopsy record straight. Thus was I able to present a clean, concise set of notes to the pathology professor as soon as the day's classes had come to an end.

I am certain the professor was surprised by the clarity of my notes.

*

All of my frustrations and troubling experiences at this time did not emanate only from my school-related problems. One such wrenching, strictly non-scholastic encounter occurred one rainy Sunday afternoon when Dr. Park's waiting room was crowded with patients.

Dr. Park, the nurse, and I were exhausted; we had already seen over fifty patients, and there was no letup in sight. I was at the point of losing my reasoning abilities, when the housemaid entered the treatment area and whispered in my ear, "You have a personal visitor at the front door."

Surprised, I turned from what I was doing and saw through the glass window in the door that a woman was standing outside, in the yard. The rain was torrential and the wind was pasting her wet hair across her face and eyes. On her head she carried a large bundle. This caused me to assume that the stranger was an older woman. Who could it be? Something about the woman's shape and carriage, some spirit flowing from her to me dredged up dark memories from my cherished past. Then I knew. It was Yim Ok-wha, Father's discarded concubine from Harbin days.

Not since 1946, during that brutally cold winter week when she invaded our home in Chu-ul before vanishing so mysteriously, had I seen her nor heard anything about her. She had disappeared from my life completely, like an apparition in a dense fog.

The accumulated animosity because of the unhappiness she had caused our family—especially my beloved mother—and the bitter memories of Father's absence from our home on her account, all welled up within me, like a genie brought forth from a bottle by magic. So intense was my feeling I hesitated about even asking her in out of the drenching rain. Then I saw before me a tiny, age-defiled, miserable woman in her mid-fifties. Pity claimed me and I opened the door, motioning her to follow me to my room. Upon reaching there and entering, the first thing she did was to open the bundle she had carried on her head and take from it a package of my favorite treat of childhood—rice cakes stuffed with jujubes.

Ok-wha was childless and had always doted on my older sisters and me. All the nice clothing I had as a young boy had come from her. Now here she was, once again appearing in my life, bringing a sackful of goodies. Softly she urged me to eat the jujube-stuffed rice cakes.

I think I had always disliked Ok-wha, but I am certain her affection for me was genuine, because, I suppose, I was Father's child. Regardless of her kindnesses to me when I was a boy, I was too aware of the suffering Father's defection caused Mother and, of course, for that we blamed Ok-wha. My devotion to Mother prejudiced me against Ok-wha and although we had been taught to show her respect as demanded by our strict Korean upbringing, we were not encouraged to accord her affection or love. Until that rainy Sunday at Dr. Park's clinic, I had never considered my true sentiments regarding her. Always it was the proper form we were taught to observe. And form, I have come to learn, often obscures the truth.

It was Cousin Chun-duk, that patriotic maker of maps, who gave her my address. I was confused as to how to act or what to say. I quickly related the events that had brought me to Seoul. I told her of my last meeting with Father and how I had been unable to locate him anywhere in the south. I think we both instinctively believed that Father perished on the grueling trek from Chu-ul.

The longer I talked, the stronger grew my bitterness. Finally the hostility overwhelmed me. I was through telling her about myself and didn't want to hear any more about her.

It was at that point that I asserted my manhood in my own eyes. "It is best you leave now," I said in a steady, level voice. "Never return to my life."

She rose, saying not a single word, and shambled out the door. Tears had glistened in her eyes as she made her brief, silent passage from the room.

At the moment I was not affected by her emotion. But later, after she had disappeared into the streaming rain, I regretted my stunning rudeness, realizing she had come to me because of her love and devotion to Father, whose identity, I'm sure, I was assuming during our brief painful encounter.

That rainy Sunday in 1957 in Dr. Park's clinic was the last time our paths were ever to cross and no word of her has since reached my ears.

It was as if, there in Dr. Park's clinic, I successfully amputated a very real and malignant growth within me. For I do not think I sustained any longer the hatred I had harbored, replacing it with pity.

*

My days passed quickly. I slept little and studied hard and, in time, I felt that I was progressing beyond my initial handicaps. My comprehension of English-laced lectures was improving and, much to my amazement, relief and pleasure, I realized that my classmates were beginning to ask me to help them with their studies.

Now I knew I was no longer a refugee. Was I not now just as good as any native southerner? I had earned equality by my hard work yoked to my native talent. Fulfilling my duty to the ROK Army's demands gave added strength to this equality.

But the capstone of it all was in fulfilling the demands of Dr. Koo—that tough-talking dean of admissions and professor of pathology. This was clearly brought home to me when one of my first and heartiest congratulations came from Dr. Koo!

The first semester examinations in all my courses were completed by the first week in September. No longer treading on shaky ground, I was enthusiastic on going into each one, and met each with confidence.

I was successful in passing them all and knew I was in the higher ranking class standings. But it was the

Donald Chung, M.D.

A I achieved in pathology that was most gratifying, for it was considered to be the most important sophomore course. But even my confidence in my academic ability did not prepare me to learn I had attained the highest grade-point average in my class of one hundred twenty sophomores. This insured the lifting of my probationary status. An even greater—and totally unexpected—achievement was being awarded a 50,000 won scholarship, almost half of the junior year tuition. Only one such scholarship was given to each of the five classes comprising the student body. But as I had long realized, happiness is an amalgam of pleasure and pain, and in this case my joy was tempered by the fact that the previous winner had been a young lady from an extremely poor family. Not having the scholarship which she probably expected might deny her access to the remainder of her education.

Gone was my role of second-class refugee which I felt had been thrust upon me since my first day in South Korea. The momentous news of my academic success completely dissipated the insecurity and apprehensions—mostly false—I had harbored and nurtured during my struggles.

I was basking in my newfound glory when at lunch the next day, Hwang Ki-suk, a male classmate about ten years older than I, came over to congratulate me on my achievement. He then asked if I would be willing to move in with him and his wife; he would provide me with room, board and even some spending money in return for my helping him with his academic work. He explained that he owned a small clinical laboratory in the southern section of Seoul and that this might prove helpful to my education.

Hwang Ki-suk seemed to be sincere in his offer and I was inclined to accept as soon as I heard the proposal. Frankly, I was feeling sorry for Dr. Park since I was increasingly unable to turn in an adequate performance at his clinic. As I had thought at the outset, something eventually had to give. It had, in my mind, been the quality of my work. By the time my glory days at the end of my first sophomore semester arrived, I felt guilty because Dr. Park was so uncomplainingly sensitive to my needs. However, he needed a full-time assistant and that I could not be. I was taking up valuable time and space and, worse, living off his labors. If anything, I knew that I would be able to maintain my class standing only if I had even more time to study.

I told Ki-suk that his offer was satisfactory and that I accepted pending Dr. Park's reaction. I spoke with Dr. Park the next day when he had the time. He accepted my resignation, he said, with regret and total understanding. My own feelings of guilt were somewhat assuaged by the obvious pleasure he received from having been my mentor.

I moved a few days later at the beginning of our summer vacation. Ki-suk and his wife rented a spacious room on the second floor of a commercial building. The room was divided by movable partitions into a large clinical laboratory where many kinds of blood, urine and stool tests were conducted. Behind the lab was the living area where the Hwangs cooked, ate and slept. My bed and a small table had been placed in the hallway between the lab and the main living quarters which we also used as our study area.

Ki-suk was a fellow northerner, a native of South Hamgyong Province, but he had moved to Seoul immediately at the conclusion of World War II. This exempted him from being seen as a refugee. Ki-suk's wife was from South Kyongsang Province in the south. She was a very sweet, very gracious lady who spoke with the typical lilting southern accent. Though she was five or six years older than I, she accepted me as a friend,

I suppose out of gratitude for the help I would be providing her husband in attaining his goal to become a medical doctor. She was so gracious and thankful that she even shined my shoes every morning!

Though I knew I was at the head of the class, I used many hours of my vacation to dip into texts that would accompany upcoming lectures. Ki-suk had to run his laboratory, so he did not have time to study with me. I knew that my getting ahead would accrue to his advantage and I wanted desperately to give him even more than he was buying. When I was not studying, I was relaxing, because I felt I had about used up my reserves in attaining my newfound status.

My daily life became less pressured from the first moment with the Hwangs. I had nothing to do except be a medical student.

CHAPTER TWENTY-FOUR

I came back to earth with an audible thud.

Despite the golden opportunities afforded me by my superior academic performance, there still remained the question of obtaining the 70,000 won I needed to make my full second-semester tuition payment. I certainly was not going to make it on the small cash stipend that went along with my room and board at the Hwangs' home.

By this time, Yi Jung-gi, my former roommate, had graduated from the Seoul National University College of Medicine and had completed his surgical internship. He had already moved with his wife to Sokcho, on the east coast near the 38th Parallel, to establish his new general medical-surgical practice. I had recently received an enthusiastic letter from Jung-gi in which he described the glories of his first independent surgery, the successful repair of a bleeding ulcer. Included in the letter was an invitation to visit him and his new clinic. I wrote back to say that I would indeed visit because there was a matter of great urgency that I needed to discuss with him. I then borrowed my bus fare from Hwang Ki-suk.

The journey was difficult and time-consuming. Although Sokcho was only 150 miles from Seoul, it took the bus many hours to cover the distance. The country roads were narrow and could be traversed only at slow speed; they became even more hazardous as they wound upward to the highest point in the Taebec Mountains, the great central cordillera running from the Korean peninsula north to Manchuria. At the highest point, Taeguallyung, the whole expanse was green and beautiful in the bright September sunlight. There was a chill in the air at the high altitude, but it was exhilarating and refreshing after my lengthy exposure to the atmosphere of Seoul.

This was where, during the winter of 1951-1952, my reconnaissance company had spent many nights thrashing around in hip-deep snow seeking out the Communitst guerrillas who posed a nasty threat to the United Nations forces. This was where my hands and feet had been mildly frostbitten, grappling as I was through darkness and snow, pursuing the enemy. We caught few guerrillas, but did force them to flee before our approach leaving their warming fires in otherwise hidden bivouacs to guide us in our search.

Contrasting the memories of those dark times and disastrous events with my present circumstances considerably strengthened my spirits. The sheer natural splendor of the verdant mountainsides of late summer encouraged me to believe that even as those turbulent times had passed and were followed by a putative peace, so my present crisis would somehow be met and my future studies secured.

Finally, after ten hours of riding on the bus, I arrived at Sokcho. It was evening and I had no real sense of direction for finding Jung-gi's clinic, so I wandered about for some time before reaching my ultimate destination. Many of the buildings throughout Sokcho, which was hardly more than a large village, had been destroyed in the see-saw battles that had raged through the area during the war and few of them had been repaired. Rather, the destroyed structures had been supplanted by a string of one-story homes strung out along the main road through town. Most of the new buildings were straw-thatched, but several were built of wood or even aluminum panels. The edge of the town was set right up against the beach from which local fishermen launched their boats to collect the pollack, cuttlefish and crab that abounded in the waters offshore.

Jung-gi's clinic and home occupied a one-story wood-paneled building just a few hundred yards north of the tiny bus station. There were glass sliding doors at the entrance and a vertical wooden signboard inscribed in black brushstrokes, "Dr. Yi's Clinic." I knocked on the door and was immediately greeted by Jung-gi's wife, Kim Kyung-suk, my old medical school classmate and Jung-gi's old girlfriend from Chongjin, the one who had broken a tied basketball game by scoring at the last moment for the other team. This was the first time I had seen Kyung-suk since 1950 and she gave me an excited smile and a warm welcoming embrace. "Welcome," she said.

Jung-gi was right behind her. He heartily embraced me and set right off to show me proudly around his clinic. It was only one room, less than three hundred square feet, with a pounded-earth floor and one oil lamp for light. In one corner stood a table with Jung-gi's surgical equipment and medical supplies and, in the center of the room, stood the metal surgical table, the symbol of my friend's many years of schooling. This was the waiting room, consultation room, operating room, and everything else besides. Jung-gi and Kyung-suk lived in a pair of even smaller partitioned rooms behind the clinic area.

Jung-gi, justifiably proud of his first surgery, glowingly described it in minute detail. With only Kyung-suk to assist him and only the light of that single oil lamp to guide him, he had had to remove two-thirds of his patient's stomach because of an intractable bleeding ulcer. He told me that, afterwards, he had become a "big man" as news of his success quickly spread through the region.

Kyung-suk, who had put on quite a bit of weight since her ill-starred basketball days, was now the mother of two, a girl not quite ready for school and a newborn baby boy.

265

Donald Chung, M.D.

Dinner that night was ample and festive and we stayed up very late exchanging remembrances of our days at Chongjin Medical College. Naturally, we all had a good laugh as we relived Kyung-suk's last minute basket for the opposing team. One thing we did not discuss—then or ever—was how Jung-gi and Kyung-suk escaped to the south during the war. I am not sure why I never asked, but I sensed then and later that they did not want to speak of it.

As always when refugees met, our talk eventually turned to our lost homes and families in the north. This reunion was no different in that regard, so our exuberance was somewhat dissipated by midnight when Jung-gi suggested we go out to a small noodle stand for a snack.

The stand was located right behind the beach so we had a clear view of the bright, starry sky and could feel the cool sea breeze which carried the inshore smell of fish and rotting seaweed. Even as we walked along the beach, I was lulled by the gentle, rhythmic splashing of the waves in the dark.

We entered the noodle shop and seated ourselves on the *on-dol*, a Korean-style raised floor with flues running beneath the surface to carry heat from the stove throughout the room. Though it was quite late, other diners were seated around the room, eating noodles or sipping from bowls of rice wine. In the cooking area, the grandfather was bearing down heavily upon the noodle press, extruding buckwheat noodles right into a vat of boiling water, from which the grandmother fished the finished product and served it up with broth and seasonings.

This sharing of midnight noodles, made and eaten in the traditional style, was the most relaxing, emotion filled moment I had encountered in years. I felt the terrible weight of those years drop from my body and soul

266

as I basked in the warmth of the *on-dol* with Jung-gi and Kyung-suk.

I spent the remainder of my month-long vacation working as Jung-gi's assistant. There was no appointment system in this tiny rural fishing and farming community; the doctor had to wait for his patients to show up for whatever treatment they might require. Interspersed with days of sheer bedlam were many days when not one patient showed up The practice was especially slow in the evenings, so Jung-gi and I often went off to the town recreation hall to play game after game of billiards.

At Jung-gi's suggestion, I signed up for a class in social dancing. We all agreed that I could use some added polish, so I blanketed my fears of looking the fool to venture out on the first appointed evening. The class met on the wooden floor under a dim blue-red light in the home of one of the student couples, one of five or six couples who danced to a worn collection of Western phonograph records. I noted at the outset that everyone—including me, I suppose—seemed to be in a romantic mood. Jung-gi and Kyung-suk introduced me to the instructor, who took me aside to teach me a few basic steps, about all I could manage that first night. I did not learn enough to even begin dancing with a partner. I went again, alone this time, to another private home two days later, and the instructor immediately suggested that I try dancing with a young lady. We had only just gotten started on a slow foxtrot when the owner of the home rushed in shouting, "The police are coming!" As everyone else grabbed their shoes and took off through the back door, I stood for a moment trying to figure out why the police would be interested in a group of private citizens taking dance lessons in a private house. Terrorized lest I be unwittingly involved in some heinous crime, I grabbed my shoes and followed the crowd down the dark beach. I arrived back at the clinic, out of breath and scared. Only then did Jung-gi laughingly explain that such dance classes in private homes had been made illegal by a local ordinance and that anyone caught participating could be fined or even jailed. Despite this, or perhaps because of it, I went to several more of the roving sessions during my stay.

Far too soon came the day of my departure. With no patients to tend, Jung-gi accompanied me to the bus station. Just as we stepped out of the house, he silently pressed a thick envelope in my hands. Instinctively I understood this was not to be opened until I was on the bus and on my homeward way. After a profound embrace in the Korean manner, I boarded the bus and vigorously waved good-bye from the rear window until turning a corner, I lost sight of my friend who was a life-saver in more than the medical way.

Only then, in keen anticipation, did I open the envelope I had been given. Just as I suspected, it contained a thick wad of cash. Counting it out as unobtrusively as possible in the half-empty bus, I realized that my dear friend had in all probability given me all the money he had saved since opening his clinic. Even now I cannot find words adequate to express the feeling of gratitude and love that overwhelmed me at that moment.

Ten hours later I arrived in Seoul far more secure than I had been in years. I had a home to which I could return. But even more important and significant, I had a worthwhile career to pursue which in time would enable me to earn my passage through life's stormy seas.

*

My travel arrangements, and the time it took to complete them, changed at the start of the new semester.

It now took over an hour to travel each way by bus between Hwang Ki-suk's lab and the medical college. When there was time, I spent many mornings taking the streetcar and walking for about thirty minutes each way from the transfer point—just so I could save the cost of some of the fare. Since classes usually ended at three o'clock in the afternoon, I walked home whenever possible, a trek of about three hours. Every bit of cash that I saved could be used to purchase the things I needed to help with my education, beginning with books.

I worked hard to maintain my position as the class honor student, and I was able to advance to the junior class in April, 1958, with the same ranking and the same scholarship arrangement. By that time, I was becoming quite proficient at reading—and comprehending—the English-language medical texts that dominated our curriculum. In time, I began translating American- and Japanese-published texts into Korean and selling them to other students. I even edited two question-and -answer workbooks for the medical school entrance examination and sold them to would-be medical students.

I did my writing and editing late at night and over the weekends. I made enough money from sales to hire fellow students to type the manuscripts, and I had the books printed on cheap pulp paper. This made for a lot of hard work and loss of rest, but I managed to stay afloat. The books and workbooks were quite popular, and I usually sold out each edition as soon as it was delivered from the printer. My enterprise also made me extremely well known within the student community.

By this time, I had been able to retire my paint-stained black-dyed army uniform in favor of several changes of modest but presentable clothes. I even bought my very first pair of leather shoes—nice, black ones—to replace my disintegrating white rubber shoes. Things became so good that I was able to go to the barber once a month for a haircut, and, most important, I was able to join my classmates from time to time to play pool after classes, or even eat out in the company of fellow human beings.

As my notoriety spread, I was frequently invited to conduct many of the weekly workshops sponsored by the school. Most of the students who attended were women from the freshman and sophomore classes, usually in small groups of from four to six. We would meet at the home of one of the students, and there would always be refreshments served after the study sessions, an important adjunct to my diet. Although the women were usually several years younger than I, they all seemed quite mature and had active social lives. I, on the other hand, felt that I had remained socially immature. In all the time I attended the medical college, I had few dates and only one of these developed into anything remotely like a love affair. Still, I was doing better than I had in the past. At least no one at the school addressed me as "Sergeant Chung" any longer.

I advanced into the senior class—my final year at Soodoo Medical College—on April 1, 1959, still the class honor student and, thus, still the recipient of the crucial scholarship. Many of my classmates whose grades were barely passing had me on retainer as a tutor, so I began conducting workshops in their homes in order to help them pass their medical board examinations upon graduation. Passing these boards was required of every medical school graduate in order to practice medicine in South Korea. Overall, the failure rate was under ten percent, but the results actually varied from school to school, depending on how tough the members of each board chose to be. I usually tutored a group of three or four seniors early in the morning before classes began and another group of three or four after classes in the afternoon. I not only increased my earnings, I built my own knowledge to the point where I knew I would be unassailable when the time came to take my own board examination.

Toward the end of my senior year, one of my tutorial students invited me to join him on an outing to a high-class, tailor shop. This man's grades had improved under my guidance from a "D" to a "C+" average in only six months. When we reached the shop, he bought me a fashionable new three-piece Western-style suit as a token of his appreciation. The suit was of a substantial material, a solid light brown. It was the first suit I had ever owned and though I would have been proud to wear it as soon as it was done, I quelled that impulse and set it aside to be worn on graduation day.

Whenever Hwang Ki-suk passed an exam— which was always, now—he invariably took me to a good restaurant as a special treat. The better he did in the exam, the better the meal!

*

My senior year progressed from day to day without a hitch. Finally, the day of the graduation ceremonies loomed on the near horizon. I was profoundly aware that at the end of that day I would at long last be entitled to be addressed as Doctor Chung! Meanwhile, as all preparations were being finalized, the college dean informed me that I was chosen to be class valedictorian. Even though I cannot in all honesty say that this singular honor was unexpected inasmuch as I had been the class honor student since my first semester, still I was ecstatic.

I had evolved a custom which would prove to be lifelong. On the eve of all the momentous days of my life I would spend the last hours before sleep thinking of the many events and people that had brought me to the pinnacle on which I stood. On this most significant eve of graduation, I thought of my childhood in Harbin, how it had contributed to making me what I was about to become. I thought of my family's arrival in Taehyang at the end of World War II, then relived our move to Chu-ul and my halting steps toward maturity and adulthood. I thought of the difficult first semester at Chongjin Medical-Technical School and the eventual transition to medical college. I thought of my first attack of puppy love with Hae-jean, and of how it represented all that I had missed in all the ensuing years. I thought of Uncle Kil-yong and his death at the hands of his Communist keepers and of the hundreds of nameless residents of Chongjin whom I had seen die in the cataclysmic bombings early in the Korean War. I saw before me the faces of my fellow medical students, some safe and secure in the south, some dead and buried in the war's wasted battlefields, most lost to me forever, but for the memory I yet retained of them. I thought a great deal about war and death. I thought of my three sisters: of beautiful, gentle Moon-hee; of brash, abrasive Ok-bong; of sweet, young Jung-hee, whom I had hardly known at all. Above all, my thoughts—all of them—were suffused by Mother's ethereal presence. I felt her in my soul that night, as I had on many less secure nights during the war. It simply broke my heart to realize that the son she had sent away for three days had been gone for ten years. Was she still living? I felt she was. Did she know that I was still living? I felt she did.

With thoughts of Mother still in my head, I turned my attention to the future. I had long dreamed of completing my studies in America and, from there, of finding some way to get word to my family that I lived and prospered and had achieved all my dreams but the one I held most dearly in my heart—a return to my home, to those I dearly and truly loved and who I knew loved

me more dearly and truly in return than anyone I had ever
known or would ever know.

*

I had no more than an hour's restless sleep when
dawn roused me from my bed. It was March 21, 1960,
graduation day.

I carefully dressed in my virgin light brown, tailor-
made three-piece suit, which I set off with a brand new
necktie of alternating wide brown and white diagonal
stripes I spent extra time shining my new chocolate-
colored leather shoes and brushing my newly-trimmed
hair to a blue-black sheen.

I was as happy as I had ever been as I strode
through the gates of Soodoo Medical College, my head
held high and my chest thrust out in sheer pride looking
for all the world like an overgrown pouter pigeon. The air
was fresh and clear, but still quite cold this first day of a
brand new spring. There, in the courtyard, I hailed several
of my South Korean cousins, who had come to hear me
speak and see the title of "Doctor" conferred.

As I received my valedictory award at the
conclusion of my speech, many in the audience applauded
loudly, including, of course, my relatives. It is n o
exaggeration to say I swear I heard Mother's voice
whispering in my ear, "Son, you have done a good job.
You made me happy; I did not waste my life on you." As
the words echoed across space and time, I saw Kim Ki-
bok's face, with its brown and wrinkled skin and her
gnarled hands which had never touched me with anything
less that total love. This was Mother's day more than it
was my own.

*

Donald Chung, M.D.

After having my photograph taken together with my professors, friends, classmates and relatives, my cousins took me to a small graduation party they had arranged in my honor at a nearby Chinese restaurant. I nervously downed several glasses of strong Chinese wine and ate only a little of the food. As a result, after the party, I returned to my room and fell right to sleep, a combination of exhaustion and the wine.

That evening, just as it was growing dark, I was awakened by a sharp knock on the door. I found waiting a gentleman who introduced himself as a reporter for one of Seoul's major daily newspapers. I invited him in and he explained that he had come to get background information on me for an upcoming feature news story. I summarized my life for him, then he shot questions at me over the next half-hour. He concluded his notes by writing, "This North Korean refugee medical school graduate now has the dream of going to America some day for further study." Then he took my picture and left.

A few days later, a long story, including my photograph and the concluding sentence the reporter had written in my presence appeared in the newspaper.

The main result of the news feature was that I received several letters through the newspaper. One was from a seventy-year-old man, a former Northerner, who had made an extremely large fortune and risen to national prominence since coming south after the Communist takeover at home. He invited me to a sumptuous dinner at his Seoul mansion, ostensibly in celebration of our common roots, but really to marry me off to his homely granddaughter.

I declined the offer in part because I had a more-important priority at that time. I needed to earn enough money to purchase a $600 airline ticket to the United States, for I had every intention of finding an internship position there.

My determination to study in America came largely as a result of my exposure to and admiration for one particular professor, Dr. Suh Sun-kyu, a cadiologist trained at Johns Hopkins University Medical College. I had worked directly under Dr. Suh for most of my senior year and I had become enamored with the idea of pursuing advanced credentials in cardiology. Dr. Suh had had a great deal of influence upon my desire to study in America; he urged me to get there any way I could while assuring me that high standing at Soodoo Medical College would open many doors, at least at the outset of my quest.

Before I could go, I needed the price of passage. To that end, though no position in America had yet been offered, I accepted a job as an unpaid rotating intern at the Soodoo Medical College Hospital beginning June 1, 1960. On nights and weekends, I also worked at one of the internal medicine clinics in the neighborhood. Meantime, I passed my Korean Government Medical Boards, as did every one of my tutorial students.

I managed to work for many weeks under the guidance of Dr. Suh, who was named Chief of Cardiology at the medical school hospital shortly after I joined the staff. He took me under his wing and reinforced my desire to eventually seek a career in his medical specialty. At the conclusion of my one-year internship, I was accepted as a cardiology resident and, thus, worked full time under Dr. Suh.

*

I took examinations administered by the Educational Council for Foreign Medical Graduates, based in Evanston, Illinois, at the beginning of 1962, after completing my Korean hospital internship and one year as a cardiology resident. I was notified a few months

275

later, in March, that I had passed the test and was now qualified to seek an internship position at a qualified U.S. medical facility. By June, 1962, I had saved enough money for my airplane ticket and what I had learned would be enough to live on for a few months in America. The South Korean government would issue me an exit visa when I applied since I was a citizen and had completed well in excess of the required two years' military service. All I needed was an American hospital to take me in.

One day in late June, I was poring over the job listings in the *Journal of the American Medical Association* when I finally found what I was looking for in an ad that read: "Immediate opening for a rotating internship. Missouri Baptist Hospital, St. Louis, Missouri. Room and board with a stipend of $250."

I was overjoyed to find such an opening so late in the year since training programs of the sort I needed usually began around July 1 each year. I was late, and my finding anything was a real longshot. Of course, I only knew of the opening; I did not have the position secured.

I sent out a brief resume to the hospital's education director and requested an application form by return mail. I received a response in two weeks' time. When I opened the bulky envelope, I was amazed to find, instead of the requested application, a letter of acceptance together with immigration papers and a one-way airplane ticket to St. Louis. A cover letter explained that I was to report for work as a rotating intern as soon as possible.

*

There were farewell parties in my honor night after night, when friends from the army, friends from school and relatives vied to outdo one another in celebrating my good fortune. One sad observation struck home when I realized that I was the only survivor of my reconnaissance company's original refugee contingent to complete medical school; all the other former medical students from the north had died or fallen by the wayside. True, it had taken me fifteen years since the day I began classes at Chongjin Medical-Technical High School to reach this plateau, but reach it, I had!

Finally, in the middle of the morning of September 17, 1962, I met the passengers for my flight in front of the Bando Hotel, one of Seoul's finest and largest, a place where American businessmen usually stayed. In fact, the group which I joined contained numerous Americans. We boarded the airline bus for the drive to Kimpo International Airport, where I found a crowd of friends and relatives waiting to say one last good-bye.

As I shook hands, slapped backs and embraced these well-wishers, my mind turned to the most important of those missing, Mother. As always on overpowering emotional momentous occasions, I could see her face and hear her voice: "Son, take good care of yourself. And hurry home as soon as you finish your training. We will be waiting for you, to live together at last, happy once again."

The airliner took off shortly after noon. It was the first time I had ever flown, which added a whole new element to the excitement I had been feeling for days. I looked down through my window and watched everything on the ground grow smaller at an ever-increasing rate. Soon, the entire city of Seoul, which was a huge, sprawling metropolis, was well within my view. Then the city was gone and the mountains seemed little more than heaps of slag. In little more than three hours, the plane began descending into Tokyo International Airport. It had taken me ten grueling hours to get from Seoul to Sokcho to visit Yi Jung-gi in 1957. Now, in 1962, I was in another country in one-third the time!

Many of the Korean and Japanese passengers alighted from the plane in Tokyo, and many Americans boarded there during our two-hour layover. During that wait, I thought of how, as a young boy in Harbin, I had dreamed of venturing to the imperial capital to seek my fortune. Tokyo had been a vague and distant place then. Now it was merely a transit point on my way to a far more potent vague and distant place: America.

Evening overtook us as we flew out over the vast Pacific. As dinner was being served, the pretty blonde stewardess came by and asked me something, but I was lost in reveries and she startled me; thus, an entire language fell from my mind. She seemed to be asking what I wanted for dinner, but I was unable to comprehend the nature of the choices. I finally figured out what she was offering by simply looking at the trays of food arrayed on her cart. I chose some strange-looking fish and asked for hot tea. I don't know why, but I was suddenly overcome by embarrassment and kept glancing at other passengers to see if I was handling my knife and fork in an acceptable manner. This was my first taste of culture shock and the peculiar brand of paranoia it breeds. The meal was no success, for my nerves, combined with the feeling of weightlessness that accompanies some flights, induced a sensation of helpless nausea. Of course, my discomfort bred upon itself and I was soon waiting hopefully for Death to seek me out.

The hours droned on, but I was unable to sleep. Rather, as usual when I was going forward, I dwelled upon my past and all the lost souls of my life. As the distance between me and Korea became greater, my past drew closer. I napped fitfully, but I was sensitive to each bump in the air, so constantly reawakened and confronted some fleeting vision of a past moment.

Fifteen hours out of Tokyo, I was flying over the United States. Soon the airliner began descending toward

Anchorage, Alaska, where we landed in midmorning. All the passengers had to pass through customs and the foreign nationals had to clear a check by the U.S. Immigration and Naturalization Service. I was particularly struck by the friendliness and cooperation shown by these petty government officials; it was so different from similar contacts in Korea. I felt, finally, that I was really in a free nation.

The last leg of the flight from Anchorage to St. Louis brought on fits of uncertainty. After grappling with my lunch, my thoughts turned to all the difficulties I was certain to encounter in adjusting to life in St. Louis. I read English fairly well, but I doubted I could speak it well enough to be understood; my trials with several shifts of friendly, patient but nonetheless incomprehensible stewardesses had substantiated that fear. All non-Caucasians who could read knew that America suffered at the hands of racial bigots; I was an Asian, so I would be in trouble. How was I going to live, and where? Was there Korean food available in St. Louis, or would I have to experiment with a whole new class of gastro-intestinal outrage? But that was not the real worry: How was I going to get to Missouri Baptist Hospital? The plane would get me to St. Louis, but where was my real destination in relation to the airport?

Finally, after countless hours of discomfort and sub-vocalized fear, I fell dead asleep as we were making our final approach to my destination. I was awakened by the screech and bump of our landing and soon repeated the traditional and usually uncomfortable off-loading of wan-smiling, thankful passengers that I am sure has followed every safe landing in all the years since man first paid to fly.

At long last, I stood upon free American concrete: St. Louis, Missouri, U.S.A.!

Donald Chung, M.D.

The only money I had was the fifty dollars the South Korean government allowed its nationals to take from the country plus all the belongings I had been able to fit into one suitcase.

It was still the middle of the afternoon of September 17, 1962, the same date, but not the same day, on which I had left Seoul to fly across the International Date Line.

I stood safely in America, and the rest of my life stood before me. In more ways than I could count, I had truly arrived in the Land of Opportunity.

PART IV
The Land of Opportunity
(August, 1962 - February, 1982)

CHAPTER TWENTY-FIVE

I walked through the door from the airplane taxi apron and immediately saw that an Asian man with an expectant, tentative expression his face was looking me up and down. He broke away from the crowd of waiting people, strode right up to me and asked in Korean, "Are you Dr. Chung?"

All my fears dropped away at the sound of his words. I told him that I was indeed Dr. Chung, and he introduced himself as Dr. Oh Se-uk, a surgical resident at Missouri Baptist Hospital for the past four years. The hospital director had asked him to meet me and drive me to the hospital.

I picked up my heavy suitcase and followed Dr. Oh to his brand new avocado-colored Pontiac Tempest. As we drove down the freeway and then through an old section of St. Louis to Missouri Baptist Hospital, we spoke of his life in America. In the background were the soft strains of popular tunes emanating from his car radio. I was too excited to take in all of what I could see from the freeway and the city streets and too excited even to form a first overall impression.

Missouri Baptist, a four-hundred-bed facility, was housed in a four-story building. It was one of the oldest medical-care facilities in St. Louis. Dr. Oh parked the car and led me directly to the doctor's lounge, where he introduced me to the educational director, the young general surgeon who had written my letter of acceptance to the approved intern training program. That done, Oh led me to the interns' quarters, my new home. Minutes later, as I was unpacking my suitcase, my countryman brought me my lab coat and a pair of pants, my work uniform. Next, he conducted me on a brief tour of the hospital, stopping in each department to explain the important features. He explained that my duty as a rotating intern would begin the next morning, at eight o'clock. Since it was by then dinnertime, Oh invited me to his hospital-provided one-room apartment, which was only a few blocks away. He lived there with his wife, mother-in-law and new baby son.

My head was awhirl and jet lag was on the verge of taking its toll. However, my head cleared as soon as I walked into Oh's apartment, for my nose was struck by the pungent, familiar smell of *pulgoki*, Korean barbecued beef. I saw that the table was already set, and there was a place for me. How lucky I felt! Just a few hours earlier, I had been nervously anticipating an overwhelming encounter with an alien society. Now, much to my surprise and pleasure, I had entered a little enclave of home.

I went back to the hospital early and fell into a deep, contented sleep. I had no worries. Dr. Oh came by my room early the next morning and led me to the hospital staff cafeteria. I was put off by the unfamiliar array of foods along the gleaming stainless steel serving line, so I just pointed to Dr. Oh's tray and said "Same-same." My memory transported me back to my first encounter with an American food line on my trip to Taegu in 1952.

*

I received my three-month assignment to the internal medicine department after breakfast and met the chief resident, a Greek woman who spoke fluent English but, of course, no Korean.

Now I was on my own, for I had to function, professionally at least, entirely in English. After orientation and a tour of the department, the chief

284

resident assigned me to minister to a patient who had just been admitted to the department by her private physician. It was my duty to take a medical history and conduct a preliminary medical examination. I was then to treat the patient under the supervision of her own family physician.

Mrs. Joyce Casey was a Caucasian female in her early thirties, a Baptist pastor's wife from Festus, Missouri, a little town about thirty miles south of St. Louis. She sensed right away that this was my first day on duty and it was painfully obvious at the outset that my spoken English was not very good. She was very patient with me, speaking slowly and clearly, repeating anything she felt I had not gotten right the first time. Still, I had a great deal of difficulty understanding her. At length, she took up a paper and pen and wrote the answers to my questions, the reason she had been admitted and her past medical and family histories. She seemed to have an excellent sense of the sort of questions I would be asking if my English had been up to it. I suppose this was a result of her previous medical consultations. In the end she wrote out nearly a full page of notes. I had absolutely no trouble comprehending the written information, and I quickly copied what I needed onto the patient chart. She was a literal godsend—intelligent, kind, and sensitive to my embarrassment and feelings of inadequacy. I had no trouble conducting the physical examination since I had performed countless such in Korea, and I was able to write my findings in English without the slightest difficulty or hesitation.

Later in the day, Mrs. Casey's attending physician paged me to join him in the doctors' lounge to go over the case. He commented that the history I had taken was well done, and that I appeared to have conducted a thorough examination. I could not admit that I had had little to do with collecting the data.

Donald Chung, M.D.

During Mrs. Casey's two days in the hospital, while I conducted a complete diagnostic work-up, she consistently exhibited concern over my foundering verbal abilities in English. In fact, she told me of her concern that I was so new to her country. When she was ready to leave the hospital, she offered me her phone number, which I accepted, and asked me to visit her and her husband whenever I could get away. I was overwhelmed with delight. Was *this* how Americans treated foreign guest? If so, I had definitely made a good choice. (In fact, I have not felt the burden of discrimination at all during my years in America. If anything, native Americans have consistently gone out of their way to help me, and particularly during those early days of confusing transition.) I eventually took Mrs. Casey up on her offer, and I shared years of warm friendship with her and her husband.

*

I met nearly all of the twenty-five interns and residents during my first week at Missouri Baptist. Every one of them was a foreign medical-school graduate. They came from all over the world: Canada, Mexico, Brazil, Turkey, Greece, Italy, the Philippines, Korea—all over. Being a member of this group was a bit like living in an international bazaar. Because of the heavy workload heaped upon interns, I did not get away from the hospital building very often. My early exposure to America, then, was through sharing foods and conversation from around the world. I did not then have the opportunity to see if the larger America beyond the hospital walls was truly a melting pot, but I certainly lived in a melting pot that had little contact with that larger America other than through the patients we treated.

I had had to come to St. Louis "to see the world". It was all very strange and, in the beginning, I was very lonely and homesick. Fortunately, Dr. Oh had me to dinner from time to time; the pleasure and relief I felt from speaking my own language, eating familiar food and sharing a common heritage is beyond description.

The laws governing such things at the time provided each foreign medical intern and resident with up to five years to complete his studies before he had to return to his home country. I never anticipated staying in America; I had come solely to obtain the best educational opportunities. So had my colleagues. In many ways, we had no need to become immersed in the American culture; except for alleviating curiosity, there was little purpose in doing so.

Most of the interns were like me: old, poor and single. I doubt that there were many love affairs between members of our group, and I am sure there could not have been more than one or two serious relationships taking place between interns or residents and native Americans. This made for a socially introverted environment, long on desire and very short on sexual release. Fortunately, we were worked so hard that sex was little more than a forgotten dream for most of us. The only thing that probably saved some of us from total deprivation was the hospital nursing school. Typically, the young ladies who had not yet found dates for the weekend were on the prowl every Friday afternoon. I cannot guess how many of these young women had decided after only a few months of nursing school that marrying a doctor was preferable to working for one. The fishing was not particularly good at Missouri Baptist, but I am sure many of the ladies ended up trolling those shallow waters just for the sport. Several of my colleagues took advantage of the situation, but I rarely had the time or inclination to

deal with those predatory youngsters on any but a
professional level.

*

Interns drew night duty every other night. When
we were on-call, we had to sleep in the on-call room, a
cold, stark sort of place with an uncomfortable bed and a
perpetually untidy appearance. On my second or third
night shift, I was jarred awake by the phone and listened
tiredly as the night operator mumbled something about
my being needed at "the nursing station". I was still
disoriented, so I said, "Yes", and hung up. No sooner
done, however, than I sat up in stark terror: I had no idea
which nursing station had been mentioned nor which
patient had been named. I roared out of the room and ran
to the elevator, where I was brought up short by the
realization that I had not learned how to operate this
wonderful contraption. I charged through the stairwell
door, arbitrarily decided to go up rather than down, and
climbed the stairs as quickly as my short legs could carry
me. I ran through every medical department on both top
floors: "Did you call Dr. Chung? Do you need a doctor
here?" Nothing. I ran down to the second floor, on which I
had started and ran through all the corridors asking if I
was needed. Nothing there either. I ran to the first floor
and, after a total of thirty minutes of breathless sprinting,
located my quarry. As I fought for air, the nurse primly
announced, "Oh, doctor! You didn't really have to come
all the way out here. The patient only needs a laxative.
You could have handled it over the phone." In fact, as I
blushed from my deep embarrassment, I only then
realized that I could have saved all the breathless
running by simply calling the night operator back and
asking her to repeat her message.

From that night forward, I never hung up a telephone before I had a complete understanding of the message, even if it meant asking the caller to repeat himself several times.

Ah, America!—the land of confounding ease!

*

My years of intern and residency status at Soodoo Medical College Hospital had exposed me to the workings of cardiology, and I had decided to make that discipline my medical specialty. Every evening, Dr. James Hutchinson, one of the attending physicians affiliated with Missouri Baptist and a clinical professor in the Department of Medicine at Washington University Medical Center-Barnes Hospital, read electrocardiagraphs taken during that day. I made myself known to this eminent professor and made it a point, as often as I could, to join him at the heart station as he read the EKGs. At times, with his tacit urging, I commented about particular readings or on one of his interpretations. Mainly, however, I simply showed my interest in the work. Dr. Hutchinson received my attentions with great warmth, and I soon had the impression that he had actually come to look forward to our frequent sessions together.

I made my mark one day in October, after I had been in the country for less than two months. I was paged by Dr. Hutchinson, who was calling from his private office. "I'm sending over a patient for you to see. She's a young female with an acute heart problem; please take charge of the case, it appears to be critical." I said I would do what I could and report back.

I was notified as soon as the patient was brought into our emergency room, at about eight o'clock that evening. I conducted a brief preliminary examination and

sent the young woman to the medical floor, where I soon
joined her and undertook a very thorough examination.
My English had improved considerably through the thrust
of daily use, and I was able to conduct a cogent interview.
The patient was Caucasian and thirty-eight years old.
When examined earlier by Dr. Hutchinson, she had
registered an extremely high blood-pressure reading.
This was confirmed by my findings; in fact, the reading
was the highest I had ever seen. She complained of a
pounding headache and overall weakness, and her skin
was cold and clammy to the touch. During the
examination, she suddenly began having chest pains. All
the information pointed to a chemically-induced condition
of some sort. This was years before drugs were in
common use, and she responded to questions on the
subject by saying that she was not on any sort of
medication. That left some sort of chemical dysfunction in
her body, but there was no way as yet to determine what
that might be.

I remained at her bedside all that evening and into
the night, closely monitoring her progress, recording all
my findings in detail. Soon after admission, her EKG
showed that she was having a "heart attack" involving
the front part of the heart muscle. soon, her blood pressure
began dropping and her heart beat became steadily
weaker. There was little I could do for her except monitor
her condition and treat her symptoms. Shortly after
midnight, she groggily asked me to inject something to
relieve the pain in her chest. At that point, I began
hearing a new sound, a murmur, from her heart, and she
was having great difficulty in breathing; she was gasping
audibly for air. Suddenly, her body relaxed and turned an
ashen color. There was no pulse, blood pressure or
respiration, so I pronounced her "dead" after little more
than four hours of constant care.

We had no intensive care units at the time, not nearly the technical expertise we have today, but I had done all I could for her. There really had been no hope. My final comment on her chart read, in lay terms, "It seems likely this thirty-eight-year-old lady had a tumor of the adrenal gland, on top of the kidney. Heart attack is very unusual for such a young lady, but it is possibly related to her tumor. If she has one, death was brought on by the rupture of the wall dividing the right and left ventricles (lower chambers) of her heart following damage to the wall from the heart attack."

When the body had been taken to the morgue, I made the final entry in the chart and went to the on-call room to sleep.

At six o'clock in the morning, as I was beginning my regular daytime duty, the chief of pathology paged me. I picked up the nearest phone and identified myself. He told me in an excited voice, "Hurry down to my office." When I got there, he looked up from the chart I had filled in and submitted upon the death of my patient and asked me in an excited voice, "Chung, how did you know all this? You came up with a correct diagnosis of an extremely complicated problem using observation, and without using any lab equipment!"

Then, more calmly, he explained that his autopsy had shown the predicted tumor at the top of her left kidney, and that death had indeed resulted from heart failure caused by the rupture of the chamber walls— precisely as I had written in my closing remarks.

The truth of the matter is that I had made an inspired guess. I suppose it might have been prompted by the sum total of knowledge a physician accumulates as he is exposed to a constantly-growing and increasingly-varied cross-section of ailments. Indeed, such a broad-based knowledge is precisely the rationale for intern and residency programs. In later years, research revealed

that adrenal tumors occasionally cause the release of
doses of adrenaline so large as to prove lethal when they
damage the heart muscle. Something I must have seen
and unconsciously stored away in Korea contributed to
my purely empirical diagnosis, for I was years ahead of
the published research data.

The case study was presented at the next
hospital teaching conference, and I achieved an instant
notoriety as the Korean doctor whose poor spoken
English did not prevent him from rendering spectacular
diagnoses. Needless to say, I never came close to
repeating this feat during my time at Missouri Baptist.

*

The months passed quickly, and happily. I went on
to fulfill my surgical internship requirement and then I
was assigned to the obstetrics service.

I had had no prior practical experience with
delivering babies in Korea, where we were very long on
theoretical training and very short on actual patient care.
However, if a private physician sent his patient to
Missouri Baptist in the middle of the night because she
was well along toward delivering her child, I, the on-call
intern, had to do what had to be done. I found I had no
aptitude for delivering babies, which, on the surface,
seems a natural enough process. Even with practice, I
could never tell with any assurance how far along the
birth was, nor even how far along in the birth canal the
baby might be. I was always relieved and grateful when
an experienced obstetrical nurse provided me with all the
information I needed to monitor the progress of labor.
When the time came, I did my best to have an
obstetrician on hand, in which case I passed along all the
information provided by the nurses and stood as far out of

the way as I could get. Thanks to the nurses, I never called the attending obstetrician in too early or too late.

*

Spring, 1963, found most of my intern colleagues busily writing letters to the hospitals at which they wanted to become residents in their chosen specialities. Usually, the entire community of interns moved to new hospitals on July 1. I had learned since arriving at Missouri Baptist that the best resident programs in all fields were usually filled a year in advance, almost before the physicians who had been accepted had begun their intern programs. Moreover, it was more difficult for a foreign medical school graduate to win the best positions than it was for graduates of American schools. I had long since settled upon internal medicine as my speciality for the resident program, and I had sent applications to many fine hospitals in Missouri and throughout the United States. By spring, I had received only three replies, all from non-university hospitals, all negative. I interviewed for a new position in April, but I came away feeling that I had not made much of an impression. It seemed to me that my poor command of spoken English was working against me, and that that factor alone might prevent me from obtaining a position at one of the better teaching hospitals.

One evening in late May, just over a month before the new residency programs were to start, I was working at the heart station with Dr. Hutchinson when he asked me what my plans were and where I would be going. I explained to him that I had been turned down everywhere I had applied and that I assumed this was because I had served only ten months as an intern (the implication being that I was a substandard last-minute fill-in) and because my English was not deemed sufficient to take on the added responsibilities of a residency. He replied with his usual warmth, "I just can't understand why someone with your background can't find a good resident program." He patted me on my shoulder and said, "Let me see if I can do something for you."

The following afternoon, I was paged to the phone to speak with the chairman of the Department of Internal medicine at Washington University Medical Center-Barnes Hospital. The man wanted to see me as soon as possible. We arranged an interview for early the following week.

I arrived at the appointed hour, resume in hand, and did my best to answer his rather pointed questions. He was neither particularly warm nor particularly distant, just cordially businesslike. I had the distinct impression that he did not think much of my English, but he did offer me, then and there, a position as a first-year resident effective as of July 1. He told me that the issue had been decided "on the basis of the recommendation of one of our trusted professors"—Dr. Hutchinson, of course.

I was simply dumbfounded. I had just been accepted to one of the most-coveted residencies offered by one of the world's finest and most-prestigious medical-training centers—after having been rejected by every one of the countless second- and third-class hospitals to which I had frantically applied over a period of many months. This was the first time that I saw how very important it was in America, as in Korea, to have an influential ally in your corner. More to the point, I had first-hand evidence that influential allies are won through many days and nights of hard work.

I moved to the new hospital setting on July 1. Washington University Medical Center-Barnes Hospital was considered huge by the day's standard and still is. It housed over one thousand beds and had a service in each and every medical branch. Over fifty interns and residents were employed in the internal medicine service alone. The majority of my fellow internal medicine residents were graduates of America's most-prestigious medical schools, including many from Columbia, Harvard and Yale. Indeed, I was the only foreign-school graduate on the service. This, more than anything, convinced me that, when excellence really counts, racial or national origins are simply not considered, that opportunity derives from who you are rather than who your parents might have been. I was the son of an illiterate peasant mother and a man who had parlayed a fourth-grade education into a series of petty bureaucratic jobs. But *I* was the thirty-one-year-old war veteran who had earned his medical education and valedictory award through hard study and numerous survival schemes; *I* was the yellow-skinned foreigner who had excelled thus far in his chosen profession; but *I* had been chosen only on the basis of my performance, and for none of the other ways in which I could be accurately but incompletely described.

Any feelings of inferiority I might yet have harbored were gone forever by the time I put my head on my pillow and fell into a comfortable, secure sleep the night of July 1, 1963.

CHAPTER TWENTY-SIX

I had a cousin living in Seoul who had been a classmate of mine at Chu-ul Junior High School in 1946. Like me, she had fled to the south with retreating ROK troops in 1950. She had married a few years later, and she and her husband had often invited me to their home during my post-war army and school years. She was thus my nearest contemporary among my relatives in the south and, I would have to say, my closest friend in the family. We remained in close touch while I was in the United States.

One day, during the summer of 1964, I received a letter from my cousin.

"Dear Dong-kyu," it began, "I know that you are trying hard to reach your goal of becoming a good doctor, but I cannot help worrying that in the process you will miss the opportunity to start your own family. You are already thirty-two years old, and you must marry soon, before you are too old to raise your own children. Your father, my first uncle, was the eldest of eight, and you are his eldest and only son. It is your responsibility to carry on the family line. With this in mind, I have been keeping my eyes open for any likely candidates to be your bride, and I think I have finally found just the one..."

This was just the sort of letter to which a dutiful Korean male would have to respond. My duty was before me.

The letter went on to explain that my cousin had recently been visiting a close woman friend of good family when they were joined by the friend's younger sister. My cousin had been attracted to her in my behalf at first glance that day. The sister was twenty-three years old and a college graduate with a major in history. She got on well with my cousin, who had gone back to her friend's home the next day to find out all she could about her.

"...She is very pretty, even by your impossible standards. She is pleasant, open-minded, intelligent, and waiting to find a good candidate for a husband. Her name is Kim Young-ja."

Several photographs, taken by my cousin, were enclosed with the letter. Getting the photographs taken had been something of an ordeal, my cousin admitted, because Miss Kim had a mind of her own and apparently did not consider herself bound by millennia-old traditions; it had been very difficult for my cousin to get her to agree to have her picture taken. In the end, they had met at one of the old royal palaces in Seoul, where my cousin took numerous color photographs of Miss Kim posed against exquisite backdrops. As I was reading, I kept glancing at the pick of the photos.

In closing, my cousin urged me to write to this Miss Kim before I lost what she considered to be a golden opportunity.

*

I had been exposed to many women in the years since I had entered Soodoo Medical College, where, after all, female students outnumbered males by about thirty-to-one. Since arriving in St. Louis, I had been in daily contact with literally hundreds of females—nurses, nursing students, doctors and patients. I had unwound a bit since joining the Washington-Barnes medical staff, but I had never in all my life had a serious protracted liaison and certainly no relationship that could be considered a "love" affair. My priority remained, as ever, my medical training. On the other hand, I sincerely hoped to marry, and my mind was firmly set upon finding a woman of similar heritage. Doing so in St. Louis, I knew, would be almost impossible, in part because there were many more Korean male students—and nearly no suitable Korean females—arriving each year.

Miss Kim's acquiescence to the idea of corresponding with me seemed fine on the surface. I thought it over for several days and decided that nothing could be hurt if I tried to get to know this person through an exchange of letters. So I began my end of the exchange late one night, just after coming off duty. Drawing my inspiration from my earliest puppy-love contact with Hae-jean in 1947, I spent several very late hours composing and recomposing my first letter to Miss Kim.

I waited anxiously for her first reply. Mail between Seoul and St. Louis took an average of a week each way. After three weeks of waiting, I finally received my first letter. Like mine, it was an introductory letter, and very brief. It was apparent that she was shy about writing under these circumstances, and to a total stranger at that. Somehow, my interest in this intelligent, straightforward and self-expressive young lady grew out of proportion with each exchange. We moved ahead swiftly and were soon exchanging intimate details of our feelings about life and personal plans and goals. After our first five or six exchanges, I found myself looking forward to her letters and growing steadily more impatient over the two-week minimum delay imposed by the mails. I found myself reading her old letters over and over to help me through the long intervals. Within a few months, I was writing Young-ja at least a brief note every single day, and she was doing the same.

We had come to know one another in intimate terms within three months, though we had never met and despite the usual cultural restrictions regarding such matters. I had never been good at conversing with women, but when it came to writing to Young-ja, I found that I could organize and express my feelings without any strain. My letters made sense. Too much sense, as it turned out, for Young-ja eventually pointed that they tended toward the practical rather than toward the romantic.

It eventually came out that I had proven to be a better candidate for marriage in Young-ja's eyes than might have been evident on the surface. She proclaimed herself to be a very modern thinker, cognizant of tradition but, as my cousin had pointed out, not necessarily bound by cultural patterns. I sensed, in answer to my questions regarding her inability to find a suitable husband, that she was just too strong-minded for the average Korean male living in Korea's male-dominated society. I, however, had been exposed to American women and was beginning to feel somewhat at ease around those free and free-thinking creatures.

There was another very important factor in Young-ja's consideration of me in favor of a convenient marriage at home. A new Korean bride traditionally owed the groom's family a year's service ostensibly for purposes of education. During that year, the bride lived under the new mother-in-law's roof, doing all the hard labor and undesirable work. Even a new mother-in-law living in the most poverty stricken circumstances had at least one year when she could feel she was the lady of her manor. Young-ja cringed at the notion of this sort of submissive servitude and had frankly been seeking a man without a family matriarch. Indeed, she had put marriage from her mind for several years beyond the Korean woman's traditional wedding time partly because she could not find a bachelor who was suitable in this regard. I eventually learned of Young-ja's attitude from the cousin who had "introduced" us. It naturally saddened me that Mother was not a physical presence in my life, but I found Young-ja's resultant interest to be the only factor I ever encountered that softened the blow of that central truth.

I finally decided that I wanted to marry the young lady in the photographs. After consulting her parents and elder sister, she consented to a proxy wedding. These things were not unheard of in Korea, and we facilitated the paperwork in a very short time. There was a wedding ceremony in Seoul, followed by a huge banquet at the home of Young-ja's parents, with whom she would continue to live for the time being. I was not there, but my relatives and many of my classmates attended, and memorial photographs were taken, with copies soon bound for America.

*

By then, I was well into my second year as an internal medicine resident. My stipend was $275 per month in addition to room and board. From this minscule budget, I was paying out $98 per month for my new Pontiac Tempest. I waited several months, until September, 1964, to invite my bride to come to America to live with me. I hoped she would be able to settle her affairs in Seoul in time to attend the hospital's annual Christman party with me.

My plan did not go well. The staff of the United States Embassy in Seoul could not comprehend the idea of a marriage by proxy, so Young-ja could not get a visa. I was still writing to her every day, but there was a sudden break in the letters caused, as I later found out, by her inability to come to grips with our mutual disappointment—even though I did not know of the difficulties she was encountering. After several days without hearing from her, I decided to telephone Seoul and speak to her—for the first time, ever. Telephone communications in Korea and particularly between Korea and the outside world were technically very poor. I had to shout at my wife to be heard. "Young-ja," I yelled in several sorts of frustration, "what is happening? I haven't had a letter from you in days; all the letters you sent must have been dropped into the Pacific." She laughed and told me what the trouble was and that I had better resign myself to going to the Christmas party alone, as I had in previous years. After that, whenever there was a break in the flow of letters, I called and yelled the same corny line into the phone, and she always laughed.

Young-ja called me on April 2, 1965, and shouted the good news that the U.S. Embassy had finally granted her a visa. She would be arriving in St. Louis—the following day!

The break had finally come through the influence and hard work of my good and dear friend, Pastor Eugene Casey, of Festus, Missouri, the husband of my very first patient at Missouri Baptist Hospital. I had been the guest of Gene and Joyce Casey on many holidays and numerous weekends the whole time I was in St. Louis, and they had taken great pleasure in going to work in my behalf. I doubt that the wheels of bureaucracy would have turned anywhere near as fast, if at all, without the support of my native-American friends. They told me often that they considered me a full-fledged member of their family, and they never treated me as anything less than that.

I phoned the Casey's as soon as I finished talking with Young-ja. I was in a panic; there was no time to plan anything, much less arrange for Young-ja's arrival. Joyce Casey calmly took matters in hand. "Bring Young-ja to Festus directly from the airport," she ordered. "Gene will be thrilled to perform your wedding ceremony." I thought this was particularly touching because neither I nor Young-ja were Christians.

The rest of my day was spent rushing around getting wedding invitations printed and mailed to all my Korean friends in St. Louis, arranging for time off from work, completing, updating or turning over the records of patients in my care, rearranging my finances, and finally getting my clothing in order and packing it and everything else I would need in Festus.

*

Young-ja arrived in the middle of the afternoon of April 3, 1965. I was standing at the exit gate, just where Dr. Oh had met me when I arrived nearly three years earlier, when the Northwest Orient jetliner landed. I watched each passenger alight from the ramp, hoping to catch an early glimpse of the beloved face I had seen only in photographs and dreams.

There she was! Young-ja wore a traditional Korean dress, peach-colored, with a thin, blue-silk overwrap. We recognized one another from afar without any difficulty and embraced as soon as she stepped into the waiting room. I felt at that instant as if we had been husband and wife all our lives and were just ending a years-long separation. I knew her only from the more than one hundred fifty letters we had exchanged over the past year, but I sensed that I also already knew more than those letters had ever conveyed in mere words. I felt, from the first touch, that we were *truly* husband and wife.

We rested at the Casey home in Festus for two days, then drove back to St. Louis to take care of shopping chores. I bought a black suit and black tie and had my best black shoes resoled and polished for the wedding ceremony. Young-ja had brought an exquisite wedding dress from Seoul.

303

Donald Chung, M.D.

On the afternoon of April 11, only nine days after our first embrace, Young-ja and I were married in the Second Baptist Church of Festus before Reverend Casey and thirty friends and members of the congregation. What a difference between my parents' wedding and my own! Or was there, really? For Festus was an agricultural community, as was Taehyang. Moreover, my parents' marriage had been arranged after an exchange of photographs—just as mine and Young-ja's. My wife and mother were both picture brides, and my father and I were both elder sons. I hoped and prayed that all similarities stopped there, except that Young-ja would love her children as much as Mother had loved me and my sisters.

The congregation gave us a wedding reception, complete with a traditional American wedding cake. Unfortunately, only a dozen black-and-white photographs were taken.

We left immediately after the reception to begin our honeymoon at Kentucky Lake. I had promised Young-ja in my letters that I would take her to Niagara Falls, but doing so was so obviously beyond my means that the subject was never really broached once she joined in making plans. All of our wedding gifts were packed in the car when we reached our destination the following afternoon. The weather was chilly, but it was off-season and thus very quiet—just what we needed.

As soon as we had checked into a small motel, we decided to take a drive around the side of the beautiful mountain that dominated the area. Early that evening, the car got stuck in deep sand as I attempted to ford a tiny, shallow creek. We were deep in the mountains, at least five miles from town. I had had no experience in driving in this sort of terrain—little driving experience at all, in fact—and, as I tried to rock the car back and forth, it just sank deeper and more hopelessly into the sand. At length, Young-ja suggested, "Should I walk into town to get help?" But I insisted, "I'm the man. *I* will rescue the car!"

After a few more tries, I asked Young-ja to help unload all the gifts and help scoop the sand out from under the tires with her hands. When we reached what appeared to be a solid footing, I asked her to push the car from the rear while I gave it the gas. By then, our faces, hands and clothes were spattered with mud and dripping water, and our strength was about gone. Her efforts to push us free failed time and again, and it was beginning to grow dark and cold.

We had been at it for nearly three hours because I kept insisting that we would save ourselves. As the chill night wind hit our wet clothing and sweaty bodies, I finally relented. With a beaming smile and a very small voice, Young-ja asked, "Is it time to walk to town for help?" At last, my honor more than fully requited, I relented.

I later heard a lot about that essentially humorous incident. Young-ja told me that I exposed my stubborn streak to her as we wallowed in that creek bed; that my sweet letters had in no way prepared her for my willfulness. She also observed in time that my stubborn streak probably saved my life many times, and pushed me through to my goals in life. Conversely, Young-ja revealed much of her underlying strength, for she had patiently allowed my stubbornness to spend itself before reintroducing the perfect solution, which she had seen at the outset, three grueling hours earlier than I had.

CHAPTER TWENTY-SEVEN

Our first son, Richard Sae-woo, was born August 29, 1966, at the Jewish Hospital in St. Louis. At the end of June, 1967, I completed my professional training at Washington-Barnes, the last two years of which had been devoted to cardiology. This milestone arrived just nineteen years after I had entered Chongjin Medical-Technical School.

In theory, it was time for me to return to South Korea; my training was complete and my exchange visa was due to expire in August. I had been corresponding with an American medical missionary who established a major hospital facility in Taegu, and we had more or less agreed that I would start work there as chief of internal medicine upon my return. The salary we negotiated was excellent, and perks included free family quarters, furniture, and a car of my own.

I had mixed feelings about leaving. I had struggled mightily to live in this strange, wonderful country, and I had pretty much succeeded. I was comfortable with America and Americans, and I liked living here. I had friends and status, and Young-ja and I knew that as a medical family we had an opportunity to enjoy a far better life in America than we could hope to enjoy in South Korea. The law, however, was clear; we had to live outside the United States for a minimum of two years before we could reapply for admission, and there was no guaranty that we would be allowed to re-enter under any circumstances.

Pastor Gene Casey went to work on the problem as soon as I articulated our desire to stay. He and a fellow clergyman petitioned their local congressman and created just enough interest to provide an extension to our visas pending a solid ruling by the Immigration and Naturalization Service.

Personally assured by the Missouri congressman that I would eventually be granted permanent-resident status, I accepted a job at the Veterans' Administration Hospital in Long Beach, California.

*

Young-ja, Richard and I left for Long Beach in July, 1967, in our four-cylinder 1962 Tempest. I purchased a water-based cooling box which I attached outside one of the rear windows, and we packed all the furniture that would fit in the trunk and atop the car. We had all of about $1,000 cash and enormous hope to see us through.

After a hot, grueling, wonderful trip, we checked into a small hotel and I reported in to the personnel office at the VA Hospital. I was expected, which was nice, but I was also asked for my "green card", the INS document that indicated my legal-alien status. These were the same people who had hired me after I had made full disclosure that my ultimate status was pending; they were being paid their salaries by the same government that was reviewing my status at the behest of the Missouri congressman; and they were the same people who told me how sorry they were that their agency's hiring guidelines prevented them from putting me to work for pay. However, nothing prevented them from offering me an *un*salaried position at the VA hospital. I was angry and confused, but I grabbed at what appeared to be a lifeline; I accepted the job and hoped that all would be made right by me in the end.

Since I clearly needed money, I also went to work for the cardiology department at the University of

308

California Irvine School of Medicine. The pay was miserable, but it was enough for us to squeeze by on.

During our first days in Long Beach, I made contact with the then-tiny Korean community by way of a miniscule Korean Baptist congregation. Young-ja and I were from Buddhist families, but we gravitated toward the Christian congregation and were welcomed by it because of our cultural affinity. The pastor of the church was particularly good to us, and very giving of his time despite his responsibilities to his congregation.

No one ever pressured us nor even suggested that we become Christians, and we felt no calling to do so until one particular Sunday when we left the morning service and stepped out to the street with the congregants. I am not sure I know just what happened, but something of the peace and tranquility I felt set off an internal reaction. Young-ja somehow felt the same thing and we discussed it taking into account our long and warm friendship with Pastor Casey, himself a Baptist minister. Finally, and quite easily, we decided to convert and we were baptized at the earliest opportunity.

After two months, the local INS office sent me a letter demanding my appearance for an exit interview pending our departure from the United States. I'm not sure why I reacted thus, but I placed an immediate phone call to another Korean-born cardiologist with whom I had struck up a close relationship at Washington-Barnes, Dr. Edward Chung. Edward had completed his training in 1965 and had achieved immigrant status shortly thereafter. I thought if anyone knew the system Edward would. He was then an assistant professor in cardiology at Meharry Medical College, in Nashville, Tennessee. I quickly outlined my problem and asked for advice. Edward said that he had a few ideas and would be back to me in the morning.

Young-ja and I spent a pensive night, to put it mildly. And then Edward called with a job offer from Middle Tennessee State Hospital. It paid $1500 per month and was for an immediate opening; I would be put to work as soon as I could get there, and no one would ask me for a green card.

I resigned from both my jobs that day and collected my outstanding salary from UC Irvine. Next morning, Young-ja and I packed our meager belongings and paid our bill at the motel. As an afterthought, we drove to downtown Long Beach, where I stopped at the post office to buy stamps for letters I had written to tell friends where we could be reached. Richard began crying while I was gone, so Young-ja took him out of the car and walked him to the end of the block to pacify him. When she returned to the car, her purse, which contained all but about $100 of my savings and earnings, was gone.

If the drive from St. Louis to Long Beach had been grueling, then there is no way to rate the drive from Long Beach to Nashville. The car was underpowered, the stops were few and far between (one way of saving limited capital) and the meals were awful (another money-saver). We arrived somewhat the worse for wear, but we did arrive. Edward had obtained a one-bedroom apartment for us and even loaned us some money to live on until my first paycheck was issued. We were relieved and excited, and looking forward to a useful fulfillment of all my dreams and aspirations immersed in the good life America had to offer.

*

The next two years were dream years; we were utterly happy. And our joy increased, for, in November, 1969, our second son, Alexander Hyun-woo, was born.

His arrival naturally placed constraints upon our limited financial resources but we still felt we were doing fine.

We continued to have difficulties with the INS, but we beat back each attempt to get us to leave the country. Unfortunately, our excuse was a real medical problem. Young-ja had two babies, one before Richard and one before Alexander. We tried to have at least one more, but doing so nearly killed Young-ja several times. We stopped trying, but we frankly used her underlying medical problem and its treatment as an excuse to stay while, during the same period, we continued to petition various influential people to intercede in our behalf. The medical excuse and the infrequent intercessions were barely enough to keep us is the States, but at least we remained.

Eventually, a change in the immigration laws favored our ongoing petition. It was no longer required that we leave the United States for two years before reapplying for immigrant status. Though our immigrant status had not yet been granted, the change in the law resulted in our receipt of official papers granting us an unlimited stay pending a final resolution of our petition to apply for citizenship. We could no longer be deported unless we committed an out-an-out crime.

The dream continued, and got better. Edward Chung moved on to become a full professor in cardiology at the West Virginia University School of Medicine, in Morgantown. As soon as he was settled, he helped me find a well-paid position with the local Veterans Administration Hospital, in nearby Clarksburg, as well as an appointment as Assistant Professor in Cardiology, also at the West Virginia University School of Medicine. This was my first paid teaching job and while I would continue to enjoy clinical work more than anything in my professional life, I soon discovered an unknown talent for teaching; indeed, I became quite a good teacher.

311

Donald Chung, M.D.

Young-ja and I finally received our green cards in spring, 1972, and we immediately began counting the days to our full naturalization. In our minds, and in the eyes of the law, we were virtually assured the fulfillment of that dream.

I had by then helped Edward in the writing of a cardiology textbook, which was bringing in some extra money and enhancing my reputation in my field. Edward had recommended that I Americanize my name for promotional purposes. It was a difficult decision, really quite wrenching. However, by then, I was used to being called "Dong" by Koreans and "Don" by my American colleagues and friends, so I had my name legally changed to Donald K. Chung.

My green card also provided me with an opportunity to take state licensing examinations, which I would need if I wanted to go into private practice. I took tests from several states and was thus fully licensed to undertake the private practice of medicine in West Virginia, New York, and Pennsylvania.

*

Since we were free to live and work anywhere with few constraints, we decided to give Long Beach another try. We had good memories of the weather and lifestyle, if not the job situation and moral responsibility of all its residents. Besides, we had heard that Long Beach had long since become the center of a growing, vital Korean community in metropolitan Los Angeles County. The notion of living among Koreans, with familiar food, culture, language and ideals was very appealing at that time. We loved West Virginia and its people; we had flourished there, especially my two sons, and we had even had our own house built for us, a small place, to be sure, but our very own. We would hate to leave this happy place, but we craved at least a taste of home.

I searched the classified sections of professional magazines for a job in the Los Angeles area, preferably in Long Beach. I finally obtained an interview with Dr. Carlton Waters, an established Long Beach internist who wanted to take in a partner for his thriving practice. We met in Indianapolis, where Dr. Waters was attending a convention, and we hit it off. I was just forty, still up and coming, and he was fifty-nine, ready for some leisure. He invited me to come out to see the practice, and suggested I apply immediately for a California medical license.

In 1967, when I had thought I would be settling in California, I had been refused a medical license because they said I was not qualified. This time, I was granted the license without being tested, on the basis of my having met licensing requirements in three eastern states.

Since there was nothing tangible holding me back, I flew alone to Long Beach as soon as I could get away. I only intended to look over Dr. Waters' practice, get an idea of how much housing might cost, and then fly home to West Virginia to discuss the whole thing, pros and cons, with Young-ja.

Dr. Waters' offer was so good that I accepted the job on the spot. I happened to find the perfect home while driving around Long Beach the next day. A new housing development, aimed at professional people, was under construction, and a unit that had been previously sold had suddenly come back on the market at a "distressed" price. I had just one chance to jump on what appeared to be a superb deal, and I did so without a hint of hesitation—though I had no money with which to consummate the purchase, and would not be able to afford it unless I could quickly sell our home in Clarksburg. In fact, even with the proceeds from the sale of our Clarksburg home, I would be plunged deep into debt. However, I had no qualms about my decision. The only aspect of the transaction that brought me up short was facing the need to call Young-ja and tell her what I had done without affording her an opportunity to influence the decision.

Fortunately, Young-ja was merely surprised. She flew to Long Beach to confirm my decision and sign the loan papers. She turned out to be happy with both the house and her headstrong spouse. I must have done the right thing, for we still live in the house.

The Clarksburg house sold quickly and at a good profit, and we shipped our belongings. We also decided to drive back to California. It was September, and the weather was perfect. I had sufficient cash this time, and owned an air-conditioned Ford LTD, so we made the journey in considerably more comfort than we had, both ways, in 1967.

*

I worked with Dr. Waters for a year, then decided to establish a full-time cardiology practice on my own. We parted cordially and remained friends. I opened my own practice with patients Dr. Waters graciously allowed me to retain, though our contract would otherwise have prevented me from seeing them. I lived for the first three months on my portion of the accounts receivables from my share of my very limited partnership with Dr. Waters.

During my first year in Long Beach, I became affiliated with Long Beach Memorial Hospital, a large non-profit medical facility with over eight hundred in-patient beds serviced by over five hundred attending physicians. I was one of the few foreign-born physicians affiliated with the hospital, and one of the few graduates of a foreign medical school. However, these factors have in no way darkened my professional outlook. Though I was engaged in private practice, I craved to carry on with my teaching—in one form or another. I volunteered for the hospital teaching service and thus gave a weekly lecture in cardiology to interns and residents. In addition, I was retained as an assistant clinical professor at the University of California Irvine School of Medicine. I thoroughly enjoyed my role as a teacher, and I soon received ample recognition, for my interns and residents at Memorial Hospital voted me "Teacher of the Year" only seven months after I joined the hospital staff.

*

I received a call one day in early 1975 from Joyce Casey, the very first patient I had attended upon my arrival in the United States in 1962, the wife of the pastor who had officiated at my wedding. We had kept in touch through the years, by phone and mail, and by way of several mutual visits, and the Casey's had been of enormous help in fending off the Immigration and Naturalization Service.

Unfortunately, the news this time was not good. Joyce's husband, Gene, had just been admitted to the local hospital as an emergency patient. Joyce was sobbing as she relayed to me the opinion of the local physician that Gene's weakened heart probably would not survive for as long as six months. Of all the people with whom I had come in contact in America, Gene and Joyce had been the constants, there whenever I needed them for whatever reason. I felt my own tears begin to flow, for Gene Casey was a brother to me.

As soon as I had done what I could to calm Joyce and get her off the phone, I placed a call to Gene's attending physician, explained my interest in the case, and received a full briefing on Gene's condition. Fortunately, the attending physician and I agreed that Gene could be safely transferred to Long Beach Memorial Hospital, as Joyce Casey wished.

I made immediate arrangements and oversaw the Caseys' flight. I met their plane at Los Angeles International Airport and accompanied them from there directly to the hospital—all within twenty-four hours of Joyce's initial call.

Gene was brought to the cardiac catheterization lab the following morning. The weakened muscle stopped once during the procedure, but Gene was resuscitated immediately. Sadly, I found that his heart muscle was well along in the process of deterioration and, in addition, there was a considerable blockage of the heart's nerve-conduction system. Within days, a surgical colleague implanted a permanent cardiac pacemaker and I prescribed a proper schedule of medication.

I monitored Gene's heart over the following months and years by means of a telephone link between his local hospital and Long Beach Memorial's Cardiology Department, and I stayed in regular close touch with Gene's attending physician.

The Caseys returned to Long Beach in 1978, three years after Gene's emergency pacemaker implant, this time for a full battery of tests and an adjustment of his medication. A few weeks later, while vacationing with Joyce in Florida, Gene's heart stopped—forever.

Several years later, Joyce Casey succumbed immediately at the onset of a cerebral hemorrhage.

*

By 1979, there were nearly 100,000 Koreans living in the Los Angeles area, and over two hundred fifty physicians belonging to the Korean Physicians Association. In June, 1979, during my two-year term as chairman of the Korean Physicians Association, I was chosen to speak on a cardiology subject at the Fourth Joint Scientific Meeting of the Korean Medical Association and the Korean Medical Association of America, to be held in Seoul.

I returned to South Korea for the first time with Young-ja in the company of other medical families and in the care of gracious Korean flight attendants—a far cry from my 1962 flight in the opposite direction.

My three sisters-in-law and two of their husbands were waiting to greet us as we landed in a driving rain. This was the first time I had met any of Young-ja's close relatives. I also met my widowed mother-in-law for the first time.

Seoul struck me as having become a modern metropolis, and had a population of over seven and one-half million. It boasted many Western-style hotels where English was the most-spoken language, and Western food and drink was available throughout the city.

On my first full day back, I visited Dr. Park, my old mentor. He was extremely proud of me, particularly since I was to deliver a paper at so august a gathering. We reminisced about old times, then got on to discussing a vague notion I had about somehow returning to visit North Korea. "I know the Communists well," he cautioned, "and if your mother is still alive and you find her, your visit could hurt her well-being, or even endanger both your lives. If you truly love her, don't visit or disturb her in any way."

I also visited Yi Jung-gi, who had divorced his first wife, my classmate, and moved his practice to Seoul a few years after I left for the United States. I was well up on his life because his daughter, who had been seven

years old when I visited Sokcho during my first year at
Soodoo Medical College, had taken her degree at Long
Beach State College. This was the first time Jung-gi and
I had met face-to-face since 1962, seventeen years
earlier. He was overweight but appeared healthy to my
appraising, concerned eye. He said he was happy. (Six
months later, he was diagnosed as having liver cancer,
and he died at age fifty just a few months later. Like me,
he had been an only son. And, like me, he had had no
word of his family since 1950.)

I delivered two lectures, one each in Korean and
English, and had numerous positive comments,
particularly from Soodoo Medical College classmates
who came especially to hear me, which was particularly
gratifying. I was impressed by the general level of
education I found among medical students and young
physicians, but the teaching and care facilities I saw
seemed to be ten to fifteen years behind the facilities at
my disposal in Long Beach or in most large American
cities.

Young-ja and I, and nearly all our Korean-
American colleagues, were treated to a three-day tour of
South Korea sponsored and paid for entirely by the
Republic of Korea government. We had an opportunity to
visit many familiar places, including a few I had fought
over from 1951 to 1953. One of the eerier aspects of the
journey was repeated every time my excitement got the
better of me and I related wartime stories to my younger
colleagues: they exhibited no interest whatsoever in my
ancient historical accounts. I could not believe that the
war was all but forgotten, and particularly by educated,
prosperous Koreans!

During a stopover in Pusan, I planned a visit to
the clinic of Dr. Kim Pung-u, the surgery professor who
had encouraged me to evade conscription into the North
Korean People's Army. I learned that he had died several

years before from cancer of the colon.

We were in South Korea for two weeks, and I managed to locate many of the people I had hoped to see, particularly the old Chongjin Medical School comrades who had helped to stake me to my medical education. However, I was not able to locate any of my wartime comrades, including Lieutenant Kim.

*

I came away from this essentially sentimental journey with an uneasy sense that there still remained one major hurdle to true happiness. I had broached the matter with Dr. Park, and he had strongly advised against my following through on my heartfelt desire of visiting North Korea. Thus, I put my emotional needs aside once again and returned to Long Beach, an essentially confident and happy man, but an incomplete one.

I dampened any renewed desires to explore the roads that might lead home until the night of February 6, 1982, my fiftieth birthday. In the end, my thoughts turned to Yi Jung-gi, who had died in his fifty-first year, as unfulfilled in his longing for home as I was in mine. It was then that I decided to face up to the consequence of my inaction—and every possible consequence of my overt action.

I decided, then and there, to fulfill the last promise I had made to Mother.

PART V
The Promise Fulfilled
(February, 1982 - July, 1983)

CHAPTER TWENTY-EIGHT

One of my first ideas in my quest to find my family in North Korea was to contact the North Korean delegation to the United Nations. However, to start with, I had no idea how to initiate the contact, nor even if doing so was acceptable or even legal. After some months of fruitless consideration, I wrote to my congressman and asked if his office could make the contact or find some other way to inquire into the whereabouts and well-being of my family. I sent the congressman all the information I could, including the names, ages and last-known addresses of my mother and three sisters. I waited for several months without receiving a response and despite several phone calls to my congressman's Long Beach office.

While I was waiting, I took to reading Korean-language newspapers published in Los Angeles and Toronto. I thought these might offer some insight into a solution to my dilemma, particularly since the Toronto publication frequently carried news from North Korea. Eventually, I came across several articles written by Koreans living in the United States in which were described journeys to North Korea and reunions between themselves and "lost" family-members. The impression I gained from these articles was that I might indeed be able to find some members of my family and, in fact, actually safely visit North Korea to see them. This small encouragement based upon the experiences of like-minded strangers caused me to press ahead even harder.

In July, 1982, I sent identical letters of inquiry to several agencies cited in the articles I had been reading and others: the Committee for Aiding Overseas National of the North Korean Government; the mayor of

Chu-ul; even the chief of Taehyang, where I had been born and where Mother's brothers had been living in 1950. I had no idea if any of my letters would even be forwarded to North Korea by the U.S. postal authorities. I felt strongly that these shots into the dark were well worth the effort and waiting, for I realized how precious time had become; Mother would be around eighty years old if she was still alive.

In early autumn of 1982, I contacted a Korean Christian pastor who had journeyed from Los Angeles two years earlier to visit his sisters and see his mother's grave in North Korea. After sharing cherished details of the trip, he gave me the most valuable piece of information, the Toronto phone number of the Organization for the Reunification of Separated Korean Families. I immediately telephoned the man heading this group, Mr. Chun Chung-lim—who turned out to be the publisher of the *New Korea Times*, one of the newspapers I had been monitoring since the beginning of the year.

Mr. Chun told me that his organization had thus far succeeded in reuniting over two hundred former North Korean nationals living in the United States and Canada with members of their families still living in North Korea. He assured me that every one of the visitors had returned home safely.

I gave Mr. Chun all the necessary information and he told me he would immediately initiate inquiries.

It was during this period, which was marked with wildly alternating rising and sinking hopes, that I began to write this chronicle of my life—both to relive and recall the important moments of my past and as a testament to Mother's eternal love for me and mine for her. I hoped, one day, to be able to show Mother the fruits of my labors. The task turned out to be easier than I had anticipated; the story simply flowed out of some secret place deep within my soul's memory. I had been telling war stories to incredulous patients and colleagues for years, whenever I was asked about my exotic background, and I had even given an occasional lecture on my Korean War experiences. Thus, I had kept my past alive. Using those familiar tales as a basis, and my compulsion as a driving force, it took only a few months of steady work to get the first draft on paper. It helped pass the time and smooth out the extremes in my emotional pendulum. The intense work also bolstered my resolve.

Also during this period, other developments impacted on me and my quest. One evening in April, 1983, Young-ja and I invited to dinner Dr. Poo Mu-ming, a former Taiwanese whose wife, Wen-jen, was a resident physician at Long Beach Memorial Hospital and who himself was a physiology professor at the University of California Irvine School of Medicine. During the course of our conversation, I shared news of my quests with the Poos, and Mu-ming revealed that he was planning to be in the People's Republic of China for a month that summer to participate in a lecture series at a research institute in Beijing. He asked if I would be available to deliver lectures on my way to North Korea—as if my going was a foregone conclusion. I told him that I would certainly take part in the effort and echoed his sentiment that this was a superb way "to kill two birds with one stone."

I only wish I truly shared his optimism as to the availability of that thus far elusive second bird.

*

May 17, 1983, was the saddest day of my life.

I had just finished examining the last patient of the day when my receptionist-nurse told me that Chun Chung-lim was calling from Toronto. I rushed straight to my office and excitedly picked up the phone, certain in the core of my being that the newspaper publisher had solid news of my family.

"Dr. Chung," he began, "I have just received news from the government of North Korea that it has located two of your sisters. They are both in good health."

My heart leaped with joy, but I sensed there was more to be said. I waited to hear the rest.

"I am sorry to have to tell you that I have also learned from the North Korean authorities that both of your parents have passed away."

There it was; the dreaded news.

Mr. Chun went on to say that efforts were being made to locate my third sister, but I was engulfed with the anticipated, but no-less-tragic news that Mother was dead—gone sometime in the thirty-three years it had taken me to garner the courage to make the necessary inquiries and seek her out. I cursed my timidity, for I had been a man of means for ten of those years and could have faced up to my responsibilities sooner had I merely had the courage to do so.

"Dr. Chung?" Mr. Chun pulled me back from by dark thoughts. "I have the pleasure of informing you that the government of the Democratic People's Republic of Korea will be extending an official invitation to you to visit with your sisters."

I thanked Mr. Chun for his efforts. He said he would get back to me as soon as he had more news on my third sister and details of the trip.

I spent the rest of the day in a dazed state; I was in despair over the news that Mother had died, but I was also buoyant with thoughts of meeting at least two of my sisters, though I had no idea which two.

The first draft of my memoir had been completed a few weeks earlier, and I had not had the heart to re-read it in that time, not without some news from home. Now that I had the news, I read every word, relived every deed, felt again every emotion. I counted the hours until Mr. Chun's next call.

*

I received an official letter from the North Korean government at the end of May. It confirmed the news of my parents' deaths and went on to say that all the rest of my family was safe and well, and anxious to see me. The letter contained an official welcome to my proposed trip and advised me that I would be contacted by representatives of the North Korean embassy staff upon my arrival at the airport in Beijing in early July. At that time, firm arrangements for the remainder of my journey to Pyongyang would be presented to me. I was to consider myself a guest of the North Korean government.

Within days, I had confirmed my participation in the Beijing Medical College lecture series and had purchased my round-trip airline ticket between Los Angeles and Beijing. I was to leave on July 3, 1983, eight days after the thirty-third anniversary of the outbreak of the Korean War and twenty-four days before the thirtieth anniversary of the signing of the armistice ending that fratricidal conflict.

On June 13, I received my official invitation from Beijing Medical College in which I was cordially invited to tour the school hospital facilities and deliver a lecture entitled "Pacemaker Therapy—An Update."

This simple progression of events, not always in sequence, but always oriented in a forward direction, left me in an increasingly excited and uplifted state. I never pressed my luck by asking, not even asking myself, why I was being treated so well.

327

Donald Chung, M.D.

*

The mail that reached my office late in the morning of June 24, 1983, included an envelope bearing Mr. Chun's return address in Toronto. Inside that envelope was a second envelope bearing the imprint of the Committee for the Aid of Overseas Nationals of the North Korean Government. This I opened with shaking fingers, only to find yet a third envelope. In this was a four-page letter, handwritten with a ballpoint pen in a neat *han-geul* script. There was no date or return address on the letter.

"To My Dearest and Only Brother From Your Eldest Sister, Moon-hee—"

My first inclination was to doubt the authenticity of the letter. Could this really be from the sister I had last seen as she stode purposefully from our tearful departure beside the Chongjin Medical College playing field thirty-five years earlier? Or was it a clever ploy advanced by the Communists to lure me back into their clutches, to get even for my defection? I frantically searched over the neatly-written characters on that first page, seeking a firm clue that would assure me the letter was a fraud—or what it purported itself to be. Tears formed in my eyes, from joy and frustration and a deep sense of loss.

Halfway down the first page was the proof I sought:

"...We almost lost you when your inflamed appendix ruptured just before the end of World War II...How is that awful scar of your right groin that we thought would never heal?"

There followed Moon-hee's description of how poor we had been because of Father's failure to support us while he lived with his concubine. Every line revealed other intimate details, details whose memories wrenched my heart anew, yet at the same time gladdened me

328

because it was proof positive my sister was the one whose hand had held the pen, putting the words on paper.

As the memories flooded over me as if for the first time, I became overwhelmed that I had in my hands a letter that had not long before been touched by my beloved sister's hands, had probably been moistened by her tears, and undoubtedly was freighted with the love the absent years had only strengthened. I finally could read no further. I carefully folded the treasured testament I had longed to receive and placed it in my pocket. I then rushed into the bathroom to bathe my face and eyes and compose myself in order to examine the last two patients of the morning who had probably arrived for their appointments. Then, the examinations over, I would have my two-hour lunch break and could resume reliving the past as well as discovering a fragment of the present in my far-off homeland.

When I had completed examining the last two patients, I drove to the ocean and parked at the edge of the beach. I walked along the shore and sat on a large rock. For some moments I gazed westward, conjuring up before me out of the distant horizon the steep cliffs of my native land, lapped by another distant sea, yet well within my purview. Lulled by the soothing susurration of the waves washing on the shore, I took from my pocket Moon-hee's letter and with studied calmness began reading it from beginning to end. Then, with rising emotions, I reread it, now with wonderment that what I had felt was my impossible dream was on the verge of coming true. Then, like the sound of some giant wave crashing on the shore, it dawned upon me that by virtue of what I held in my hands, that "impossible" dream was now realized.

It was with some trepidation that I began to study the three photographs that had been tucked into the envelope. One was of Father, taken when he must have been about forty years old. The second was a fairly recent photo of Moon-hee and my baby sister, Jung-hee; the third was of Mother, showing her as she had looked in her mid-sixties. The letter did not state when our parents had died, nor under what circumstances. I continued to presume that Father had perished on the road to Songjin, after our last meeting in Kilchu, during the great retreat of December, 1950.

I learned that Moon-hee, seven years my senior, had two sons and two daughters. Ok-bong, who had been twenty-one and married when I left home, had five sons. And Jung-hee, the baby, had two sons and two daughters. Suddenly I had become the uncle to nine nephews and four nieces I had not known about until this moment. My family in Korea was far larger than the one I had raised in America and, according to Korean custom, I was its patriarch!

I spent a great deal of time over the next two weeks preparing for my departure. I was particularly busy purchasing and packing gifts for my sisters, their husbands and all their children, not to mention for cousins and their families. All that joyous activity and focus upon my generation and the next did nothing whatever to dispel the sense of loss I had felt since learning that Mother was gone.

CHAPTER TWENTY-NINE

July 3, 1983.

The morning of my departure was warm and sunny. Young-ja and 16-year-old Richard drove me the short distance to Los Angeles International Airport, getting me there the specified one hour before departure time. The worry both Young-ja and Richard were experiencing was etched on their faces: both; were deeply concerned about my venturing to a Communist country. I, too, was anxious and apprehensive and it deeply annoyed me to have to sit around for an hour—then another hour, and another. It was impossible for me to sit still; I prowled through the international departure area like a big cat stalking small game.

We finally took off at nearly one o'clock in the afternoon and, according to the pilot, climbed to 31,000 feet as the Pan American 747 circled toward the distant Sierra and then out over the wide Pacific. Less than half the seats were taken, so I decided to restore body and soul following a weeklong bout of acute insomnia and nervous exhaustion. I moved to a vacant row and stretched out, asleep before a whole minute had passed.

During the exhaustingly long flight there flashed across my mind an odd assortment of scenes from the past, scenes so realistic as to make my skin crawl.

I saw, as if receding into the nearby cloud bank, the railroad bridge stretching across the Tumen River, the last barrier the train carrying my family must cross before reaching our homeland of Korea on our flight from Harbin. I felt Mother's warm hand gripping mine as she led me along the narrow dirt path to Grandmother's home, when I went into hiding from the dreaded Security Police. Once again I was held fast in Mother's embrace on that dreadful day of departure—December 2, 1950—and I heard loud and clear little Jung-hee's plea not to leave them all alone. I felt the salty tears freeze solid on my cheeks as I thrust myself away from them and stepped onto the roadway that would all unwittingly take me on this thirty-three-year circle. I felt again the sinking pain in the pit of my stomach as I hefted my meager belongings over my shoulder and strode away forever from the 3rd Medical Battalion Compound in 1956. And even over the steady drone of the plane's engines I heard distinctly the pounding surf on the beach at Sokcho as Yi Jung-gi and his wife led me to the noodle stand to seal our hours-long talk of undying friendship. Just as distinctly I heard Mother's ethereal voice commending me as I accepted my valedictory award upon graduation from medical school. Then, through the drift of the years, I was once again in St. Louis, greeting my paper bride from Korea, and felt our first tender embrace.

But running over and above all these recollections was the insistent, dull ache of irretrievable loss, as intense and real as the moment it first took hold, when I knew for certain that Mother was no more.

I thought a great deal about my departed friend, Yi Jung-gi, and felt deeply that at least a small part of the pilgrimage on which I embarked was for him. I would be going to Chongjin Medical College to deliver a lecture, and I felt sure I would see at least a few of the places where Jung-gi and I had played and worked and eaten— perhaps the playing field on which he had earned his reputation as a star athlete, or the railroad station from which he had departed, disheveled and hung-over, for his service in the North Korean People's Army Medical Corps.

Tears flowed freely from my eyes long into the endless day as we hurtled sunward across the vast gulf I had placed between myself and my roots, between an insulated reality I had created from fear and timidity and the ultimately pain-filled fulfillment of the most necessary promise I had ever made.

It was ironic, of course, that one of the two movie features that day should have been *The High Road to China*. Then, eleven hours, three meals, several snacks and two movies after leaving Los Angeles, the Pan American 747 clipper landed at Narita, Tokyo's new international airport. It was, by local time, two o'clock in the afternoon, July 4, 1983.

I hung around the boarding area until just after five o'clock that evening—I had lost track of my own personal time—and then boarded another Pan American 747 for the relatively short hop to Beijing. This flight was completely filled, largely with business-suited Japanese and Americans come to reap the huge bonanza from the world's most-populous nation. Here and there were American tourists, come to reap the cultural heritage of the world's oldest existing nation-state. We arrived over our destination shortly after nine o'clock, local time, and made a quick, smooth landing in the dark under control of what our proud American pilot described as the most-advanced aerial computer-guidance system in the world.

*

I was just stepping off the escalator preparatory to entering the customs office when two Asian men in ill-cut business suits walked up to me. Startled by the swiftness of their approach, I recovered as soon as I saw small badges depicting Kim Il-Sung on their lapels. I sensed that these were the North Korean embassy greeters I had been told would be meeting me in Beijing to facilitate my departure for Pyongyang, so I asked them in Korean, "Are you looking for Mr. Chung from the United States?" The two nodded and smiled perfunctorily. The younger of the two who appeared to be in charge, explained that they had to meet several other passengers from my plane, then they would see us all through customs and on to the airline ticket office to collect our tickets for the next-day's flight to Pyongyang. I tried to sense any feelings of hostility in these two, but they were businesslike and cordial, just two functionaries doing a routine job.

The Chinese customs officials appeared to be soldiers. Every one of them I could see had small red squares affixed to his lapels, and no insignia rank I could detect. As I waited my turn, I asked the older North Korean, who turned out to be an embassy driver, how one could tell the officers from the enlisted soldiers. He flashed a knowing smile and explained that one had to observe the cuts of their uniforms; officers each had four square pockets on their tunics while the tunics of the enlisted soldiers had only two large pockets at waist-level.

The customs inspection was thorough, but courteously done. I sensed that the presence of the North Korean embassy people somehow shortened the process.

Purchasing my ticket to Pyongyang required an exercise in international currency exchange. The cost in U.S. money was $98, but I first had to convert the required amount of cash to Chinese Yen, which were going for a rate of 195 Yen for $100. I noticed that most of the currency clerks did their figuring on popular-brand Japanese-made electronic calculators, though a few were sticking with the traditional Chinese abacus.

We were accosted by men yelling "Taxi! Taxi!" as soon as we walked out of the building. I learned from my guides that all the taxis in Beijing were government-owned, but that fact did not seem to dampen the ardor of their drivers. As we cut through the throng on the way to the embassy limousine, I saw that many people were carrying bowls filled with steaming rice-wheat or steamed dumplings. I also noted that everyone was dressed in rather dumpy clothing, not better and perhaps not as good as the clothing favored by Chinese laborers in Harbin during World War II. It was a fleeting impression of a nation about which I realized I knew very little.

*

The embassy limousine took us to the Beijing Airport Hotel, only a few minutes from the terminal. There, as I was checking in, I met Chun Chung-lim, the editor of the *New Korea Times*, and his wife. Though I had spoken with Mr. Chun many times and at great length by phone between Long Beach and Toronto, this was our first face-to-face meeting. As soon as I had signed in and received my room assignment, the Chuns took me to meet several Korean-American professors who would be accompanying us to Pyongyang on the morning flight. The six professors had just come from Kyoto, where they had attended a symposium of Korean reunification. I had been invited to attend the symposium, but I had not wanted to become politically involved. Besides, Young-ja, a native southerner, was a bit worried about the South Korean government's reaction to my participation.

One of the six was Professor Choe Ik-hwan, the former Chu-ul High School student body president, now an English professor at a Seattle-area community college. Ik-hwan and I had met many times since 1951, when our two infantry companies had passed on a dirt road near the 38th Parallel, and we had often spoken by phone many times, particularly within the past few weeks.

Donald Chung, M.D.

The growing excitement over my pending reunion with my sisters, the throes of jet lag, the incessant drip-drip of an imperfect showerhead only a few feet from my bed, the churning memories—all these robbed me of my sleep that night. As four-thirty rolled around, I finally ventured out into the corridor and on down to the lobby in the hope of finding a fellow human being with whom I could share some of my time. Too long had I been living with ghosts! I found only the night watchman, a pleasant young man I judged to be in his mid-thirties. He was bored with sitting, so willingly listened as I stuttered out some ill-spoken memories of my life in Manchuria years before he was born. I had hoped that my Harbin-acquired Chinese had withstood the test of time, but he was unfamiliar with the dialect and I became flustered, so I quickly left for a walk around the hotel grounds.

Outside, I found several older women walking and several older men, either walking or going through the intricate, measured movements of Tai-chi as part of their morning exercise rituals. I joined the group of walkers and breathed in the morning air as the sky to the east gradually brightened. By full sunrise, I could see that numerous joggers had arrived in the small park in front of the hotel. Within an hour, the main thoroughfare beyond the park was teeming with cars, small trucks and bicycles.

I was the first hotel guest to enter the dining room when it opened at seven-thirty. However, I was soon joined by five of the six Korean-American professors and Mr. Chun and his wife. The conversation was animated, but I felt that, like me, most of my companions were masking an inner nervousness.

*

336

After all of the formal lectures had been given, the North Korean embassy minibus picked us all up at one o'clock in the afternoon and drove us straight to the airport departure terminal. We were told that there were two round-trip flights per week between Beijing and Pyongyang: North Korea Airways on Tuesdays and China Airways on Fridays. Since it was Tuesday, we boarded a four-engine Russian-built North Korea Airways airliner, which perfectly suited my need to transit by bits and parts into North Korea itself.

The day was extremely hot, and so was the interior of the crowded airplane, which was carrying at least eighty passengers. I took my seat between Mr. Chun and his wife and was issued a paper hand-fan to cool the sweat on my face.

We took off at two o'clock and were immediately addressed over the loudspeaker by the senior stewardess. I was a bit taken aback by her accent. Though it was the accent I had spoken from my earliest years, I had been living mainly among southerners for three decades and was used to hearing their distinctive tonal inflections. At that moment, there seemed to be a lot more to this going-home business than merely weathering some grueling air travel.

Three stewardesses began distributing snacks about thirty minutes into the flight. They were a long way from me, so I had an opportunity to watch them for quite a while. The girls were beautiful in their pink uniforms, but there was not one smile on any one of their faces. Rather, their expressions were fixed and neutral—wooden. I pulled out my Polaroid camera, which I had purchased along with a 35mm camera and a huge supply of color film especially for the trip and took several quick photos. The girls noticed the flash and looked up to see what I was doing. A wave of curiosity passed over their faces as I showed them the instantly-developed photos from afar. Mr. Chun, who had an unusual sense of humor, asked each of them to sit beside me while he snapped photos in which I naturally smiled for the camera and in which they maintained their expressionless composure. In return for favoring Mr. Chun and Dr. Chung with their time, the three managed to walk off with everyone of the photos. This was in sharp contrast to a similar experience in Beijing, where the hotel dining room waitresses had posed with huge, beaming smiles and asked for only their half of the photos we took. Fortunately, Mr. Chun also took several shots of me with the stewardesses with my 35mm camera.

My next bit of "cultural shock" arrived with the snack, which consisted of a boiled egg, a green apple and several rice cookies. This again presented me with a contrast; I thought of the heaping portions of food I had received on my 1962 flight from Seoul to St. Louis. I had been uncomfortable then with too much food, but my decades of life in America caused me to crave something more substantial than this meager offering. I began indignantly thinking that this fare might be well and good for the average Korean, but it was too little and too plain for the seasoned American air traveler—me!

*

We began the descent toward Pyongyang at about four o'clock. My heart began to thud heavily and my mouth became dry while my throat muscles constricted. Dipping lower and lower, I could see through the little window on my side of the plane the green fields and the vague cityscape of the capital of North Korea spread out below me. Down there, I thought, reaching up to me through the intervening space, was the fulfillment of my dreams. Down there was home!

The cityscape became more clearly defined as we made the final approach. Tall, modern buildings, amid vast expanses of green forests, resembled a vast city standing in a lush park rather than the traditional asphalt metropolis dotted with small green areas. Still lower, I saw well-tended green rice paddies stretching into the far distance. It all seemed so peaceful, yet I knew that this very city had been blasted to ruins by over 40,000 aerial bombs nearly 32 years before.

As I braced in anticipation of the airliner's wheels touching the runway, Mr. Chun leaned over and delivered his last and best surprise by whispering, "Two of your sisters will probably be among the welcoming party at the airport."

Ever practical, he controlled my soaring spirits by coolly offering to carry my cameras so that he could take pictures of the long-overdue family reunion. I nodded my assent and handed over my two cameras and some extra film. Then, as a practical afterthought of my own, I shifted my handkerchief to my right coat pocket, where it would be in easy reach as soon as I needed it.

The landing gear thumped once and the pilot backed the airliner's engines. I was on home ground.

CHAPTER THIRTY

July 5, 1983.

We landed at Pyongyang's quiet, surprisingly small airport at four-thirty on that scorching afternoon.

As soon as the rolling stairway was in place and the cabin door opened, two North Korean officials strode briskly aboard the airliner and one called out, "Mr. Chung Dong-kyu, from the United States, please come forward."

I had been told to anticipate an early recognition of some sort, but all the same I was quite apprehensive because I did not know what was going to happen next. Mr. Chun squeezed my arm to reassure me, then I climbed over his legs into the aisle and walked forward to an uncertain fate.

Both of the officials nodded greetings and shook my hand before briskly leading me down the stairs. I could see a knot of about a dozen people gathered below, obviously a welcoming delegation. Many of the waiting people had the look of the government dignitaries, but I could also pick out several middle-aged women dressed in traditional finery. All of them had apprehensive looks on their faces, but if any were my sisters, I could not tell.

When I reached the ground, I shook hands and exchanged brief greetings with the dignitaries, but my eyes were by then fixed upon the faces of a pair of extremely nervous-looking women who were standing in the rear of the group. Somehow, they did not seem to be a part of things, and yet they looked as if they very much were. Both of the women seemed to be following my every move with deep concentration.

When I finally reached the end of the receiving line, the elder of the two women rushed up to me. "You

341

must be my brother, Dong-kyu." I knew then she was Ok-bong, my middle sister. Before I could answer, the younger—Jung-hee, the baby—also rushed to my side, cried aloud and placed her head on my shoulder—just as she had done at the moment of parting over thirty-three years before.

We three joyous souls hugged each other and cried our eyes out. It made no difference to me—with my amalgam of Korean and American diffidence—that there were people standing about staring. We were all so choked with emotion that we could not say a word for a very long time.

I realized that Jung-hee, who had been eleven years old on the day of my departure, was now forty-four. Ok-Bong, who had been a married lady of twenty-one, was now fifty-five. By my American way of reckoning ages, both appeared to be ten years older than their actual years. Like Mother, they both had weathered, sun-browned faces, and the palms of their hands were rough and work-hardened. It dawned on me, also, how alien I must look to them; I was hardly the boy to whom Jung-hee had clung on that snowy December day of our parting in 1950. I considered myself fit but I had acquired glasses and, I hope some dignified bearing and carriage that age can impose. Nothing could erase the lost years, nor the ravages of time. But neither was there anything short of senility and death that could erase the flood of fond memories we three siblings silently shared at that moment of reunion.

These thoughts, and a million others, flashed through my mind in those opening moments of that heretofore impossible reunion.

*

Mr. Chang, secretary of the Committee for Aiding Overseas Nationals, escorted us to the VIP waiting room. On the way, I noticed for the first time the huge, heroic portrait of President Kim Il-sung which utterly dominated the spartan building. It also registered that all of the notables I had just met were wearing Kim Il-sung lapel portraits identical to the ones my greeters in Beijing had been wearing. I was soon to learn that portraits of Kim Il-sung were everywhere—literally everywhere in North Korea.

Once in the waiting room, Mr. Chang introduced me to Mr. Kim Won-ho, a government-paid employee of the Committee who had been assigned to guide me throughout my stay in North Korea. Mr. Kim seemed friendly and perhaps a bit over-eager to please. I knew that he would be my constant companion for as long as I remained on the soil of the Democratic People's Republic of Korea.

Following a half-hour delay in the waiting room, my sisters and I were escorted by Mr. Kim to a well-maintained black Mercedes Benz 220. My sisters and I were ushered into the back seat and Mr. Kim got in front beside the driver. We were then driven into town along a smoothly-paved, nearly empty freeway as good as any I have driven on in California.

The streets of Pyongyang were immaculate, wide and clearly well-maintained, if a little under-used. I was frankly surprised to see so many tall modern buildings rising above the beautiful tree-lined sidewalks. The main thing that struck me then, and throughout my stay in the capital, was the oppressive feeling of isolation from my fellow human beings. We saw few pedestrians and very, very few other cars on this initial drive. Pyongyang had all the earmarks of a science-fiction city that had been abandoned in mid-beat by its entire population. I felt then and throughout my stay there as if I were being conducted on a tour of an artifact. I could not have felt farther from my home in teeming, automobile-dominated Los Angeles County.

Every building, every intersection, seemed to have its dominating portrait of an ageless Kim Il-sung.

To help pass the time, I asked Mr. Kim to tell me a little about himself. It turned out that he was a native of North Hamgyong Province, my own home province, and had probably been chosen as my guide because of our common origins. Other than this bit of news, he told me very little about himself, and I did not pursue the matter, for I was quickly immersed in gray thoughts.

I could not stop the inevitable workings of my mind. This sterile cityscape reminded me of thoughts I had had over the weeks since Moon-hee's letter about the utter control the government of North Korea had over its citizens. Where else in the world, I had asked myself, could one locate three married women after a thirty-year interval, and in so relatively short a time? I had long tried to imagine the infinite tentacles of such a government, but my life in the West had rendered me incapable of imagining the implications of such a thing—until I was first driven through the eerie place that is that nation's capital city. I shivered despite the oppressive heat, for the monolithic themes that dominated this potentially-warm, outwardly-beautiful steel-and-cement place so utterly devoid of its populace—and its humanity—resonated cold chills to the core of my being.

*

It took us about thirty minutes to reach the Changgwang-san Hotel, in the center of the city. This was one of several Pyongyang hotels devoted to foreign guests, neither the best nor the least desirable of its type. There were over one hundred government-hosted

newspeople from around the world staying at the hotel. I
think I groaned when I heard the theme of the gathering;
it was the "Conference of Journalists against Imperialism
and for Friendship and Peace."

My bright, spacious suite consisted of a bedroom,
sitting room and a full bath. The porter made a big deal
out of showing me the 16-inch Japanese-made popular-
brand television, the small Japanese-made refrigerator,
and the Korean-made Chollima Model 67 radio. See, he
seemed to say, all the modern conveniences.

Thankfully, the obsequious Mr. Kim left me to my
sisters almost as soon as we got to my suite. The three
of us sat on the sofa beneath Kim Il-sung's portrait,
holding hands and chattering madly to try to catch up on
every moment of the past thirty-three years. We burst
into laughter now and again, but in the madcap
conversation faltered many times as one or another, or all
three of us together, burst into tears.

Most of this first real family meeting was devoted
to shared memories, as if we had arranged in advance to
start on familiar ground before embarking upon the
needed journey to fill in the years of separation.

I found myself speaking mainly from my heart and
I was sure that Ok-bong and Jung-hee were doing the
same.

We were interrupted by Mr. Kim's return at
around nine in the evening. The dining room would be
closing soon, he told us, and dinner was waiting. I was a
bit startled to learn it was so late, and only then did my
physical hunger catch up to me.

We were the only diners in the hotel's ample main
dining room. Since Mr. Kim was with us, we tacitly
decided to turn our conversation to small things, mainly
to my career in medicine. This is where we reached the
gulf that separated us in the objective world. The road I
had traveled had taken me light years from Chu-ul, while

my sisters had merely grown older along lines we all could have anticipated then. The city beyond the hotel doors was not the only alien presence I encountered that day, for I began as well to truly face my years of separation from the mainstream of my family and my culture, and not just what my culture had become.

As the conversation became increasingly awkward, I turned to Mr. Kim for the first time and asked why Moon-hee had not been able to join us. He smilingly indulged me by saying that he had heard that she had some sickness of advanced age that prevented her from riding the train just then. I was assured that I would be spending ample time with her as my trip progressed; painstaking plans were in the works and I would enjoy the company of my entire family very soon.

I kept glancing at Ok-bong and Jung-hee during Mr. Kim's smiling recitation, but I could not see any clues in their faces, neither acceptance nor rejection, neither resignation nor anticipation.

We returned to my suite after an excellent dinner I barely noticed I was eating. I hoped that Mr. Kim would again leave us to our memories, but he smilingly reminded us of the time and said that my sisters were scheduled—not "had to" but simply "are scheduled"—to return to their hometowns on the midnight train. Oh, how I wished we could spend the entire night dismantling the barriers time and distance had imposed, but I had not yet divined the nature of Mr. Kim's outward friendliness, so I was afraid to state my desires. I am sure that stating their desires was quite beyond my sisters' comprehension, who both hugged me long and hard and assured me that we would have plenty of time to catch up on things at the family reunion to which Mr. Kim had earlier alluded.

Thus ended my very first day back in my native land.

CHAPTER THIRTY-ONE

Mr. Kim came to my room at eight o'clock on the morning of July 6 and suggested that we take a short walk before breakfast. He showed me a large international sports arena directly across from the hotel. There, we watched an East German table tennis team conducting its morning workout; it was attending an international competition, no doubt of eastern bloc and neutral nations.

The streets were not very crowded considering it was the morning "rush" hour. I saw several buses, many electric trollies, an occasional taxicab, and only a few pedestrians. Mr. Kim explained in response to my question that all the buses, trollies and taxis were government-owned and that the majority of rush-hour movement took place on the government-owned Pyongyang Metro System, one of the most modern in the world.

I had a better opportunity to take a close look at the dining room when we returned than I had allowed myself the night before. There were about eighteen round tables, each seating four to six diners. It seemed fairly cosmopolitan this morning, as I heard languages from around the world. The waitresses were well-trained and mannerly if a little cold, as had been our air stewardesses the day before. Each waitress had several years of college and was capable of speaking and understanding English, Spanish and Japanese with some fluency. Each was assigned to specific guests who were assigned to specific tables during their stays. Upon completing one meal, the waitress took orders and a reservation for the next meal, which was typically ready to be served as soon as the diner arrived. The menu offered a surprising variety of well-prepared and ample Korean, Japanese, Chinese and Western dishes and prices for each full meal ranged from ten to twenty won, the equivalent of five to ten dollars.

After breakfast, I was visited in my suite by Mr. Chang, the executive secretary of the Committee for Aiding Overseas Nationals, who was to brief me on the North Korean government and answer political-type questions. (It had been made clear by then that Mr. Kim was simply a tour guide and companion and that he was not available to respond to questions having a political context.) Mr. Chang first emphasized that the post-war reconstruction of the North Korean industrial, commercial and housing base had been made possible only as a result of the brilliant leadership of President Kim Il-sung. He then detailed Kim's concept of national self-reliance, The *Juche Idea*: "The masses are the masters of the revolution and construction. They must retain their position as master and perform the role of masters in revolution and construction. To maintain their position as masters, the masses of people must maintain an independent and creative stance." Mr. Chang then explained that the *Juche Idea* is in accord with the concepts of Marxism-Leninism, that it is a creative theory serving the principles of the Communist movement.

My one and only reason for coming to North Korea was to visit my family. I had in no way equipped myself with any special ideological or political ideas, either for or against the concepts underlying Chang's recitation. I consider myself a medical doctor, a healer of the ill, and I have maintained little more than a layman's passing interest in matters such as Mr. Chang was broaching. I made up my mind then and there that I would simply listen to Mr. Chang and those sharing his convictions for as long as I was a guest in North Korea. I would offer no questions during nor any comments after such recitations. That decision, however, did not make it one whit easier to sit through the pedantic hour-long presentation.

This took us nearly to lunchtime, following which Mr. Kim escorted me to Mangyongdae, a remarkably beautiful spot about eight miles southwest of downtown Pyongyang. At the foot of the hill stands an old, low house with a thatched roof. It is said to be the home acquired over one hundred years earlier by Kim Il-sung's great-grandfather, when he took a job as a graves-keeper for the family that owned the land and the hill.

Our guide told us, "In this home, the great leader of our people, President Kim Il-sung, was born on April 15, 1912, the eldest son of Kim Hyong-Chik and Kang Pan-sok." She went on to tell me that "the young general's spirit of resistance to Japanese imperialism rose in storm and stress. At the tender age of thirteen, he walked out of the wicker gate at his home at Mangyondae with the firm resolve not to return before Korea became an independent nation. For twenty years, he waged his hard-fought revolutionary struggle against the power of Japanese imperialism before he was able to return to his home and long-awaited reunion with his beloved family and relatives."

Following this orientation lecture, I was led through the Mangyondae Revolutionary Museum and shown the school, park, restaurant and visitors' facilities.

We next traveled a short distance from Mangyondae to one of Pyongyang's two elaborate amusement parks. It was the middle of the workday afternoon, so I did not expect to find the park filled with visitors. But neither did I expect that Mr. Kim and I would be the *only* visitors!

A lovely guide was waiting for us at the gate, at which point Mr. Kim cheerfully volunteered the news that a light drizzle that afternoon had prevented the park from being opened until that moment and that we were thus the first visitors.

The park was quite large, about the size of Knotts Berry Farm, near Los Angeles, and set within an area otherwise dominated by tall, stately evergreen trees. All the familiar amusements were in place: merry-go-round, monorail, dodge-'em cars, water-log ride, an exciting 360-degree "revolutionary" rollercoaster, scaled-down rides for very small children and an elaborate shooting gallery.

The shooting gallery presented me, I am sure, with an inadvertent early look at another side of North Korean society. While Mr. Kim served as a cheerful photographer, I responded to my guide's challenge of seeing who could get the highest score for the fifteen-shots of light fired by each rifle. I had survived service as a combat infantryman thirty years earlier, but I had not handled any sort of a weapon since. I scored four miserable hits for my fifteen shots. The young lady—and Mr. Kim, when his turn came—each scored a perfect fifteen hits for fifteen shots. Later, when I asked Mr. Kim how they had managed to do so well, he looked at me in amazement and said that all young men and women in North Korea were trained to defend the homeland against invasion or subversion, and that the skills were maintained through regular refresher courses. He ended by quoting the famous line, "A hundred of the enemy are no match for one of us."

My dead-eyed guide explained that the amusement park had come into being "under the profound loving care of the great leader, Kim Il-sung, whose great love for the people is shown in everything he does for them. " Mr. Kim proudly added that this park was one of the best facilities of its kind in the world and that all citizens could enjoy its wonders free of charge. The park was fine, but I knew that neither Mr. Kim nor the guide had ever been abroad, nor was it likely they had ever seen any films of Disneyland, Busch Gardens, Sea World or Knotts Berry Farm. However, there was no point in antagonizing them with news of the wonders—albeit expensive wonders—of the outside world.

I was dragged through the park and made to have fun for the rest of the afternoon. The end of the light drizzle that had preceded my arrival failed to produce a single other patron until my tour was nearing its end, so my general feelings of dislocation in Pyongyang were considerably enhanced by my being the only rider on literally every amusement in the large place.

A late dinner was provided that evening by Mr. Chang and included myself, Mr. Kim, Mr. Chang and Mr. Chang's assistant. Though only the four of us were ensconced in a tiny private hotel dining room, Mr. Chang rose to deliver an expansive and flowery welcoming speech, as if to multitudes, and to offer a toast. The liquor was ginseng wine, which is far stronger than the infrequent glasses of wine to which I am accustomed. I felt it was incumbent for me to reciprocate Mr. Chang's gesture, so I rose to deliver my speech of humble gratitude and to propose a toast thanking all those who had helped in the effort to locate my sisters and arrange my family reunion and tour of North Korea.

My dinner partners proved to be both heavy drinkers and generous hosts who pressed glasses of domestic whiskey, beer and wine on me whenever one or another of them needed a refill. The food arrived in great abundance and variety, all highly seasoned in the North Korean fashion. My stomach was unfit for the onslaught of liquor, and I had been away from spicy foods for decades. Usually, I had a simple salad, a small steak and tea for dinner each night. I managed the meal without embarrassing myself, and I was quite thankful when Mr. Kim said he thought we should be getting to bed because he had a busy day planned. I allowed him to escort me to my room without asking what he had in store.

*

July 7, my third day in Pyongyang, dawned clear and cloudless, the nicest weather so far. When Mr. Kim and I emerged from the hotel after breakfast, we found our black Mercedes Benz 220 awaiting us at the front door. We turned immediately into Chollima Street, Pyongyang's broadest main thoroughfare and proceeded directly to the Tower of the *Juche Idea*, arriving at the stroke of ten o'clock. As always, a guide was on hand to greet us.

As we made our way around the tower, the guide explained its symbolic value: "The Tower of the *Juche Idea* mirrors the will and desire of the Korean People to advance under the Juche Idea rallied close around the great leader, President Kim Il-sung, and the dear leader, Comrade Kim Jong-il."

When we had gotten about halfway around the tower, I noticed that several more black Mercedes 220 s had pulled up. From these alighted the six Korean-American professors I had met in Beijing. We exchanged quick "Hellos" and "See you soons" in passing as our respective guides hurried us along in opposite directions.

The next stop that morning was the *Arch of Triumph*, at the foot of Moran Hill. This was the place, according to the latest in our series of waiting guides, "where our great leader, President Kim Il-sung, first extended his greetings to his people after his triumphant return to Pyongyang in October, 1945, after he liberated his country through the victorious anti-Japanese revolutionary struggle he had waged for twenty years."

I then learned that the arch had been unveiled on the occasion of Kim's seventieth birthday, on April 15,

1982. It is sixty meters high and fifty-two meters wide an imposing architectural edifice made by joining over 10,500 pieces of choice granite. The arch itself is twenty-seven meters high and eighteen meters wide, and it is framed with seventy azalea flowers each symbolizing one of the president's seventy years. The columns display the dates "1925" and "1945", the beginning and end years of Kim's struggle to replace Japanese rule.

The guide concluded, "This arch, built because of our people's unanimous wishes, is the great monument to our era; it will emblazon our great leader's revolutionary exploits forever."

At four o'clock in the afternoon, following lunch and a nap, we visited the Korean Central Historical Museum. Mr. Kim explained that office workers in North Korea take a three-hour lunch break between noon and three before returning to work until seven in the evening. This, to once again explain why the streets and the museum were so devoid of human presence.

The museum displays provide a record of the Korean people from the paleolithic age through the commemoration of the Independence Movement of March 1, 1919, the first—unsuccessful—attempt to throw off Japanese rule. (The attempt began in the farthest part of South Korea, though it did spread and take hold in the North. The result of the effort was further repression, but the first true Korean anti-imperialist revolutionaries fled to China, where they were joined by the teen-aged Kim Il-sung in 1925.)

The three main halls were each devoted to a separate era. The first was given over to the primitive age, the second to the middle ages, and the third was devoted to the fight against foreign invaders including but not only the Japanese. The guided tour of the displays, and particularly the relics and materials associated with the anti-imperialist phase, took over two hours.

Donald Chung, M.D.

*

Without stopping for dinner, Mr. Kim and I proceeded to Kim Il-sung Square to attend a "Soiree of the Working People in Pyongyang." This was given mainly in honor of the journalists attending the world conference, but odds and sods like me and the six professors were drawn in, as were over 6,000 local people, mainly young men and women.

The mass-dance program opened at eight-thirty to the music of the Korean People's Army Band. Most of the introductory songs were new revolutionary compositions which I did not know, but the program included one popular song of my era, "Nodulgangbyon", which brought a mist to my eyes. The band-accompanied choir sang for the first fifteen minutes, then the crowd filling the square arranged itself in circles of twenty or thirty men and women each and began to dance something like a polka to strong Korean dance rhythms.

When the master of ceremonies urged all the foreign guests to take part in the soiree, Mr. Kim immediately pulled me down from the bleachers and pushed me right into one of the dancing circles, where he found me a partner, who gripped my hand tightly in her own. I had hoped this might happen since I thought it would provide me with an opportunity to mingle with ordinary North Koreans.

I was quite nervous at first. It was all I could do to watch my partner's feet and try to follow her steps without falling down. After about ten minutes, I was able to catch the rhythm without looking down, and I felt myself gradually relax, but only to a point. With my fear and vertigo now under control, I was able to look directly at my partner.

354

She was a beautiful young lady with classic features and fine, light skin. She wore the traditional Korean white summer dress and just a hint of make-up. I took her to be in her mid-twenties, but I also noticed that her hands were as rough and strong as had been my sisters'.

Despite my years-long regimen of golf and vigorous sets of tennis several days each week, I was soon breathing heavily from the exertion of the fast, non-stop dancing. When I could catch my breath, I shouted exultantly above the music, "I just came from the United States of America and found my sisters after thirty three years of being separated. They came to meet me at Pyongyang Airport, and we hugged each other and cried."

The young lady danced on without a word in response, her unchanging bland smile pasted to her lovely, unfeeling face. She reminded me of the three stewardesses on the flight from Beijing. They also had shown no emotion in their otherwise pleasantly-composed faces. I also noticed that this woman's face was not even damp from perspiration despite the warmth of the evening and the vigorous exercise.

My face was pouring sweat, and I could feel that my light summer shirt was pasted to my chest and back with sweat. However, the music went on and on without a hint of letting up—for nearly ninety minutes!

I desperately wanted to stop dancing, but I was quite frankly held in my place by a powerful irrational fear of the consequences of going against the current, of angering the authorities I was convinced were monitoring my every move, my every thought. I kept dancing despite physical pain and the cardiologist's classic fear of succumbing to a coronary incident.

When the music finally wound down and the dancing stopped, I staggered to find a seat. Only then did I notice through the haze of my exhaustion and hunger that none of my fellow dancers was sweating or breathing hard. I suppose they had been conditioned to such physical feats by a lifetime of similar events.

The program ended at nine o'clock when the crowd obediently dispersed on cue. After stopping by at a tailorshop to try on a suit I had ordered the day before, Mr. Kim and I returned to the hotel for a long, soothing shower. A needed late dinner was served at eleven-fifteen by our regular waitress, who had remained on duty with the entire dining room staff. They had had to remain on duty to serve a warm dinner to all the hotel's exhausted guests.

*

It was drizzling outside when I awoke early on the morning of July 8. Since it was doubtful that I would be walking in the park across Chollima Street from the hotel, I turned on the radio for the first time since my arrival. I found only two stations broadcasting on the middle band. The one I settled on had the Mansuda Orchestra playing a piece called "Our Belief is One", which was followed by song after song on the revolutionary theme.

I was still listening to this station when Mr. Kim arrived and asked if I would enjoy having a haircut. It did seem like a good idea, so I accepted. Then I told Kim, "You know, this is the first time since my arrival that you've asked me what *I* want." He smiled in response, then volunteered information about himself. He told me that he lived in Pyongyang with his wife and two young children, but that he had been staying in the hotel, only two doors down from mine, and had not had a moment's time to see them since my arrival.

After breakfast, we dashed across Chollima Street, through the rain, to the Changgwang-won Health

356

Complex. This lavish building stands facing Chollima Street on the edge of Potong River Park, upon the bank of the Potong River. The building houses many and varied public and private baths, hairdressing salons, soft-drink stands and other amenities aimed at promoting the health and cultural inculcation of Pyongyang's working people. The complex is open each day from eight in the morning until eleven at night. As usual, we found the vast building empty but for a group of swimming pre-schoolers, for this was a workday. Mr. Kim proudly showed me the indoor Olympic-sized pool, with its over 2,000-seat viewing stands, as well as numerous indoor and outdoor public swimming pools. He told me that the public and individual baths can and often do accommodate up to 10,000 people a day. The place was overwhelming and impressive, perhaps because it was empty of people.

The barbershop, which was clean and surprisingly modern, was staffed by young ladies, all in their twenties. One of them offered me a chair and then went to work, carefully clipping my hair. Following a vigorous shampoo, the young barber shaved the hair on the back of my neck. Next, she covered my face with soothing, aromatic hot towels and massaged my head, shoulders and arms, first with her hands and then with an electric vibrator. The treatment was topped off with a silky-smooth shave and some blow-dried hair styling.

The whole treatment consumed an hour, during which I took the opportunity to extract a bit of information about her job. Though reluctant to provide details about herself, she told me that she treated six or fewer customers on an average day, for which she was paid a good living wage by the government. I was charged only three won, which was equivalent to $1.50. Thus, on a full day, she took in the equivalent of $9.00, or $54 for a full work week. I estimated that she took in, at most, 512

357

won or $216 per month. I did not ask what her monthly
wage was, but I was sure it was far less than 512 won.

Our next stop was the city's indoor ice arena, just
a block down Chollima Street from the health complex.
Like the health complex, it had been opened on April 15.
1982, President Kim Il-sung's seventieth birthday. The
arena is conical in shape and of the following heroic
proportions: 25,650 square meters, 63.5 meters high and
135 meters in diameter. The building seats 6,000
spectators and is kept at a constant 18-20-degrees
Celsius the year around for spectator comfort. The ice is
maintained in the temperature range of 3-5-degrees
Celsius. I saw only one young boy on the ice during the
time I was there.

The last stop of the morning was the likewise
impressive Pyongyang Metro, which was first opened in
September, 1973 and completed in 1978 to a total
route of thirty-two kilometers served by fifteen
exquisitely decorated stations. Mr. Kim and I were led on
a tour of the Kwangbok Station by one of the Metro
managers. From there, we decended to the platform by
means of a hundred-meter-long escalator and rode on the
clean, bright train to several other stations. The
lighting—chandeliers bolstered by recessed incandescent
ceiling fixtures—complemented the architectural forms
and decorations. Sculptures and mosaics, murals and
reliefs filled the walls, and the floors and pillars of each
station were clad in patterned marble granite. The entire
Metro routing scheme is aimed at carrying huge numbers
of people quickly between home and work, but also to
provide easy access to. museums, theaters, stadiums,
parks and other communal recreation centers. The air in
the underground is as clean and fresh as it is on the
surface. The manager told me with evident pride that the
system carries an average of 28-30,000 passengers each
day, and over 40,000 riders on holidays, which did not

begin to approach the designed-in upper limits. Trains averaged 37-45 miles per hour. The fare, I was told, was the equivalent of ten cents for each ride. Not surprisingly, this metro system was the one North Korean achievement that truly impressed me, for I was once—just once—an inmate of the New York subway system.

The evening's entertainment was a "revolutionary" opera entitled "The Flower girl." My program notes indicated that the story was based on a classic of the same title which had been written and first staged in 1930, during the period of anti-Japanese revolution led by Kim Ol-sung. Mr. Kim told me that this original North Korean opera had been performed on many East European stages. However, no mention was made that the whole story line was based on a folk tale hundreds of years old.

*

After dinner that evening, I met a Korean Japanese businessman in the hotel lobby while I was waiting for Mr. Kim to return from a trip to the men's room. During the course of a brief casual conversation, this experienced traveler told me, "Dr. Chung, you can make a phone call from your hotel room to your family in America. The best time to call is after midnight." This was joyous news to me.

Time moved extra-slow that night, but the longer arm of the table clock beside my lonely bed finally moved beyond the midnight hour. I lifted the telephone receiver in my sweaty hand and dialed the operator as my heart pounded a rapid tattoo in my chest. I dimly realized that I was hyperventilating, but nothing short of death was going to keep me from this call.

Donald Chung, M.D.

A woman's voice sounded in my ear. "This is the operator. May I help you, Dr. Chung?"

My voice quavered its rehearsed response, "May I place a long-distance call to my family?"

"Where are they, sir?"

"In America." And I blurted out the area code and phone number before she could protest.

"Dr. Chung, would you please hang up and wait? I'll call you back as soon as I have made the connection."

Time stood still as I anxiously awaited the sound of my loved ones' voices. At long last, the phone on the bedside table issued a long, jolting ring.

"Dr. Chung," the operator began, "your wife is on the line."

"Hello! Hello?" I heard myself shouting, as if that would close the gulf of miles. "Young-ja? Hello? Can you hear me? Are you there? I am in my hotel room in Pyongyang. Hello?"

At first, I only could hear the noise of static, then I heard a distant, panicky voice break through. "When are you coming out from there?"

"I will see you soon, Young-ja. Everything is okay." The part of my mind that compares things dredged up a clear recollection of the first time I had ever spoken to Young-ja, when I had called her in Seoul from St. Louis. A week before I left Long Beach for North Korea, I had called a friend in Seoul, and he had sounded as if he was speaking on a phone in the next room. However, the part of me that cares for things could not have been more pleased to hear anything that sounded remotely like my wife. I am certain that my joy was far surpassed by her relief at hearing my words.

I paid $18 for the privilege of yelling "Hello? Hello?" across the ether at my wife for three minutes that night. No money was ever better spent.

Ironically, a call the next morning from a government official in Pyongyang was of no better quality than my call to California.

(The postcards I mailed daily from Pyongyang arrived home two to three weeks after my return from North Korea and China.)

*

The morning tour on July 9 began at the Museum of the Korean Revolution, which stands on Mansudae Hill on a piece of ground measuring 240,000 square meters. The sum of the ninety exhibit halls is 60,000 square meters. The separate halls are organized around the stages of the revolution: the anti-imperialist, anti-Japanese struggle; the anti-imperialist, anti-feudal democratic struggle following the ouster of the Japanese in 1945; the initial transition to socialism; the Great War for the Liberation of the Fatherland (1950-1953); laying the foundations for socialism in the post-war years; and the struggle for completion of socialist industrialization.

According to our guide, "The Museum of the Korean Revolution is a university and a palace for education in the *Juche Idea*; a place where you will learn about the immortal revolutionary ideas and profound revolutionary theories of the respected and beloved leader, his wise unique leadership which so admirably implemented these ideas and theories in all fields of the revolution and all phases of reconstruction, his rich experience gained in this arduous and complex struggle, and his lofty character."

We visited only the first twenty-seven halls of the museum. These were devoted to mementos and materials relating to the revolutionary history of Kim Il-sung, "The great revolutionary leader who organized and led the glorious anti-Japanese revolutionary struggle to victory and was successful in attaining the historic goal of national liberation." The fact that Korean independence was the result of the Anglo-American victory over The Empire of Japan in the Pacific and Southeast Asia was not mentioned.

Following a break for lunch, we viewed a film commemorating Kim Il-sung's seventieth birthday, "Victorious Great Commemoration."

Nearly two hours of the afternoon were devoted to a stultifying lecture delivered to me alone by one of the vice-chairmen of the Fatherland Unification Committee. He set about explaining how agriculture, industry and standards of living had all improved in the thirty-eight years following Korean liberation. Agricultural production, which aggregated 9,500,000 tons in 1946, was expected to rise to 15,000,000 tons annually by 1990; the tax system had been abolished in 1962; education was compulsory through the eleventh grade; the number of college graduates would increase to 1.1 million out of a population of 17 million by 1986; and universal free medical care had been available since January, 1953. According to the lecturer, four master plans were in current operation: reclamation of tidal lands on the west coast; an increase in arable lands throughout the nation from one-fifth the total land area to one-quarter by 1990; construction of canals connecting the east and west coasts; and construction of numerous new hydroelectric plants.

After listening to this long lecture, I was fed an excellent and well-deserved dinner and sent on my way. My last full day in Pyongyang had finally ended.

*

Mr. Kim and I left for Ok-bong's home in Myongchun, North Hamgyong Province, on the ten o'clock evening train, July 9, 1983, five days after my arrival in Pyongyang. A family visit had of course been the first priority on my personal agenda when I had made out my request for a visa some months earlier. I was filled to brimming with words relating the deeds of Kim Il-sung, and sick to death of political orientation lectures and traipsing through the heroically-proportioned, bizarrely-depopulated showcases of the people's revolution.

Mr. Kim insisted upon carrying my bags along with his own as he led me briskly to the rear coach of the train, an exquisitely clean sleeping car in which each compartment was designed for four passengers. Mr. Kim told me that I would have the compartment to myself as he had been booked into a similar compartment next door. He then set bottled beer and soft drinks he had brought from the hotel and left me to myself.

CHAPTER THIRTY-TWO

By four o'clock in the morning of July 10 I could sleep no longer. I arose, dressed, and went into the corridor, bent on finding out where we were. I was anxious to at least get a passing glimpse of Songjin, for somehow it had become extremely important that I retrace insofar as it was possible the route I had taken as I fled to the south.

Gazing from the fast-moving train I saw I was far too early. At about five o'clock the train raced through the port city of Hungnam where, in 1950, the ship carrying me south had stopped to board a new contingent of ROK soldiers.

At Hungnam the train veered almost due north, following the eastern coastline. Since I had failed to pack a map, I had to rely on a hazy memory to tell me where we were. The speeding train made it even more difficult to recognize anything racing backwards as the train raced forward. I was not even sure of the train's route, but since I had never been this far south on land, I realized there would be no familiar landmark to give me guidance.

Mr. Kim emerged from his compartment at around seven and asked me why I was standing there, watching the eastern sea. I could have told him I was there for the view, but I decided to hold nothing back: "I'm eager to see Songjin as we pass it. I left North Korea from there thirty-three years ago." Mr. Kim silently nodded his head and returned to his compartment. We could never be friends, but I sensed that he had finally come to see some things through my eyes.

The train entered the outskirts of Songjin at around eight o'clock. The town had been pretty well destroyed during the war; there was nothing on its site but some ruined buildings. However, a new town, Kim Chaek City, had risen on the southern arm of the bay. This was a new, highly industrialized monument to the *Juche Idea*, but I had no interest in it. It evoked no memories as did even the ruined remnant of Songjin. I aimed my 35mm camera and took many pictures of the ruins as we clattered past.

We reached Kilchu, where I had joined the volunteer youth group and where I had also last seen Father, at about ten o'clock. We were nearly eleven hours out of Pyongyang and had reached our terminus. (I later compared notes with other travelers in North Korea and we discovered that we had all traveled long distances across the interior only at night. Speculation ran heavily toward this being a ploy by the government to mask the underdevelopment in the interior regions of the country. But, since it was always too dark to check our beliefs, our views remain speculative.)

Mr. Kim piled our bags across his shoulders and under his arms and waddled off down the corridor in my wake.

*

As soon as my feet touched the platform, I recognized Moon-hee coming toward me. Mr. Kim had prepared me. He told me that Moon-hee and her family had been brought to Ok-bong's home in Myongchun with her family the day before and then she came back to Kilchu by car in order to accompany me the rest of the way to the reunion.

I must admit that I was able to recognize my sister only because of the photo she had sent with a letter that had reached me only a week before I left Long Beach. I was happy to see that she was wearing a *han-*

bok, the old-style white silk blouse covered by a black scarf.

My eldest sister was now fifty-nine years old and was tiny, weighing less than one hundred pounds. My mind instantly flashed backward to the countless times she had cared for me when I was a child, while Mother was out scraping together a living. I had not seen my beloved older sister since she left home in 1948. We hugged one another tightly and cried our eyes out in joy and sorrow.

We had had to leave the train at Kilchu because there was no station in Myongchun, where Ok-bong lived. A county official joined us, explaining that he was our host and would be seeing to my stay in Myongchun. He directed us out of the station, where we found a black Volvo waiting for us. I climbed into the rear seat after Moon-hee, while the official climbed in beside the driver. Mr. Kim packed our luggage into a smaller second car and climbed into it for the twenty-five mile drive.

The brief drive through Kilchu was another heart-wrenching experience. Father's face loomed large before me on every hand. Gone were all the old animosities, the bitternesses, the pain. Intently I sought the spot whereon I took my final leave of him. Somehow I felt, seeing that long-abandoned place, I might recapture a bit of Father to take with me to the reunion. Finding no familiar sign, I sorrowfully acknowledged to myself it perhaps was better thus. I could not undo the past and a ghost is not always welcome at a festive occasion. But somehow I felt unburdened, uplifted, for I had come at long last to terms with accepting Father for what he was and no longer would I try to force him into an alien mold.

The road between Kilchu and Myongchun was unpaved and exceedingly rough, particularly where ruts had been gouged after a recent rainstorm. Repair crews were at work down the entire length of the road and I also saw many farmers working their plots under the hot sun and in the humid air. It looked to me as if they were all using traditional farming methods.

I had not come all this way merely to gape at the scenery, but I found myself staring longingly out the window, as if the peaceful bucolic scenes were a call from a distant past. This was the same road I had tramped in ice and snow during my harrowing, lonely walk south from Chu-ul. I had seen hundreds of refugees mired in snow and freezing mud, many dead or dying by the wayside. As we now topped hills or crossed streams, my revitalized memory leaped into the past, overlaying long ago scenes of privation upon the empty roadway, scenes I had thought the flow of time had long since washed from my being. Since this was summer, everything I saw was green and growing; life replacing death with each blink of my eye, but the effect was eerie and disturbing, even to the absence of the familiar thatched roofs of olden times, now replaced even in this remote area with brightly-colored tile.

We reached Ok-bong's house at noontime. It was in the center of Myongchun, to all appearances a remote but prosperous farm town. I was ecstatic to have finally reached the ultimate goal of this long and arduous journey—the reunion with my long-lost family. I was also supremely relieved to be out of the Pyongyang showcase, soon to be surrounded by ordinary people.

The families of both of my elder sisters greeted me as I stepped from the car. Except for Ok-bong's husband, the former security policeman she had married in 1948, and two cousins who had come from their homes near Chu-ul, all my relatives were strangers. Still I was overjoyed to be with them. I was introduced to each and every one of them and got right down to the serious business of remembering which name belonged to which body. Since many of the new faces and names belonged to children, there was both joy and laughter in the impossible matching-up game.

It was also impossible to tell these humble, inquisitive relatives very much about my life in America; the necessary frames of reference did not exist in their quiet lives. Also, I did not want to seem to brag, so I simply conveyed the facts that my family and I were comfortable and secure, and that we lived in a nice house.

As we sat down to partake of what turned out to be a raucous, joyous family lunch I realized that I could have been happier only had Mother been sitting by my side.

After eating, I was led to a bedroom so I could take a much needed nap. Later that afternoon, Ok-bong told me, we would visit Mother's grave.

*

The county-owned car carrying my sisters and me could go only halfway up the hill on which Mother was buried, so we walked upward to the summit through fields of ripening corn. The mountain was not high, but from its peak we could look southeastward, out over Myongchun and a vast section of bountiful farmland beyond.

But I beheld a far vaster landscape—true a landscape of the mind—but one that was just as real, etched on my soul by time's mordant acids. I saw the cobblestoned streets of Harbin, where horses clattered through the city. I saw Harbin's sunlit Sungari River where on summer days I had watched the festive boat races and at times fished both for food and sport. I saw the Russian bandsmen, dressed in their dark, gold-braided uniforms, serenading each departing and returning cruise ship. Swiftly the scene shifted to the overcrowded refugee freight cars, one of which was

369

carrying Mother, my sisters, and me from Harbin southward to our native Korea. I saw the crowd of Korean refugees, ordered from the train, walking up the grade of the mountainous Taebek Plateau which the engine could not maneuver, pulling its overloaded cars. I heard again the hundreds of jubilant Korean voices daring to sing Korean folksongs, long prohibited in their Japanese-imposed captivity, as the refugees climbed alongside the train.

My memory film then froze on the arrival of the refugee train at the town of Chu-ul, our destination in northeastern Korea, which was my mother's home.

Once again, here in Myongchun, I had symbolically come home, for though this was not my childhood home, it was where Mother awaited me. Though the promise of returning in three days had stretched to three decades, the promise had been kept. I had come home to my precious mother.

In an oval grave about ten feet in diameter, Mother awaited me. There was a growth of well-tended, lush green grass growing over her. At one end of the oval was a tiny cement marker, about three feet high. Upon it were inscribed Korean *han-geul* characters bearing the name, "Kim Ki-bok." To the right of Mother's name were the dates, "July 5, 1904-September 19, 1979." More characters to the left of the name bore a statement which staggered me: "Owner of Grave: Chung Dong-kyu."

I have never felt a deeper, more profound sorrow in my entire life. I fell to my knees and clasped the stone to my chest, crying copiously and whimpering, "Mother! I could not keep The Promise. I could not return to you in three days. But I am back now, beside you."

Tears flowed freely from my eyes. I felt the warmth of the sun, smelled the odor of cultivated soil, heard the rustling breeze sing through the treetops, touched the softness of the grass carpet beneath my knees. The sun-warmed stone touching my arms and chest and cheeks and Mother's ethereal presence flooded over me the realization that I was as close to my beginnings as I would ever be again. The seeming futility of my lifelong dreams was dissipated in this moment's fulfillment.

I don't know which of these occurrences or what combination caused it, but there opened a great wound in my soul and from it there flushed out the disease that had so long afflicted me, impairing my every waking moment. The essence of my being was wholly cleansed as I knelt over the grave of the woman who had borne me.

"I am back, Mother. Back beside you. There has not been a moment in all these thirty-three years when you were not with me. The thought of you gave me the courage to survive and go on, to become a man you would have been proud to call 'Son.' You were there, Mother, leading me on, pulling me onward whenever I fell into despair, whenever I entered the valley of the shadow. We have been apart, Mother, and we will never meet again in this life. But you have been one with me through the whole of my life, when I was here with you or far across the seas and beyond the gulf of time. And I know, Mother, that you felt my presence upon this earth all the days you lived among us. I know you feel me now, here kneeling over you."

I threw back my head and stared into the endless cap of blue sky. I felt, once again, the gentle summer breeze blowing up from the valley and through the trees. I saw renewal in the distant green fields and in the young faces I had first seen over this day's lunch. And then I told Mother about my life.

I told Mother of my last meeting with Father, of the horrible freezing flight to Songjin, and the yet-more-horrid journey at sea. I told her of dead and dying soldiers, and of a years-long fear so profound as to be impossible to share even with my own memory. I told her of the soul-crushing poverty I had faced after setting forth into the world from my safe, dull army sinecure. I told her of my empty-seeming dreams, and how I had prevailed over my disastrous circumstances through unremitting luck and hard work.

I told Mother of the essence of my mission in this world—the healing of lives. I told her how each life I saved or made less-difficult was a dedication and a rededication to an ethic I had learned at her breast—how I literally evoked a memory of her each time I confronted a new patient.

I recounted to her that I retained a powerful memory of each small thing she had done to ease my transition from infancy to the frontier of adulthood. I had to tell her how profoundly I felt and treasured each tiny sacrifice she had made in my behalf.

"I have two sons of my own now, Mother. They are teenagers, partly Korean and partly American. They are good boys. We live in a nice home and I make a comfortable living. I am married to a Korean woman, from the south. We live in two worlds; we are Korean, but we are also American. I believe we fit in well. But we have not forgotten our culture or the old ways.

"I so wanted to show you proof of my achievements, Mother. I am so sorry I could not have come sooner. I was afraid, and I was naive. I was not always a man. Now I have only this grave, this stone and my memories.

"Oh, how I wish I could have seen your face just one last time before you left us!"

Thusly did I fulfill The Promise.

CHAPTER THIRTY-THREE

When we returned to Ok-bong's home, I told my sisters that I thought Mother's grave marker had been recently installed; did they know why? Ok-bong replied that the family had assumed I had perished on my way to the south or in the war, so had erected a grave marker in my honor in 1953. The original marker had designated Ok-bong as the owner of the grave. As soon as my sisters learned that I was alive, they had ordered a new stone incised with the inscriptions I had read earlier. I was designated as the grave's owner because I was the family patriarch.

I then asked how Mother had died.

She had begun having severe abdominal pains in the winter of 1978 and was subsequently diagnosed as having cancer of the liver, a common cause of death in Korea. My sisters also told me that she never once accepted modern medical treatment, medicines or pain-killers, though she did dose herself with the same sort of herbal concoctions and brews she had taken all her life. I suspect that she also resorted to magical incantations, another lifelong habit.

Mother lived on into September, 1979, "praying to see you again and asking that all would be made well for you," Ok-bong told me.

Both sisters told me over and again how much Mother had missed me. "She even slept with her head pointed towards the south," one of them told me, "just so she could be closer to you, for she was convinced that you had survived the journey and the war and were living in the south unable to return home."

Moon-hee told me that Mother had asked to be buried in Chu-ul, where most of our ancestors lay, but that the day of the funeral had been heavy with rain—"as if the heavens were crying for this mother, who had waited twenty-nine years, until her last breath, to see her only son return." It was impossible to carry her casket over the muddy, washed-out roads between Myongchun and Chu-ul, so a gravesite had been chosen atop the nearby mountain. Even then, the truck carrying the casket had been able to climb only part way up the steep road, so my brothers-in-law and nephews had heaved it to their shoulders and struggled upward along the slippery rainswept path to the gravesite. The grave marker with my name on it had been brought down from the empty grave at Chu-ul, inscribed with Mother's name and dates, and positioned over her head.

*

As the day wore on, I immersed myself in the joy of learning about my large family.

Jung-hee's husband was a fisherman who was at sea for many months at a time and home for many months following each journey. He was on a fishing expedition just then, so I would not be meeting him when I traveled to Jung-hee's home in a few days.

Moon-hee's husband, who was visiting with me in Myongchun, was director of a government-owned apple and pear orchard. I was not sure if he even knew that Moon-hee had been married twice before her troubled and troubling departure to become a prison guard in 1948.

Ok-bong's husband had retired from the Security Police years before to become a farmer near Myongchun. He was the current manager of the county farm-produce storage facilities, a very responsible job. Ok-bong's oldest son was an electrician and her second son was a People's Army officer.

I was assured that the family was doing quite well and that I had great cause for pride in being its patriarch. And so I did!

*

A special musical program in my honor was scheduled for six o'clock that evening at the local junior high school. I arrived to find well over a hundred boys and girls lined up to greet me.

The program, which was presented by the music and arts clubs of five local schools, was an hour long and very touching. The students were all dressed in their finery. The girls wore very little make-up, for their cheeks were naturally rosy and their lips a uniformly healthy red, but each of them was festooned with gaily-colored ribbons in her hair. Seeing these girls transported me for a moment to a time in 1947 when Chun Hae-jean, my first puppy-love, had danced the monk's dance at Chongjin Medical-Technical School.

The band played, the children sang and danced, and a mini-drama was presented to the utter delight of scores of proud parents. I was particularly delighted to see two of my nephews, Ok-bong's younger boys, participating in the program. Their looks of concentration mixed with smiles of pleasure and relieved accomplishment overfilled my heart with boundless joy.

When it was time to leave, I found all the students lined up by the school gate to see me off. They clustered around me, each and every one of them reaching to clutch or merely brush my hand. I heard their little voices say, over and over, with genuine enthusiasm, "Dr. Chung! Please come back. Come see us again!"

Ah, how I wish it was so easy. How I wish I could experience the joy of being among those children whenever I wanted. How I wish that people could touch one another without the politics of nations and the machinations of governments to keep us apart. If only my medical healing art included the ability to heal the whole world's ills.

The next stop was an official welcoming party at the largest government-owned restaurant in town. There were many people there: my two sisters and their husbands; one of my cousins from Chu-ul; Mr. Kim; the vice-chairman of the county unit of the Workers' Party; and several other officials. The table was set with scores of dishes filled with a vast variety of food. I had never seen so many Korean dishes, did not know what some of them were. I did see that many of the foods placed before me were my old favorites, many of which Mother had cooked especially for me on special occasions: bean-curd soup, steamed hairy crabs, seasoned cuttlefish, and much, much more. These were not the fanciest dishes brought forth at this feast, but each carried a special, fond memory of Mother, so they were the best.

What a thoughtful way to cap a day devoted entirely to the profound memories of the past!

*

July 11, 1983, was a cloudless Monday. The entire family—about a dozen Chung relatives—gathered at mid-morning and set out, along with Mr. Kim and five or six town and county officials, for a hike and a picnic on the slopes of Mount Chilpo, one of North Hamgyong Province's most-scenic preserves.

The park is only twenty kilometers southeast of Myongchun, but it took our Volvos and two trucks a gut-wrenching hour to negotiate the ill-kept county road system. On the way, I noticed that every isolated building had its bright-hued tiled roof, the thatched roofs even here seemed to be gone for good. I also saw that most of the fieldworkers were women, and that both men and women had been called out to do the heavy road repair following recent heavy rains.

We met our guide at the office at the foot of the mountain and began our hike as soon as we passed a bloc of government-owned flats and a rest house. We had to climb to about seven hundred meters above sea-level to reach the picnic area and it took us over an hour to get there. All the women were burdened with loads of food and eating implements. Some of the old ways die hard, I suppose, for none of the men carried anything during the grueling climb. However, everyone, including all the women, reached the picnic area long before I dragged myself to the objective. I explained to them, that I had often stopped to take pictures of the spectacular scenery or consult with the guide—but this was only partly my reason for being last!

Once at the picnic site, the entire family lined up for a round of picture-taking, which we did to the harmonica accompaniment of one of my nephews. I did not recognize the tune the boy played, but it stirred something within me—rousing long-dormant memories and a bittersweet feeling of home. The air was fresh and cool under the tall, stately evergreen trees, which swayed and rustled as an occasional breeze swept up from the plain at our feet. The air was suffused with the fresh odor of wild pine. It was otherwise still and peaceful on that mountain and I would have been content to live out my days there if it could remain ever so.

Following lunch, the group turned to singing and dancing. By far the happiest, most-exuberant family dance unit was composed of the three Chungs: Dong-kyu, Moon-hee and Ok-bong. We gaily divested ourselves of our extra decades and danced and sang as we had when we were children growing up.

377

Donald Chung, M.D.

On the leisurely stroll down the mountain, I noticed that Moon-hee kept bending over to pick up aromatic seeds from the pathway. I asked her what she was doing but she would only smile impishly and tell me to wait and see.

We reached the park office at about one-thirty and were served lunch in the rest house. After we had eaten again, the park director invited all who cared to to take an hour-long nap or do as we chose.

I opted for the nap, as did Moon-hee, and the guide led us to a cabin with two neatly-made beds. The windows were open to admit a cooling breeze, and a crock of cold mountain mineral water was set out on the table. Through the open window came the plaintive notes of songbirds rustling about in the branches overhead.

I lazily removed my shoes and wiggled my tired toes in the breeze, then dropped my head gently to the pillow. Moon-hee pulled up a chair and took my hand in hers, then told me to feel free to sleep, that she just wanted to relive old times for a few moments.

I tried to sleep, but my mind took me back to August, 1945, when I awoke on the morning after my emergency appendectomy. My hand had been held then too, by Mother. But I also remembered for the first time that the teen-aged Moon-hee had also held my hand that day, to relieve Mother to undertake other errands and duties around that understaffed hospital ward.

I woke with a start a half-hour later to find that Moon-hee had placed around my neck a woven garland laced with the aromatic seeds she had earlier picked up on the mountain trail. She had often done that for me when she took me for walks around Chu-ul or up to see our grandmother at Taehyang.

I was not the only one with memories and|feelings of love to express.

*

In the evening, after returning home by the same bumpy road we had taken to Mount Chilpo, we all gathered in Ok-bong's home to watch the government's only television station. I learned that the one station offered programming only between five and eleven each weekday evening, nothing on Saturday and from eight in the morning until eleven at night on Sundays. The programs were mainly news, weather, sports and a heavy schedule of lectures, plus a variety of musical programs, most of them revolutionary in nature. There were also some Chinese and Russian films with dubbed Korean soundtracks.

I was surprised to learn that there was a weekly thirty-minute English-language class on the television and, furthermore, that English was studied in junior high school. Since it was about time I began giving out the gifts I had brought from America, I decided to give Ok-bong's third and fourth sons, both junior-high-schoolers, the two English-Korean dictionaries I had brought. They were both beside themselves with pleasure, both because of the books and because they could finally try their fledgling English out on a "real American."

I opened my trunk and distributed the bounty of America throughout that happy house. I had been careful to avoid ostentation, which was undoubtedly the best choice. The presents included Seiko self-winding watches, solar-powered calculators, cameras, the English-Korean dictionaries, electric irons, neckties, shirts, blouses, skirts, cigarettes, chocolates for the adults and hard candy for the youngest children. Unfortunately, I came up a bit short, so had to issue several IOUs.

*

379

July 12 was a Tuesday, the first day of my second week in North Korea. Mr. Kim told me to take the day off and spend it with my family.

I took the time to amaze the crowd with my magic Polaroid camera, and even encouraged the use of much of my hoard of Polaroid film to satisfy boundless curiosity and a universal family desire to have everyone's photo taken with everyone else in endless permutations. We spent hours keeling over in gales of laughter. I gave away nearly all of the Polaroids, but covered myself with dozens of 35mm photographs to take home with me. Ok-bong's sons, both in their self-important teens, became quite adept with the 35mm camera in very little time and their efforts were among the best in my collection.

Ok-bong's husband approached me during a lull and reminded me that it was customary to move a grave, if it needed moving, seven years after the body had been interred, to allow the corpse to completely decay. He asked, in behalf of my sisters, that I consider returning to Myongchun in September, 1984, to take part in moving Mother's remains to Chu-ul in fulfillment of her final wishes. He mentioned that the family was depending upon me because I was now the owner of the grave.

We whiled away the afternoon comparing North Korean prices and the availability of goods with those in America. As usual, I held back. These people seemed happy, and I did not want to get them to dreaming impossible dreams or in any way to destroy the rhythms of their lives, at least no more than I already had. I feared that anything beyond my mere presence and the simple trinkets I had dispersed would be destructive or, at least, irresponsible.

Mr. Kim returned at five in the evening to tell me that my stay with my sisters and their families had come to an end, that we had to be on our way to Chongjin so that I could address the faculty of Chongjin Medical College.

The time had flown. I had been in Myongchun for only fifty-three hours, and I had frittered away sixteen of those precious hours in sleep.

Moon-hee and Ok-bong escorted me to the waiting Volvo and clung to my hands in the moments before I had to get in. We said all the right good-byes, but the real communication was passing between our three sets of eyes and along the nerve-endings leading from our fingertips to our hearts.

*

We drove out to the eastern coastal highway and followed it northward—the same road on which I had been part of the mass of refugees fleeing southward thirty-three winters before. The road was still unpaved, and I could see that many of the bridges and steep grades were the same ones I had trudged over during that dark winter week.

I finally asked Mr. Kim why the main roads were unpaved and he told me, simply, that North Koreans do not normally do their traveling by car. He also told me that the national priorities placed many things far above improving the road system. I wondered if the roads were at least in part left alone to foil an invasion from the south, the discussion of which seemed to be a national obsession in much the way the discussion of sports is America's national obsession.

Two hours and seventy-five miles from Myongchun, the Volvo nosed into Chu-ul. I knew that we had a schedule to maintain and would not be stopping, so I craned my neck wildly in search of some familiar view. The section we traversed appeared quite new; clearly it had been added since my departure. I hoped to find some landmark, some way of orienting myself, some small concession to my burning curiosity and sense of loss. But there was nothing that was the least bit familiar; no building, no road, no tree. I had no idea even which way our old house lay. On the way through, I saw that the railroad station was now housed in a large new building, attesting to the growth of the town, but I could not even tell if the new station occupied the same site as the old, the surroundings were that much changed. I snapped a few random pictures, but I don't know what they represent other than a profound sense that time and a changing world are overtaking my keenest memories.

The only old place I could pinpoint was a hill at the northern end of town. It was at the bus stop upon this rise that Mother stood to wave at me as the bus to Chongjin passed from sight when I began my twenty-five-mile commute during my first semester at the medical-technical school in 1946. My mind's eye blinked, however, and that image of Mother was left behind.

The road between Chu-ul and Chongjin was much improved, by far the best highway I had traveled since leaving Pyongyang. It was even paved, and quite wide the last few miles before the port city.

As we neared the city, I could see that despite the late hour school children were pushing little two-wheeled carts, each filled with grass, along the sidewalk. Mr. Kim broke the pattern of my solitude by droning idly into my ear that the children picked the grass to feed to the rabbits they raised as part of their extra-curricular after-school activities. Other children, he told me, were waiting at the school to pick harmful insects off the crop before the rabbits were fed.

CHAPTER THIRTY-FOUR

Mr. Kim and I arrived at the entrance to Chongjin Medical College at about ten o'clock on the morning of July 13 and were greeted there by the Dean of the College, Dr. Kim Ki-ho.

I was interested at the outset to note that the school complex, which occupied the same site as it had in 1950, was now in the center of burgeoning Chongjin rather than at the northwest outskirts. The original and familiar two-story teaching building was still there, but it was a very small part of the campus which aggregated 56,000 square meters of first-story floorspace built on 90,000 square meters of ground. There had been but one tree on the school grounds when I was a student there, the same tree beneath which Moon-hee and I had parted in 1948. To my extreme pleasure, the tree was still there, much taller and much broader.

Dean Kim read a carefully-prepared ten page welcoming speech in which he outlined the history of the school and explained its present situation. He revealed that the college was now divided into six faculties, including basic medical science, clinical medicine, oriental medicine, pharmacology, preventive medicine and oral medicine. Qualifications for entry are eleven years of primary and secondary education and a one-year college-level pre-medical course. All the courses require six years of studies except pharmacology, which confers a degree in five years. At the time of my visit, the school enrolled 3,900 students and had a five-hundred-member teaching faculty—as compared to the less-than-two-hundred students and twenty faculty-members of my era. Dean Kim boasted that sixty-five percent of the M.D.s on the faculty had additional doctoral degrees or are doctoral candidates in medical-related fields. This last was particularly important in that it conformed with the feeling in North Korea that physicians should know far more than they learn through the regular M.D. program; qualifying for advanced degrees is *expected* of North Korea's medical practitioners.

In the twenty-six years preceding my visit, Dr. Kim claimed, the college graduated 16,000 students. The medical college also incorporates a 1,400-bed main teaching hospital which is staffed largely with fourth-through-sixth-year students. In addition, the school provides student staffing at the city and provincial hospitals in and around Chongjin.

Following the conclusion of Dean Kim's briefing, I formally presented the college with a number of American cardiology text, including one of the electrocardiography text I had co-authored with my dear freind, Dr. Edward Chung.

Next on the agenda was a tour of the facilities. Our first stops were at basic-medicine classrooms and the first-year histology lab, where freshmen were learning about the spleen. Fifteen of the thirty were making slides of a spleen by slicing the organ, staining the wafer-thin slices and fixing the specimens to glass slides. The remaining fifteen students were studying the slides, each through his or her own microscope. This reminded me that we had had only two microscopes for my entire class before 1950. I noted that the histology text in use that day had been printed in North Korea. It was on cheap paper and the illustrations were not at all clear. One student had a book of electron-microscope photographs open beside him, and that prompted me to ask Dean Kim if the school made use of electromicroscopy. He replied that such valuable instruments were currently in use only at Pyongyang Medical College and that was where that one book had been fabricated.

We next returned to Dean Kim's office to enjoy a hot cup of tea and other light refreshments. As I was sipping my tea, two distinguished-looking gentlemen of about my age walked into the room and rushed straight up to me, exclaiming, "Oh! Our old friend, Dong-kyu!"

I had expected to meet old classmates this day, but I was nevertheless taken by surprise. These men introduced themselves as Dr. Chang Myung-joon and Dr. Chae Kuk-jin, both of whom I instantly recognized upon hearing their names. Dr. Chang was director of Chongjin City Hospital and Dr. Chae was chairman of Chongjin Medical College's Orthopedic Department. One of them pulled out a group photo of our class, taken on September 1, 1947, the day we advanced to the sophomore class at Chongjin Medical-Technical School, and we studied it intently for some moments, comparing our present selves with those ancient images.

This happy reunion was the work of my estimable host, Dean Kim, who had gone to the trouble of asking around the school and city medical communities until my old classmates had turned up.

At this point, I took leave with Mr. Kim to return to our hotel, ostensibly to prepare for a luncheon that was to be held there in my honor. My departure really gave me an opportunity to rush to a foreign-currency store to purchase appropriate gifts for Dean Kim and Drs. Chang and Chae, as well as several notables who would be attending the luncheon. In addition to the Japanese, American and Chinese luxury items I was seeking, the store also stocked a wide variety of daily essentials. Only U.S. dollars, pounds sterling, Japanese yen and Swiss francs could be used to purchase items in this store, so it was clearly aimed at either raking in cash for foreign exchange or employed by the privileged class of North

Donald Chung, M.D.

Korean functionaries. At Mr. Kim's suggestion, I purchased twelve good Japanese-made ink pens for $5 each.

Lunch was ready to be served as soon as Mr. Kim and I arrived back at the hotel at one-thirty. In addition to Dean Kim and my two former classmates, the meal was attended by the vice-chairman of the North Hamgyong Province People's Committee and the vice-chairman of the Workers' Party of North Hamgyong Province, who made speeches welcoming me back to their city.

We naturally skirted all political references. The two appeared to have some connections with various party organizations and that set me to thinking about how I might view the North Korean political system had I stayed. I am certain that neither of these men had particular Communist leanings when we first met as young students in 1946, and I had no way of measuring the depth of their political sentiments in 1983. It did dawn on me, however, that political systems are ultimately successful if most citizens simply "go along," and not if the bulk of the population is involved in active political foment. Judging myself through the veil of nearly forty years, I can see where I might have just gone along, as I am sure my classmates who stayed at home have done to a greater or lesser degree. I also reminded myself that Koreans, both northerners and southerners, have never known a way of life that has not included some form and some degree of political repression. I had to remember that I had become a pampered American, free to speak my mind chiefly among others of my kind. My frame of reference was one through which these two old friends could never view the world, a world view they could never even conceive.

*

386

Mr. Kim and I left Chongjin at five in the afternoon, following a brief nap. We were again bound for Pyongyang. The first stop was at the huge new railroad station I had seen as we passed through Chu-ul the preceding afternoon. There, we were joined by Choe Ikhwan, my former Chu-ul Junior High School classmate.

We put our heads together long into the evening, comparing notes and impressions and sharing the joys and sorrows of our separate rediscoveries of our homes and homeland. On that part of our journey through time, we shared things I doubt that the closest of friends can share in a lifetime of being together. My former schoolmate related how he had made a special effort to get to a particular fondly-remembered suspension bridge by the Chu-ul hot springs in order to have his picture taken. As he talked of his efforts and success, my heart was doing flip-flops. This was the same bridge I had trod with Chun Hae-jean in the long-ago days of blossoming first love. Ah, to have been there just one more time! I begged my old friend to send me a copy of that photograph upon his return to the United States. (And he did. However, the photo showed a much less-imposing span than my idealized memory had fixed thirty-five years before.)

*

Our train arrived at the Pyongyang central railroad station at eight-thirty on the morning of July 14. We strode through a light drizzle beneath a slate-gray sky to the same Mercedes 220 I had used during my first week in the capital.

This time, I was registered in the Potonggang Hotel, an exquisite place usually occupied by traveling journalists and other foreign visitors. After dropping off my belongings, I descended to the lobby and there met Mr. and Mrs. Chun, the first time I had seen my Canadian friends since our arrival. We posed for a picture together and took a short walk so I could bring Mr. Chun up to date on my adventures.

Following lunch at the hotel, I was driven to Pyongyang Maternity Hospital, a starkly modern facility which was opened in 1980. I learned that over seventy percent of the physicians were women. I also noted that many larger instruments were of Japanese or *West* German manufacture, a clear indication that the North Korean medical community places the safe and healthy birthing of its future generations at or near the top of its list of medical priorities. This tour was a tonic following so closely on my rather depressing observations at Chongjin Medical College.

On the morning of July 15, I was greeted at Pyongyang Medical College teaching hospital by Dr. Lee Tae-hyun, the assistant dean, a 1958 graduate of the college and concurrently chairman of the cardiac surgery department.

The hospital maintains two separate pharmacies: one dispenses modern medicines and the other dispenses only oriental medicines. Dr. Lee revealed that more patients each year were requesting "Western" rather than oriental herbal cures. Normally, I was told, a patient receives a five-day supply of prescribed medicines, but is free to pick up more if the condition has not improved.

Dr. Lee was particularly proud of the Intensive Care Unit, which was both his domain (and mine) and one of the few of its kind or sophistication in Asia outside of Japan or Hong Kong. The only one of the twelve monitored beds in use at the time of my visit was given over to a brain-injured patient who, much to my surprise, was not connected to a nursing station for continuous observation of his vital signs. I was surprised to note that there was no monitoring oscilloscope at the nursing station, which is unheard of in the West.

The cardiac-surgery ward, about which I was particularly interested, consists of fifty beds and is staffed by a team of seven cardiac surgeons. An annual average of six hundred cardiac catheritizations are performed. However, I was again disappointed upon learning cineangiograms—another standard diagnostic tool in the West—are performed only at Pyongyang's Red Cross Hospital. While North Koreans might suffer from different levels or even different types of heart disease than the American population, I cannot believe that the current level of only two hundred operations annually would suffice if more equipment or trained surgeons were available. Moreover, of the two hundred, approximately seventy-five percent involve congenital heart disease and not acquired life-threatening defects.

The implantation of cardiac pacemakers is infrequent, according to Dr. Lee, and employed only for seriously-ill heart-block cases. However, my North Korean colleague did not volunteer information pertaining to the underlying causes that lead to heart blocks in North Korea. He did say that the limited number of pacemakers available in North Korea were imported exclusively from Poland and East Germany. There was no time to visit the pacemaker clinic, but I was shown the surgical recovery room. It was rather spartan, another disappointment, equipped with only one defibrillator, one suction machine and one hyperbaric chamber. Unfortunately, there were no patients or staff in the room at the time of my visit.

Dr. Lee also escorted me to the endoscope examination room, where a locally-trained gastroenterologist was performing a gastroscopy with a

Japanese-supplied gastrofiberscope, a fine, modern piece of equipment through which the physician was able to identify and monitor a lesion in the patient's stomach, take a high-resolution photograph and collect several tissue samples for biopsy. Diet- or heredity-related stomach cancers are quite common in North Korea, so it is no wonder that particular emphasis is placed on their diagnosis and treatment.

I frankly could not figure out how to extrapolate all this information and the attendant impressions of spotty abundance.

*

Starting at four o'clock that afternoon, in my own hotel suite, I was provided with an intensive three-hour briefing on the state of public health in North Korea. The presenter was Dr. Chang Sin-hyuk, a 1960 graduate of Hamhung Medical College, now Director of Hospital Coordination at the central government's Public Health Department. At the outset, Dr. Chang indicated that I should interrupt his discourse at any point to ask questions. However, he began by reading from a lengthy document.

A completely socialized medical system had been in place in North Korea since January 1, 1953 and it provided completely free medical care to all citizens, including drugs and dental care. Physician-specialists were assigned mainly to county and big-city hospitals, while primary medical and dental care was available even in small villages. There is one emergency hospital, one maternity hospital and one children's hospital in each province and corresponding departments are to be found in every county, city and factory hospital.

Each North Korean province supports a medical college identical to "my" Chongjin Medical College. There is one pharmaceutical college, located in Pyongyang. In addition each province supports a four-year medical-technical high school which turns out paramedical practitioners, a provincial nursing college conferring a Registered Nursing certificate, and a provincial nurses-aide school offering a one-year course in practical nursing. Each medical college maintains an attached research center, while the nationally-endowed Medical Science Institute is located in Pyongyang.

Medical personnel are paid according to rank. The title "Medical Doctor," for example, comprises six pay levels ranging from 130 to 150 won per month, plus a significant bonus for each additional Ph.D., up to a top salary of 250 won (about $125) per month. Most doctors receive two weeks' paid vacation per year, though radiologists, whose work is considered hazardous, work half-days and receive three weeks' annual vacation. Incentives include selection of qualified post-graduate students or research-institute members to go abroad (usually to Russia, China, Romania or East Germany) for two years at a time to work as resident clinical physicians.

The statistics Dr. Chang presented were impressive. In 1982, the government spent 120 times more in health care than it did in its base statistical year, 1949. (Dr. Chang was unable to provide me with a figure indicating how much money was actually spent.) By 1960, every small village, school, mine and fishing boat had its own permanently-assigned physician or practitioner. By 1982, there were 10,000 hospitals and clinics in North Korea, as compared to less than 350 in 1946. By 1982, also, the nation supported 130 permanent hospital beds per 10,000 citizens, an increase from just one bed per 10,000 citizens in 1944, the highest rate the Japanese had been able to attain. There were 1.2 physicians per 10,000 of population in 1949 and 24 per 10,000 of population in 1982, a 2,000 percent increase. The average patient saw a doctor twenty times in 1982, either in clinical or hospital settings or, quite commonly, by doctors making housecalls.

I was reminded at frequent intervals that all medical services in North Korea are free.

Other interesting ancillary issues that were also raised included news that the retirement age is 55 for women and 60 for men. Retirees receive sixty-to-eighty percent of their closing salaries as their pension payments. Education is universal and compulsory for age groups five to sixteen and up through eleventh grade. College entrance is based solely upon examination results. All medical students receive a base stipend of 20 won per month, and they are free to use or save it, as they choose. Since the medical education is free and includes room and board, there is a strong tendency to save.

The briefing was exhaustive and exhausting, but extremely enlightening. It was clear, in sum, that North Korean healthcare delivery is still in the transition stage, that much more needs to and will be accomplished. A powerful structure is in place, and it will be strengthened considerably over time.

Though my eyes were rolling back from so massive an infusion of information, I had to rush out shortly after the briefing to catch the night train to Wonsan—for a final visit with members of my family.

CHAPTER THIRTY-FIVE

Our train arrived at Wonsan's main railroad station at seven-thirty on the morning of July 16. As soon as I alighted, I was greeted by Jung-hee and several county officials, who escorted my sister and me to her apartment.

Jung-hee's flat was located on the top floor of a five-story building near the center of the sprawling port city. As the building had no elevator, we struggled up a steep, narrow staircase. The flat consisted of two sleeping rooms, a kitchen and a bathroom. The floors of the sleeping rooms were heated by *on-dol*, the traditional radiant heat floor ducts that picked up heat from the charcoal cooking fire in the kitchen. Despite the electricity and running water and the setting in a five-story building, the flat was strongly reminiscent of a Korean farmhouse, complete with a pair of traditional iron cookpots in the kitchen. I noticed that the walls and floors had all been freshly papered and painted in honor of my visit.

I met Jung-hee's children for the first time: Kwang-ho, a thirteen-year-old boy in his third year of junior high school; Kwang-chul, an eleven-year-old in his first year of junior high; Kwang-ok, a nine-year-old girl in her third year of elementary school; and Kwang-soon, a six-year-old girl kindergartner. My brother-in-law, who was employed as a fisherman aboard a 10,000-ton tuna boat, was then at sea on his regular four-month-on, two-month-off pattern of employment.

After the introductions had been made and the children had had an ample opportunity to look me over, Jung-hee suggested that I eat a hearty breakfast. As soon as I sat down at the table in the eating room, my youngest sister brought out a battered old spoon.

"Brother, do you know what this is?" I saw that it was an ordinary chromium utensil with the English word "stainless" stamped on the back of the handle. I could divine no further significance, so shrugged my shoulders and raised my eyebrows in surrender.

"This is the very spoon you used to eat from when you lived with us. It was your spoon and Mother set it out for you at every meal for as long as we lived under one roof." Then she went on to explain, with a hint of dreaminess in her eyes and voice, "Mother insisted upon setting it out every day at breakfast time, from the first morning after you left Chu-ul until her illness forced her to take her meals in bed—for over twenty-nine years. She simply knew that you would be coming back, and nothing short of death was able to sway her from her symbolic act of looking after your needs."

As the tears poured from our eyes, Jung-hee pointed up to where an old-fashioned mirror hung from the wall. "This hung in our home in Chu-ul. Mother would often stand in front of it and cry, as if she could see your face in it."

Jung-hee insisted that I take possession of these heirlooms, but I refused, settling instead for several old photographs of Mother and my three sisters.

I could not help noticing how very like Mother Jung-hee looked and how her little mannerisms echoed Mother's. Moreover, my sister was close in years then to the age Mother had been when I left home in 1950. As close as I felt to Moon-hee and Ok-bong, with whom I had shared all my growing-up years, I realized that I felt somehow more comfortable in Jung-hee's presence. She, more than the others, looked up to me as her older sibling and that made me feel good. Being with her in her own home was an altogether uncanny sensation, both gratifying and unsettling.

The black Volvo and its driver had been left at my disposal, so after lunch Jung-hee and I were driven through the city. Although I had never actually set foot in Wonsan, I felt a certain relationship with it. For this was the point at which ROK and American soldiers and marines had entered northeastern Korea in October, 1950, launching their drive north beyond Chu-ul.

Today the city is the political and cultural center of Kangwon Province. It is a beautiful recreational center for the people of the area.

Modern buildings line the streets bordering Wonsan Bay on the North Sea. Apartment towers, some reaching twenty stories into the sky, and one- and two-story private dwellings are set in lush, well-tended gardens. Tree-lined streets of the residential areas were shady and appeared cool in the stifling July sun. What struck me immediately was that Wonsan was a warm, vibrant people city, quite the opposite of stark, peopleless Pyongyang.

The city has several excellent institutions of higher learning: Wonsan University of Agriculture and Wonsan University of Economics. Also, of course, the city is the home of the provincial medical-training complex. I was told that Wonsan is also the temporary home of many of the numerous foreign students who come to North Korea each year on exchange scholarships.

Wonsan is North Korea's leading shipbuilding center, and its commerce is largely devoted to maritime pursuits. It is from Wonsan that modern four-hundred-passenger cruise vessels routinely leave for Japan with visiting former North Korean nationals, or the younger members of their families, all now living in Japan.

Donald Chung, M.D.

*

Jung-hee and her four children and I—Uncle Dong-kyu—boarded a harbor sightseeing boat at the main maritime terminal and set boldly to sea for a cruise around the port, one of Wonsan's main sightseeing attractions. This was virtually the first time I had been to sea—such as it was—since arriving in South Korea, starved and, it seemed then, terminally seasick. The cruise turned out to be one of the gems of my return to North Korea, for it evoked in me a compelling memory of my family's cruises along the Harbin shore, in the long-ago days when all seemed right with my world.

Following the harbor cruise, we visited, among other places, Myongsasim-ri, a particularly famous scenic spot known throughout the land for its abundant crop of sweet sand roses. I had dreamed of visiting this place during my teen years in Chu-ul, but it had taken decades away from North Korea to finally land me there. I treated my sister and the children to soft drinks at the beach restaurant and took time out to shoot several rolls of photos, mainly of my nieces and nephews and, of course, my own baby sister.

That evening, Jung-hee and I went to Songdo Restaurant, a beautiful example of traditional architecture set upon a tree-covered slope of Changdok Hill. Here, the county officials who had greeted me upon my arrival in Wonsan, treated my sister and me to a particularly lavish banquet. Among the welcoming speeches were those delivered by the chairmen of the People's Committee and the city chapter of the Workers' Party. We ate, drank and talked for nearly three hours in a particularly relaxed atmosphere. Perhaps it was the knowing that my adventure was nearly over, or perhaps I was getting used to these affairs, but I enjoyed myself immensely among these laughing, friendly strangers. I even found myself trading tales of my days in Manchuria with a man who had also lived in Harbin during World War II. Jung-hee, who had been too young to recall much of those days, listened with rapt attention.

*

We finally returned to Jung-hee's apartment, where Mr. Kim left us to be alone for the first time since I had arrived in North Korea. It was then that I asked my youngest sister to tell me all that had happened to my family, particularly to Mother, since my departure in December, 1950.

The home I had known in Chu-ul—along with most of the town—was destroyed by naval and air bombardments rained down by United States forces. Subsisting there until shortly after the end of the war, Mother in July of 1953, then fifty-one years old, packed a small trunk and taking Jung-hee, left for Pyongyang.

It was Jung-hee's opinion that Mother expected to find our elusive father in the capital. She knew of his employment there as a minor political functionary before the city fell to ROK and U.S. troops in the autumn of 1950. But by 1953, the war now over, the nation was in the throes of rebuilding, and there were jobs to be had.

Although Mother knew that Father had left for the south on the same day as I had, she maintained a belief that he had never really left the north. For over a year, whenever time allowed, in all kinds of weather, Mother searched through the streets of the ruined capital, hoping to catch a glimpse of her husband. But her valiant search was in vain, and for the remainder of her life she had no further knowledge of him whatsoever.

Thus, the end of Father's story remains a mystery to us. My third uncle who was with Father when last I saw him, survived. Resurfacing after the war, he never informed my family of his being with Father and of my encounter with them in Kilchu. I was not able to see this uncle during this visit. By then he was a very old man so I could not seek the answers to the questions that plagued me.

Once in the capital, Mother found a job in a textile factory. Jung-hee, then fourteen years old, returned to high school and graduated three years later near the top of her class. Though she had qualified for college, Jung-hee forfeited the right, preferring to find a job to help support Mother. She, too, worked at the textile factory and eventually talked Mother into retiring and staying home for the rest of her days. They continued to live in their cramped one-room apartment for many years, but through Jung-hee's faithfulness and sacrifices she no longer had to spend long hours in the factory doing back-breaking work, using her poor gnarled fingers.

Jung-hee was twenty-nine years old before she found a suitable man to marry who did not have parents. (There is that tradition. The one that Young-ja had flouted in her search for a husband. Jung-hee's motivation was a determination to stay by Mother rather than going to live with in-laws.) So she married the fisherman within a short time and two years later gave birth to her first son. From then on and through the succession of newborns, Mother usually slept in the tiny kitchen with a crying grandchild on her back. Many times she told Jung-hee, "Your brother, Dong-kyu, often slept on my back like this." So even as I, far away across the sea, relived in my mind my early days with my beloved mother, so she, too, was in her own way reliving the days of my infancy with her grandchildren.

Mother's cancer was diagnosed in November, 1978. She knew that as time went on she would need more and more care, so she asked to be moved to Myongchun to live with Ok-bong. Besides the fact that Jung-hee's children were younger than Ok-bong's and needed more of her attention, Jung-hee's fisherman husband was away at sea for four months at a time. The thought of imposing herself on her youngest daughter under these circumstances and in a weakening condition added to Mother's discomfiture.

Ok-bong was more than willing to care for Mother. Her early aggressive, tomboyish manner had over the years blossomed into a sweet, gracious stability. So for the remaining months of Mother's life, she was in the loving care of Ok-bong. Although Mother refused modern treatment to the end, she readily accepted traditional herbal cures and pain-killers. Her selfless, courageous life came to an end on September 19, 1979.

Listening to Jung-hee recounting these events made me even more fully aware that it had been my responsibility to care for Mother, particularly in her dying days. Jung-hee was quick to stress in her matter-of-fact, practical way and without any trace of malice, that she had taken my place in caring for Mother. Neither she nor I berated me for the course in life I had chosen to follow. But I did then and do now feel guilty for my weakness and fear in not acting sooner to seek official permission to return to my homeland. Had I taken action earlier I might have seen Mother alive once again, assuring her that though we had been separated by oceans and mountains and plains, always she had been by my side, guiding me, encouraging me, leading me on. I could have helped Jung-hee with her burdens. Looking at her as we sat in her apartment it was apparent that she was happy and well adjusted. But I regretted that she had sacrificed herself for nearly thirty years to care for our dearly-loved mother, wishing that I could have done so.

Telling me of all these happenings and experiences lasted until two-thirty in the morning, when we fell into each other's arms amidst a torrent of tears.

*

I was awakened at five-thirty the next morning, July 17, as four neighbor ladies prepared breakfast in Jung-hee's kitchen. These women had graciously offered to help my sister with her domestic chores so that she could spend all her time with me. They were lively, friendly women who, though they asked no direct questions, appeared to enjoy being the recipients of any news they could get from me about the world beyond their city's harbor. I gladly obliged them, particularly since I found that one of them, a longtime friend of Mother's, had information I wanted to hear. I cried when it came time to oblige this dear woman's wish to pose with me in a Polaroid photo taken by Jung-hee.

The day started with a good omen: it was bright and sunshiny, the women told me, for the first time in a month. I was glad to see the sun, for Mr. Kim and I were to be off at nine o'clock on a sightseeing tour to the south.

The good omen turned to bad as soon as Mr. Kim put in his appearance at the breakfast table. The strict letter of the schedule said that I would be going to the mountains alone; no provision had been made for Jung-hee, though we also planned to return to Wonsan in two days. I asked Mr. Kim if she could come with us, and told him that I would pay any additional expenses. This was the first accommodation I had requested and, though Mr.

Kim retained the obsequious smile pasted to his face for nearly two weeks, he emphatically denied my request. I remain convinced that he exercised no personal stake in maintaining this unshakable position. He was a functionary. Like most North Koreans in his position, he had been trained to be inflexible in following orders, even lacking the personal responsibility necessary to make small, spur-of-the-moment decisions. Needless to say, the denial of my request diminished the joy in this phase of my family reunion. Under the circumstances, I realized it could not have been otherwise.

Standing on the curb beside the car in front of Jung-hee's apartment building, I kissed Jung-hee and my nieces and nephews, then climbed into the black Volvo with Mr. Kim, the driver, and my official escort, a minor county official.

*

I spent two physically exhausting days with Mr. Kim and a succession of guides. We toured impressive natural attractions in the regions south of Wonsan, going almost as far as the Demilitarized Zone between the two Koreas. A number of peaks we visited in the Diamond Mountains overlooked territory that had been the scene of heavy fighting during the Korean War.

It was here that I came face-to-face with battle-ready infantry and armored contingents of the People's Army. I am sure that just across a few peaks and ravines the territory was just as well manned by battle-ready ROK or American forces. It was difficult to believe an area of such magnificent splendor could be the leading edge of a potentially explosive war zone.

Momentarily casting aside such grim thoughts of mankind's bellicose spirit, I reveled in the beauty of the breathtaking Kuryong Falls. This wonder of nature has served as the background for countless tales, poems, and songs stretching back like a vast unwinding scroll through the centuries of Korean culture.

I was further gratified by actually visiting Samilpo Lake, an exquisite round reservoir of pure mountain water and therapeutic hot springs. I had always regretted, while patrolling the region with my company in the spring of 1951, that although we had probed towards this natural wonder, we had never quite reached it.

*

We returned to Wonsan on July 19, and arrived at Jung-hee's flat at around noon. As I was getting out of the Volvo, Mr. Kim flashed a knowing smile and told me that I would be able to spend many quiet hours alone with my sister and her family before having to catch the ten-forty-five train back to Pyongyang.

All four of my nieces and nephews had been let out of school early in anticipation of my last hours with them. They had all exhibited great interest and affection for their new-found uncle when I first arrived, and my heart was gladdened to note upon my return that, if anything, their ardor was heightened. In fact, my brother-in-law had no brothers, so these children had been deprived of avuncular affection—a very important cultural matter in Korea—until my arrival.

As these things must always go, I was particularly taken with Jung-hee's youngest, the precocious Kwang-soon. This affectionate six-year-old spent most of the day on my lap or clinging to my trouser legs. We had become fast friends upon my original arrival in her home and the relationship just took off from there. Inasmuch as I was the father of two boys, having a little girl to share my time with was a new and, to me, cherished undertaking.

As I saw this youngster in action, I could not help thinking of the universality of the human spirit. Kwang-soon was yet too young to have been meaningfully reached by her nation's political ethos. Unlike any of the scores of other countrymen and relatives I had been meeting, Kwang-soon alone asked probing questions about life beyond the sea. She was innocent of the terrors and misunderstandings and unrequited hopes that keep the family of Man fragmented into all its hostile factions. As Kwang-soon nestled in my arms, I was overwhelmed by this realization: If our fatherland and the race of Man are to be reunited in peace, it must be left to the little children to impose their clear, trusting wisdom upon their jaded elders. Without the children and their undiminished vision, there is nothing but bleak times and ultimate ruin ahead for all of mankind.

*

We used up nearly the last of my film taking photos of one another during that long afternoon and evening. I shared in a new kind of joy that day, but there was also an underlying and profound sorrow in these last acts of the fulfillment of The Promise. The heavens felt the blackness of my mood, for late in the day the sky clouded over, dismal and gray, and a torrent of cheerless rain fell upon the streets of Wonsan.

Too soon, Mr. Kim knocked at the door of Jung-hee's apartment and announced it was time to say my good-byes.

I hugged my nephews and nieces, one after another, but I clung to little Kwang-soon for a needed extra jolt of joy. As I was about to release her, the tiny child exploded in the extra-loud voice with which all young children seem to be endowed, "Uncle! Uncle! The only uncle I have! Please don't leave!"

403

Clear as a bell the words of this little child's mother, then a young child herself, rang through my mind. "Please, Brother. . . . Don't leave me." I wondered if hearing her child, Jung-hee heard herself saying almost the same words so many years ago.

Tenderly putting Kwang-soon down, I looked up into Jung-hee's face. A prescient look in her eyes accompanied her next words, "Brother," she said, "can't you come back to stay with us?"

I felt her words were more a wishful statement than a question. The look in her eyes had expressed the impossibility of the request. But something deep within her soul had brought forth the wish which, as Shakespeare said so long ago, was father of the thought. I recognized the turbulence within her calm exterior, and knew I had no skill with which to minister to her needs.

I summoned up no words for answer. A look, a shrug, a pressure on her hand told more than any words I could command.

Then, grasping my sister in a tight embrace, I followed Mr. Kim down the five flights of stairs to the Volvo waiting in the rain.

Within minutes, my heart and mind turned inward. I cried silently all the way to the railroad station as visions of my sisters flashed back and forth across the decades—first as girls, then as women. I wept most bitterly then at the full impact of having lost Mother and of having failed, truly failed, to keep The Promise.

*

But had I failed? In what did my assumed failure consist? Universal time is not measured in days or months or years. In the overall history of the Cosmos, three days or three decades are insignificant minutiae.

Only a few months before, I had thought that finding my family was an impossible dream. Now I knew that many things deemed impossible are in truth possible if we only ask the right questions or make the right demands of ourselves. I thought that perhaps my small life and the fulfillment of my dream might contribute in some way to a renewed understanding between and among the Korean people. History's great changes often result from an accumulation of small deeds. Perhaps an important breakthrough might come in my lifetime. Perhaps I might even be a part of it.

I thought of all the miracles I had witnessed in my lifetime. I saw mankind's evolution ascending on an upward spiral. My profession alone was today involved in everyday routines that fifty years ago would have been deemed as foolish will-o'-the-wisp fantasies. The revolutions in transportation and communications had shrunk the world. More people traveled the world than ever before. Greater understanding becomes possible with greater familiarity with the strange customs of strange people.

I had long since dried my tears and now contemplated the future. I was not done with the past, but it was only in the future that the past could be completely worked through.

I looked forward with new enthusiasm and vibrant hope to my eastward flight across the vast Pacific.

Suddenly the very word—Pacific—inflamed my mind. The Ocean of Peace. We have it in our power to truly make this vast sea an ocean of peace if we set our hearts and minds to it and exert our united wills, speaking with the voice of mankind.

The first major step will be to listen to the little children, to see with their clear eyes, and speak their truth unbesmirched by *any* ideology of the East or the West!

Donald Chung, M.D.

Though the timing had been off, I came to realize that regardless of life's capriciousness, I had kept The Three Day Promise.

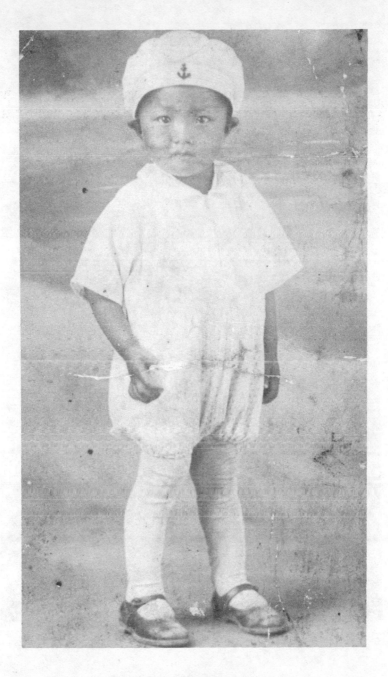

Author at age three.

Author's father at age 35.

Author's mother at age 65.

Author with Chongjin Medical College classmates in 1948.

Author as PFC in Eastern Front with Company Commander
Lt. Kim.

Author with second cousin Col. Chung Mong-ho at R.O.K. 8th Division near Hyun Ri in 1952.

Author the day of Promotion to Sgt. in 1952.

Author during assignment to U.S. 23rd Infantry Regiment Medical Company near Dong Tu Chun in 1954.

Reunion with two sisters at Pyongyang Airport after 33 years - 1983

Author Embracing elder sister Moon Hee at Kiljoo railroad
station, 35 years later. 1983.

Author kneeling to mother's grave, 33 years later. 1983.

Author with 3 sisters families during homecoming in 1983.

Author with two classmates of Chongjin Medical College
during 1946 - 1950, 33 years later, 1983

Author cruising on Wonsan Bay with youngest sister Jung-
hee and children. 1983.

Farewell to 3 sisters at Pyongyang Airport in North Korea after 18 days of visit. 1983.

Author with General Van Fleet in the General's study. January, 1988